WITCHES

an encyclopedia of paganism and magic

michael jordan

photographs by

sally griffyn

kyle cathie Limited

First published in Great Britain in 1996 by
Kyle Cathie Limited
20 Vauxhall Bridge Road
London SW1V 2SA

ISBN 1 85626 193 X

Copyright © 1996 by Michael Jordan
Photography © 1996 by Sally Griffyn
Photographs opposite pages 33 (bottom right), 113 and 160
courtesy of Spectrum Colour Library; photograph on
page 153 by Deborah Jones, courtesy of Kim Jack
Initial illustrations by Jane Maskew

Michael Jordan is hereby identified as the author of this work
in accordance with Section 77 of the Copyright, Designs and
Patents Act 1988.

A Cataloguing in Publication record for this book is available from
the British Library.

Designed by Senate
Edited by Caroline Taggart

Printed and bound in Spain by Graphycems

With some astonishing parallels, whether they have lived twenty thousand years ago in the bitter, uncompromising Europe of a receding Ice Age, or five thousand years ago on the arid deserts of Mesopotamia, or a scant millennium gone on the edge of a dark and brooding northern forest, people have found faith in the same gods. They have striven for the same clouds and bowed before the same altars.

The quest has no ending. Today's innovation is tomorrow's history. That which will remain, I suspect, is a deep and unquenchable need to reach out and feel the warmth and tenderness of the eternal mother. She is the womb of the world, and out of the womb we struggle into the world. She is the morning and the evening of our life. It was Hermann Hesse who said: 'without a mother we cannot die.'

GODS OF THE EARTH, 1992

acknowledgements

My thanks the the following for their kind co-operation and advice on specific areas of the research:

Adrian Harris

Michael Howard

Ronald Hutton

Shan Jayran

Christina Oakley

Karin Rainbird

Doreen Valiente

Elen J Williams

Steve Wilson

Thanks also to the four women who permitted me to interview them and shared their views so openly: Vivianne Crowley, Olivia Durdin-Robertson, Maxine Sanders and Doreen Valiente again.

I owe a particular debt of gratitude to Caroline Wise without whose constant advice and help, always authoritative and objective, the task would have been infinitely more difficult.

*

The publishers would also like to express their thanks to Sally Griffyn, not only for providing magnificent photographs, but for generous co-operation and sharing of her knowledge.

contents

photographer's note

Sally Griffyn is a freelance photographer based in Britain. For the past three years she has worked with Pagans and witches in an attempt to represent their varied traditions accurately and with a positive slant. All the participating witches/Pagans have given their permission for their images to be presented in this book. The forty-odd photographs included here are part of an ongoing archive s Sally has created on the history of folklore and pre-Christian spiritual practices. The Pagan contribution to European culture is extensive; perhaps these images will go some way towards clarifying the misconceptions that have led to millions being persecuted for their beliefs.

INTRODUCTION

Each year, as the sun fades on the last days of October, the flurries of falling leaves will be matched by a time-honoured bustle of activity among those of us who have not reached the mature age when clearing the local store of candles and disembowelling pumpkins lose their charm. Yet Hallowe'en, more properly the eve of All Hallows or All Saints Day in the Christian calendar, is only the popular, 'establishment' face of an event which is infinitely more profound and which shares scant common ground with the Christian faith.

31 October marks the ancient Pagan festival of Samhain and, while children play trick-or-treat on the neighbours, other rural and even suburban corners as far apart geographically as the Black Forest and Massachusetts will watch over secluded activities of a different kind. Followers of a Craft which, though predominantly attracting women, draws membership from bank managers and road sweepers, housewives and fashion models, will observe an arcane rite symbolizing the demise of any lingering traces of summer's greenery. They will bid farewell to the 'Lord of the Oak' and usher in the 'Lord of the Holly', whose role it will be to protect the natural world through the austerity of winter.

Yet the term 'Lord' risks leading us off on a false trail, because this is not a book which focuses primarily on male deities. Rather it is concerned with the worship of an ancient, and yet also very up-to-date, goddess, the Earth Mother. In the beginning of humankind's spiritual quest, many thousands of years ago, the Goddess was paramount in our worship. Her images are to be found anywhere and everywhere in the prehistoric world. But then came the male-dominated religions of Judaism, Christianity and Islam; and in some parts of the world the patriarchal male god has reigned supreme for more than two millennia.

Today, though, there begins to blow a wind of change. In the 1940s a new mood began to invade the tenets of orthodox belief. Those who held the 'Old Religion' dear but had kept their silence for fear of persecution and ridicule began to take new strength and by the early 1950s, in the more liberal climate of religious tolerance in both Britain and the United States, an almost forgotten style of worship began to re-emerge. It met with, and continues to meet with, much bigotry and intolerance, but through pioneers like Aleister Crowley, Gerald Gardner, Doreen Valiente and Alex Sanders, the 'hearth and nature' religion of witchcraft has made a come-back in Western society.

The earliest form of witch for whom we find a historical record is the *shaman*, a person of either sex, generally associated with a pre-literate nomadic or hunting tribe, whose intelligence put him or her above the rest and who consulted with, and interceded on behalf of, the spirit world for the good or detriment of the clan. In modern tribal societies those shamans who are benign are described for convenience as white shamans, those who are malevolent as black.

Understanding of the meaning of witches and witchcraft in the Western world has not been assisted by the fact that the Christian Church has always adopted a different view from that of the person in the street. For the latter a witch or wizard has been someone possessing a special innate power of influential magic for benefit or harm in society. Generally speaking the 'Cunning Person' working for social good, finding lost pigs and clearing up boils, was perceived as a wizard, the successor to the white shaman, and his or her more malevolent counterpart, once the black shaman, was a witch, but in practice the distinction was almost certainly subjective. The love-sick youth seeking a potion to charm the object of his desires may have viewed its dispenser as a 'good sort', while the luckless paramour from whom she had been wrenched might view the situation differently.

What singled out the witches of medieval Europe was that when they came into conflict with the religious strictures of Christendom they were tarred with a diabolical brush. Witches were seen as suitable targets for persecution because they practised various forms of magic and because they came to enjoy a quasi-religious popularity which roused an almost hysterical jealousy – fuelled, since most of them were women, by the Church's built-in weakness for misogyny.

In response to the threat to its street-level popularity, the Church proceeded to arm itself with massive dossiers of information on demonology and its prosecution and, on the Continent, it instigated that most notorious of ecclesiastical commissions of inquiry, the Inquisition.

Much of its 'information' was the product of gossip and rich imagination. There is little firm evidence, for example, that witches regularly joined together in covens. That is a modern notion. In James I's reign, which saw the peak of witch-hunting in England, the practitioner of the Craft was probably more often than not a solitary individual who claimed membership of no wider sorority. Yet the *Witches' Sabbat*, the nocturnal scantily clad chase to a rendezvous in honour of Diana the huntress, which probably took place only in fertile imaginations, was the stuff of medieval scandal. Tales of demonic but frisky spirits, the *succubi* and *incubi* who intercoursed with witches in the dark and small hours of the night, besmirched cleric and commoner alike. As the sixteenth-century observer Reginald Scot reported in his *Historie of Witchcraft: . . . in the night time incubus came to a ladies bedside and made hot loove unto hir; whereat she being offended, cried out so lowd, that companie came and found him under hir bed in the likenesse of the holie bishop . . .*

Reports of witches riding upon broomsticks stemmed from similar, fanciful notions, the product of over-stimulated public interest and imagination. Very few women seem to have stood accused of defying nocturnal gravity and in England only one was said to have done so astride a broom. And, as Judge Justice Powell commented when presiding over the trial of Jane Wenham in 1712, 'There is no law against flying.' On the other hand the black cat, in company with such less endearing creatures as frogs, toads, newts, spiders and rats, all enjoy a basis of historical credibility. Such beasts were the witch's familiars, animals through which occult and diabolical powers were said to be transmitted.

It would be wrong, however, to assume that, at the outset of the so-called witch-craze which bedevilled both Europe and America in the sixteenth and seventeenth centuries, witches imagined themselves in league with the devil. Most were stout Christian souls, convinced by their local priest that, because of some petty misdemeanour, they were fit for nothing better than the fires of hell. Reflecting the build-up of almost fanatical Church resentment and a propaganda campaign which fuelled public fears that some dark and sinister menace was at large, no fewer than three Witchcraft Acts were placed on the English statute books between 1542 and 1604, each more draconian than the last. As Chief Justice Anderson thundered in 1602, persuaded that the country was poised to be overrun by some haggish sorority, 'The land is full of witches; they abound in all places!'

The popular notion, however, that witches were persecuted by dedicated and over-zealous witch-hunters for many hundreds of years is deeply flawed. In England and North America, the main thrust of persecution was restricted to a fifty-year period during the latter half of the seventeenth century.

It is impossible to establish how many witches existed at any one time. It has been reckoned that about a thousand were executed throughout the length and breadth of the British Isles, but it is probably fair to say that the record of prosecutions represents only the tip of the iceberg and it also has to be remembered that for every one condemned to death, many more got off with, at worst, a one-year prison sentence. English witches also fared better than their Scottish and Continental counterparts: there existed a level of scepticism about many of the more malicious charges which often resulted in acquittal and even the award of damages for wrongful arrest. Before the miasmic surge of sixteenth-century trials very few English witches met the death penalty, and although witchcraft did not cease to be a statutory offence until 1736, prosecution effectively halted from the turn of the eighteenth century. In the USA, legislation followed the English model, but again persecution was not rife. The notorious Salem trials can be seen almost as an isolated incident whose hysteria provoked widespread revulsion and was succeeded by a mood of greater tolerance.

This public revulsion was one of a number of reasons why the witch-craze died out. Belief in witchcraft became less prevalent as philosophy and quality of life overtook it, and technical advances were making many of the back-street cures, the stock-in-trade of many witches, redundant. It also ceased to be chic at influential and intellectual levels.

In some ways perceptions of witches and magicians have changed little. Many Christian clergy still regard any form of faith healing as scarcely more than 'Devil's Work'. Though witchcraft is no longer proscribed, it still manages to receive a press which at best regards it as quaint and at worst as downright wicked. A trenchant observation of the onslaught of orthodox opinion against which the pioneers of witchcraft rebirth had to stand may be found in the words of Montague Summers, writing not in the heat of seventeenth-century fervour but in 1946; he asserted that *a witch is one who by commerce and close confederacy with the Devil has a deliberate and very determined intention of attaining his own ends.* It is perhaps not surprising, therefore, that despite legal relaxation since 1951, devotees of the Craft in the enlightened 1990s, regardless of shade, tend not to encourage public scrutiny a great deal more than did those of their predecessors who were at risk of ending up dangling from a noose.

Today's 'Craft of the Wise' – Wicca – is not so much a survival as a revival of an ancient style of worship which has been structured and focused anew to meet the demands of the twentieth century. It addresses what it perceives as the paramount challenge facing the modern technological world, the need to return to old values of revering the earth and its progeny. This book, however, is not just about witchcraft. It is a more general view of Pagans and magicians, of whom witches are only a single aspect - those devoted to the worship of the old Celtic and Germanic mother goddess. The word Paganism derives from *pagani*, the old peasant stock of the Italian countryside, but it has now come to encompass many facets of religion and magic whose adherents do not subscribe to 'establishment beliefs'. In this final decade of the twentieth century the number of Pagans probably runs into many millions worldwide. Most believe strongly that, as the new Age of Aquarius dawns, theirs is the way forward, a more relevant and believable faith than that offered by the mainstream religions.

An important point should perhaps be clarified here: those who practise diabolism are not witches. The devil is a peculiarly Christian individual and the doctrine of witchcraft rejects the Christian god. Thus all witches distance themselves from Satanism and the diabolical arts championed by such bizarre characters as Anton Szandor LaVey and the infinitely more sinister Charles Manson. Satanic masses, murderous sects and malevolent figures with horns, curly tails and toasting forks have no connection with Wicca, past or present. None of which is to claim that Satanism and other evil influences do not exist, only that they are distinct and separate. They have their place in this volume in order to serve the broad picture and to dissociate them from witchcraft and other forms of Paganism.

The very word witch needs to be treated with caution, though, because there is, as there always has been, witchcraft and witchcraft, and it is important to recognize that witchcraft embraces, sometimes to a greater, sometimes to a lesser extent, other occult disciplines, most notably those involving the magic arts. Witchcraft and magic are truly inseparable.

Many twentieth-century witches, adherents to 'The Craft', proclaim themselves firmly allied with Wicca, while others view this as little more than an exercise in semantics. There exist solitary witches and hedgewitches who claim allegiance to no one except the Goddess to whose service they devote themselves, and while nowadays few individuals would openly claim to be other than white witches working for the benefit and not the detriment of others, it would be difficult to argue, in a faith which supports the principles of anarchy, that black witchcraft is not also occasionally worked.

As far as public opinion is concerned, practitioners of the Craft may well turn out to be their own worst enemies since, while most will stoutly refute the notion that their organizations are occult, they are loth to dispense with the secrecy that remains at the heart of their ritual, and their activities and venues are not generally broadcast. They are also irrevocably bound up with the reputations of pioneering men whose undoubted courage in the face of such public hostility as that broadcast by Montague Summers was sometimes matched by their duplicity and sexual excesses. As Doreen Valiente put it succinctly, 'Alex Sanders must have had the most photographed bum in England.' Yet these same men stood full square in the face of public opinion and did great service to the cause of religious freedom.

The resurgence of interest in witchcraft was probably thrown into play most notably by such writers as James Frazer, Charles Leland and Robert Graves. What has emerged in the second half of the twentieth century, the product of imaginative and often strongly egotistical male pioneers like Aleister Crowley, Alex Sanders and Gerald Gardner, and of influential theorists such as Margaret Murray, is a loose-knit movement or assembly of movements, some Craft, some not, but championed essentially by women. In the British Isles the roll call bears the names of Vivianne Crowley, Olivia Durdin-Robertson, Janet Farrar, Dion Fortune, Leonora

James, Doreen Valiente, Caroline Wise and others, while in America it includes Margot Adler, Zsuzsanna Budapest, Miriam Simos and countless contemporaries. Today's Craft still places great emphasis on healing and charms, overlaid with a desire to return to the ancient Celtic notion of harmony with nature and her rustic deities but it is, essentially, an invented religion, drawn from scraps of history and lore combined with pure imagination and not without elements of confidence trickery.

If there is a typical practising witch in the modern age, it is likely to be someone thoroughly down-to-earth, a very normal next-door-neighbour who digs the garden and visits the supermarket without a black cat or a funny hat in sight, and who is derisive of the more fanciful notions of public perception of the Craft. Theirs is a deep allegiance to a nature- and solar- or lunar-orientated doctrine which will include observance of the major pre-Christian Celtic festivals of Samhain, Imbolc, Beltane and Lammas, interspersed with seasonal festivals at the equinoxes and solstices. It is a search for boons, guidance and strength from higher powers whose provenance rests with the ancient pre-Christian faiths. It is a working towards healing and protecting others from misfortune through spellcraft, though many will claim no special gifts of healing. They will pass on their store of knowledge and understanding to new initiates through training and workshops.

Running in parallel with the Craft are the occult societies and fraternities which arose at the turn of the century and which find their roots in Jewish Qabalism, Classical and Hermetic magic, and medieval Rosicrucianism; the most notable of these was the Hermetic Order of the Golden Dawn. These magical organizations have never attracted membership other than in small numbers and have often been marked by internal feuding, the causes of which have too often lain with bombastic individuals who, while passionately sincere in their purpose, were also strong egotists determined to impose their own doctrinal ideals and beliefs upon the rest. The same organizations have also been characterized by charter documents which, though subsequently revealed to be crude forgeries with no supporting provenance, have been claimed to originate in great and arcane antiquity. Yet does this matter? Is it important that the basis of belief is not a medieval manuscript representing a still earlier oral tradition of mysticism and magic, but the product of a fertile nineteenth-century imagination?

The drawbacks which have afflicted magical and theosophical organizations have also beset other modern occult groups. Too often there is wild inaccuracy and misinformation about historical facts which should have a direct bearing on current thinking and practice. In some cases this extends to downright mischief in distorting the truth. Furthermore some writers suffer from a tendency to couch their opinions in terms as obscure as the names of the organizations to which they subscribe. The shortcoming is amply evidenced in the introduction to an otherwise fairly lucid book on Chaos Magic by Phil Hine. On the first page, Pete Carroll observes: *Shortly after the Chaos Magic paradigm, Chaos Maths developed from the Catastrophe Theory and confirmed the Chaoist hypothesis that some mechanism must exit [sic] to scale up subatomic indeterminacy into the macroscopic world of our experience.*

One needs to look no further than Phil Hine's own opening observations for an apt, perhaps unwitting, comment on this type of pseudo-intellectual dross which does little to promote image or credibility: *Magic has become obfuscated under a weight of words, a welter of technical terms which exclude the uninitiated and serve those who are eager for a scientific jargon with which to legitimize their enterprise into something self-important and pompous.*

Notwithstanding the problems, down the centuries witchcraft and magic have demonstrated a fascinating and impressive ability to change and meet new demands and realities. Witchcraft, if treated as a phenomenon inseparable from its precursor, shamanism, remains the oldest form of worship. Today's Craft may never claim, or wish to claim, wide membership, but it may yet prove itself an enduring survivor when others fall by the wayside.

This book sets out to provide a source of reference to anyone who practises or is interested in the Craft and other aspects of Paganism and magic. It is intended to be neither subjective nor contentious, but to provide straightforward facts about people, phenomena and events. It covers history and mythology where these are relevant to contemporary practice and belief, but its focus is largely on occultism today, in Britain, continental Europe and the United States; to an extent, it also offers a stepping-off point for more detailed study.

Although the encyclopedia entries are largely committed to factual details, *Witches* also includes candid interviews with four leading Pagans whose observations and sentiments have a strong personal feel and provide a powerful insight into the workings of their collective faith. And it is faith which really holds the key because, in the end, neither the credibility of those most closely involved in the resurgence of modern Paganism nor the issue of reliable links to the past matter.

The effectiveness of witchcraft and magic, as facets of humankind's most deeply felt needs, lies not in facts or historical certainties but in that most time-honoured ingredient and test of human spirituality, the leap of faith.

AA See ASTRUM ARGENTINUM.

ABRA-MELIN An ancient Hebrew system of magic incorporating parts of the QABALAH but with allegedly Greek Iamblichan origins (Iamblichus was the celebrated neo-Platonist better known as Plotinus). This seems unlikely since the Iamblichan philosophy is PAGAN while Abra-Melin is essentially Judaeo-Christian. Practised in Europe during the medieval period and later by some notable modern magicians, including Alex SANDERS, it follows the Gnostic and Zoroastrian premises that the spiritual and physical balance in the world is established between forces of light and dark. The present-day discipline probably derives from material originating in France and dating to no earlier than eighteenth century. Abra-Melin is akin to WITCHCRAFT, incorporating many of the traditional accoutrements of the Craft but with distinct doctrinal differences. It is a very austere magic based on the assumption that everything depends on the spiritual condition of the magus. It includes 360 magical symbols, each relating to an aspect of nature.

ADEPT A leader within the occult magical disciplines generally referred to as WESTERN MYSTERIES. The term describes one who has completed training to an advanced degree and risen through the initiatory ranks. Adepts are small in number, are at the apogee of strictly hierarchical pyramids and are venerated by their followers. Such people may also be known as Inner Plane Adepti.

ADLER, MARGOT American author and NEOPAGAN whose work, *Drawing Down the Moon*, is considered by many to be the standard authoritative discourse on PAGANISM in the United States. Margot Adler is the granddaughter of the internationally respected psychiatrist, Alfred Adler. She grew up in an agnostic family and as a child developed a strong interest in Greek mythology. From this her interest in WITCHCRAFT evolved; she was initiated into a Gardnerian coven (see GARDNER, Gerald) in 1971. Her aims have included the restoration of the sacred values of the earth and the creation of a society more in harmony with nature. She is a former priestess of a New York City coven and currently lives in New York and works as a reporter for National Public Radio.

ADO See ANCIENT DRUID ORDER.

AEROMANCY The practice of DIVINATION through examination of aspects of the air and sky, utilizing weather signs, cloud patterns, appearance of comets and other astral phenomena.

AESIR The major race of deities, including a pantheon of sky gods and goddesses, in Germanic and Norse religions. The Aesir live in the mythical realm of Asgard, located somewhere on the island of Sjaelland in Denmark, and were once engaged in a war of attrition with the race of chthonic deities known as the VANIR. They are also in unending conflict with their chief enemies, the harbingers of darkness and cold, the frost giants. The leader of the Aesir gods is OTHIN (Odin, Woden) and, according to Snorri Sturluson, they number twelve excluding Othin – Thor, Balder, Tyr, Bragi, Heimdall, Loki,

Ull, Forseti, Hod, Vidar, Vali and Njord (a Vanir sent to Asgard as a hostage when the two races were at war). Several goddesses, including Frigg, Othin's wife, Idunn, Sif, Saga and the giantess wife of Njord, Skadi, also live in Asgard. Loki, being of giant extraction, is not a true member of the Aesir by pedigree.

The word As derives from the old Norse *ass*, meaning a beam or pole, suggesting that these deities were originally worshipped in the form of the 'High Seat Pillars', carved planks of wood which were erected on the shores and elsewhere as guardian totems.

The Aesir pantheon is fundamental to the modern religion of ASATRU which has a growing membership in Europe and North America, and to the London-based Pagan organization, The ODINIC RITE.

AFA See ASATRU FREE ASSEMBLY.

AGRIPPA, CORNELIUS HENRY (1486-1535) A German philosopher and intellectual magician who compiled several influential works including, most notably, *Three Books of Occult Philosophy* (English transl. 1651) and who ranked with other Continental writers, including PARACELSUS and della Porta, in his influence over contemporary philosophical and alchemical thought. He subscribed to the doctrine of correspondences, relationships between each part of the physical world, which in turn opened the way to belief in divinatory systems. A so-called *Fourth Book of Cornelius Agrippa* was translated in 1655 by Robert Turner and is held in the Sloane Collection in the British Museum. However, its authorship was questioned by various critics, including his pupil Johann Wier, and it has turned out to be fraudulent. Its content appears largely to be a regurgitation of the material contained in the Qabalistic (see QABALAH) magical manuscripts, the *Greater* and *Lesser Keys of Solomon*, including sections on extracting the names of entities, use of magical

apparatus, the precise mechanism for invoking an assortment of good and evil spirits and a concluding discourse on NECROMANCY.

ALCHEMIST A person practising the art of alchemy.

ALCHEMY The ancient mental discipline of strict ascetic control combining spirituality and chemistry through which, it was believed, the discovery of the 'philosopher's stone' or elixir of life could result. It was from this belief in spiritual sublimation that the *cause célèbre* of transmuting base metals into gold or silver arose. Alchemists pursued the formula for the elixir which it was believed, once discovered, would grant human immortality.

In the western world, alchemy derived from the ancient, second century Gnostic texts on metallurgy whilst, in the east, the alchemy of Chinese Taoism arose between the fifth and ninth centuries AD. Alchemy was practised by the Arab world in the ninth century and, in Christian Europe, reached its greatest popularity between 1400 and 1700 AD.

In England, during the Interregnum of 1649–1660, when many of the alchemical texts were published, the Puritans railed against alchemy as an activity allied with diabolism, arguing that attempts to meddle with nature played into the hands of the Devil. Many eminent scientists of the day, including R Boyle and Isaac Newton, were, however, committed to the quest. Modern interest was probably first rekindled by the psychologist C G Jung. Having been introduced by a colleague to Chinese alchemy, Jung made a detailed study of the subject and believed that he had come across an historical counterpart of his psychology of the unconscious. He published two works *Psychology and Religion* (1938) and *Paracelsica* (1942), which devote sections to the theme.

Alchemy continues to play a significant part in the magic arts and is practised widely in the Far East.

A priestess of the Order of Bards, Ovates and Druids celebrates the Spring Equinox.

A Wiccan altar showing the various artefacts assembled – crystal, pentagram, chalice and athame.

A selection of athames such as might be used to cast or consecrate a magic circle. The athame may also be used to direct or concentrate energy.

ALEUROMANCY An ancient practice of DIVINATION which began in Greece. Messages written on small pieces of paper were wrapped in flour-balls and offered as devices to tell fortunes. They form the origin of the modern fortune cookie.

ALEXANDRIANS WICCANS whose initiatory lines descend from Alex SANDERS. Divisions between Alexandrians and Gardnerians (see GARDNER, Gerald) are, in England, now largely blurred. Sanders began his Wiccan career in the area around Manchester, his group holding their coven meetings at Alderley Edge. Alexandrian COVEN practices differ from those of Gardnerian groups in several respects. The more usual three degree system of INITIATION, before the first grade of which no candidate may attend the circle, is sometimes replaced by the formal admission of novices through a neophyte ritual. These candidates may then attend rites as passive observers.

According to a biography by June Johns, at the height of its activity in 1965, membership of Alexandrian Wicca was claimed to involve more than 1600 members. However subsequent, more sober, investigation by other researchers suggests that there may have been a membership of no more than a few dozen contained within three covens.

ALMADEL A ritual device in the form of a wax talisman used in magic, inscribed with the names of divinities or spirits. It has been conventionally constructed of wax so that it can be melted down and the secret information it contains destroyed.

ALOMANCY An ancient practice of DIVINATION that relies on studying patterns of salt grains sprinkled on the floor. Allied with the superstitious practice of throwing salt over the left (sinistral) shoulder to ward off ill-luck.

ALPHA ET OMEGA (AO) An occult magical Order established in England in the early years of the twentieth century. After the effective collapse of

Golden Dawn (see HERMETIC ORDER OF THE GOLDEN DAWN) in 1903, some of its members, under the leadership of J W BRODIE-INNES and Moina MATHERS, the wife of S L MacGregor MATHERS, attempted to preserve the original concepts of the Outer Order while changing its name to Alpha et Omega. The effective demise of AO, together with the other significant splinter organization, the magically orientated STELLA MATUTINA, came when Francis Israel REGARDIE published the rituals and teachings of Golden Dawn. The AO regalia and other items were buried in the garden of a house on the south coast where they remained until the adjacent cliff collapsed in 1966. They were discovered on the beach below and were subsequently photographed to appear in an edition of the *Daily Telegraph* where they were described as having *probably belonged to a witch.*

AMEN-RA TEMPLE The Scottish lodge of the HERMETIC ORDER OF THE GOLDEN DAWN, located in Edinburgh, in which J W BRODIE-INNES rose to the position of chief until he was ejected by S L MacGregor MATHERS. In 1910 he attempted, unsuccessfully, to revitalize the lodge.

AMERICAN ORDER OF DRUIDS An organization chartered in May 1888 which held its first Council in July of that year under the Laws of the State of Massachusetts. It was founded by William Pearson and William A Dunn and opened its doors to members of both sexes.

AMORC See ANCIENT AND MYSTICAL ORDER ROSAE CRUCIS.

AMULET A protective device of ancient origin, usually in the form of a coloured stone or other natural object, often inscribed with runic symbols and designed to protect the wearer against ill-luck. This is distinct from a talisman which, by inference, offers some benefit to the wearer or owner. Popularist modern examples include the charm bracelet, four-leaf clover and rabbit's foot.

ANCIENT DRUID ORDER (ADO) A PAGAN philosophical organization founded in 1717 by John Toland (not, as has been suggested, by William Stukely). The Order originated in a climate of Deism, the existence of God perceived to rely solely on natural reason without reference to revelation, and in this it became associated with the Unitarian Church. It was influenced and moulded by elements of HERMETICISM and THEOSOPHY, and a number of other Druidic orders sprang up in its wake throughout Europe during the nineteenth century. At around the turn of the twentieth century it appears to have merged with the Ancient Order of Druids.

Although the roles in Druidry are predominantly male, aside from that of the Lady, the Spirit of the Earth, it eschews sexual discrimination and places high value on personal integrity.

It follows four seasonal rituals. The most significant, the Summer Solstice festival, is traditionally celebrated at STONEHENGE (recently the subject of restriction orders) and involves three rites following a theme of growth. At midnight on the eve of the Solstice a silent vigil takes place on a mound near the stones. The sunrise ritual on the longest day looks forward to the dawn of the Golden Age and is followed by a thanksgiving feast at noon. Two other, open public festivals are celebrated at the spring and autumn equinoxes. The fourth, that of the Winter Solstice, is held in private and is a time for reflection. Other less formal meetings are held on a regular basis and are chiefly devoted to training and guidance.

The best-known leader of ADO, who directed a successful campaign for the right to worship freely at Stonehenge, was George Watson McGregor Reid, elected in 1908.

The principles of the Order include an objective to further the evolution of mankind on the assumption that everything in the material world emanates from a spiritual source, symbolized by the sun from which descend three shafts of light, and to which the spirit eventually returns. Discovery of non-material levels, through magic and responsibly directed power, and how to act effectively upon these levels, is seen as the key to evolution. Members do not marry but cohabit.

From ADO and through the work of W B Crow, were derived The Druid Order and the British Order of the Universal Bond, or London Druid Group. A splinter faction split from the ADO in 1964; under Ross Nichols, it became the Order of BARDS, OVATES AND DRUIDS, following a path focusing on Celtic mythology and EARTH MYSTERIES. The ADO still exists and is based in London (see also DRUIDRY).

ANCIENT AND MYSTICAL ORDER ROSAE CRUCIS (AMORC) A modern American organization, based in San José, California, that claims Rosicrucian origins. It is an international Order that offers teaching to its members by correspondence course.

ANCIENT ORDER OF DRUIDS A non-religious order founded as a benevolent society in the 1780s by Henry Hurle, who is described as a working class Freemason. Today the AOD is an international organization and has generated various splinter groups.

ANGELICA (*Angelica archangelica*) One of the magical plants historically associated with witchcraft, its use probably originating in Norse traditions. A member of the Umbellifer, or parsley, family, it was said to be offered regularly by CUNNING PERSONS. In the fifteenth century, it was considered to be a beneficial herb in warding off evil spells in general and, specifically, Bubonic Plague.

ANIMISM One of the oldest forms of PAGAN religion, typical of pre-literate, nomadic and hunting tribes, incorporating the concept that all objects in nature possess souls and are controlled by spirit guardians. Animism predates the belief that individual personalities separate us, irreversibly, from the rest of the world and assumes that everything is part of a constantly veering and altering chain.

Every object, living or inanimate, is a link in the chain, but the links are fluid and can drift into one another. It is both possible and, at times, necessary for a human being to become a bird, an animal to become a rock, or a bird to metamorphose into a cloud. Moreover, a spirit-being can transmute into an object of daily life, or into another natural form. It can become a reindeer, a tree, a log of wood, a stone or even a cloud. Thus every object, at the whim of its spirit guardian, can take on another self. The SHAMAN and his or her ecstatic trance are central to animistic rites.

ANOINTING A practice among some WICCAN groups, utilizing an oil consisting of various ingredients, one recipe includes the crushed leaves of vervain and mint soaked in olive oil for twenty four hours, the oil then being strained to remove the leaves. This process is repeated several times, using fresh leaves, until the oil becomes strongly aromatic. The oil, smeared over the body, is claimed to be one of the esoteric recipes for keeping a SKYCLAD witch warm but, according to Culpeper's *Herbal* and others, vervain was a specific ingredient to protect against the plague. There is also suggestion that, in bygone times and during the periods of repression, a witch would mix the oil with soot and use the compound as a camouflage for the journey to and from a nocturnal COVEN meeting. One of the charges commonly levelled against witches was that they rendered themselves invisible at night.

AO See ALPHA ET OMEGA.

AOD See ANCIENT ORDER OF DRUIDS.

APULEIUS, LUCIUS The Roman writer who lived during the second century AD and who wrote *The Golden Ass*, arguably one of the earliest popular fictional accounts of witchcraft. It was first translated into English by William Adlington (1566) although the best known English translation is that of Robert GRAVES (1950). Apuleius was born into a wealthy family in Madaura in North Africa and was much-travelled. He was, allegedly, a priest of Isis. The main theme of *The Golden Ass* is the life and works of the mother goddess, DEMETER or Ceres, whose daughter Persephone (Proserpine) was lost to the underworld. It is this saga and its tone of invocation to Mother Nature from the depth of misery and spiritual desolation which has formed the basis of many of the Mystery Cults (see EARTH MYSTERIES) and on which many aspects of WITCHCRAFT, as a nature religion, and the modern WESTERN MYSTERIES are based.

AQUARIUS, AGE OF The coming 'New Age' of mankind, which will commence sometime in the next century, and which is the subject of much romantic idealism as a kind of anarchic world, without any kind of authoritarian or hierarchical structure, where men and women will work together and where science will be applied in a wholly benign and useful way. There is much emphasis on the conservation of, and respect for, the earth and the natural world, meditation, eating wholefoods and other vogues. The vehicle for much of this predictive enthusiasm is the cultural music and folk festival phenomenon.

The Age is depicted in the ZODIAC by a male figure bearing a water jar, and on the TAROT by a naked female figure dispensing the waters of life. Many feminists contend that this will be an age in which women will adopt a much greater influence in the affairs of humankind.

ARADIA (1) A chthonic or earth goddess of uncertain provenance invoked by modern witches and modelled on the Greek deity Persephone. The name is of Italian origin and probably derives either from the Greek mother goddess, Hera, or from Herodias, the apocryphal wife of the Biblical Herod (alternatively the daughter of DIANA), though it must be stated that its appearance is limited to the book of the same name by Charles LELAND (see ARADIA 2). The legend tells of an incestuous liaison between the goddess DIANA and the god Lucifer through which Aradia was conceived and was sent to earth to perform as the first witch. The legend stimulated a cult amongst the Italian peasants, or *pagani*, which was in direct conflict with the Christian establishment.

In Leland's *Gospel*, Aradia directs her followers to invoke the goddess Diana once in the month when the moon is full and that those participating should go naked, dance, sing and partake of a sacred meal after which they are to extinguish lights and enjoy themselves in love-making. These meetings became known as Esbats, from the French *esbattre*, to frolic. The Aradia text refers only to the monthly lunar meetings and omits mention of the four Great SABBATS.

ARADIA (2) *The Gospel of the Witches.* Allegedly a work on witchlore, derived from a variety of sources, collected and published by Charles G LELAND, the nineteenth-century occultist. He published the volume in 1899, claiming it to be based on an authentic medieval manuscript setting out the principles of ancient Italian witchcraft, *La Vecchia Religione*, a handwritten copy of which was supplied to him in 1897 by his folklore collector, MADDALENA, a young woman of Italian gypsy stock, who sent it to Leland from Colle, Val d'Elsa, near Siena in Tuscany. No original manuscript was submitted for inspection or provenancing, and it must be assumed that the exercise was probably a hoax, perpetrated either by Maddalena, or Leland, or both. Much of the content appears suspect and poorly researched and the material obtained from Maddalena is padded out with an assortment of loosely knit stories focusing on the worship of DIANA.

ARCANDAM One of the more widely dispensed handbooks of DIVINATION during the sixteenth and seventeenth centuries. Of French authorship and concerned with the teaching of personal destiny it was translated into English in 1562 by the Cambridge physic, William Warde, and was based on the classical Greek Spheres of Life and Death (generally attributed to Plato or Pythagoras). These involve a segmented circle inscribed with different destinies and calculations, utilizing numerical values of the letters of a person's name to select the appropriate section. The Arcandam was used widely by WIZARDS during the Elizabethan era and trial records indicate that the Arcandam formed the 'handbook' source of reference for a number of medieval witches.

ARTEFACTS Objects made by human workmanship, as distinct from natural objects, which may be fashioned and used for a variety of purposes.

ARTEMIS The Greek goddess upon whom the Roman deity DIANA was modelled. Although primarily a goddess of the hunt, in western Asia she was also recognized as a Mother Goddess. It was only later that she became syncretized, secondarily, with the moon goddess, Selene. Immensely popular up to and during the Christian period, much of her ethos was transferred to the Virgin Mary, both personalities enjoying major cult followings at Ephesus where Artemis was depicted as a strongly androgynous figure.

As an Asiatic goddess Artemis was often drawn winged and standing between wild animals, wearing boots and a pointed cap and carrying a torch.

In Greek tradition she was the daughter of Zeus and Leto and was honoured in a sanctuary on Delos which included a celebrated horn altar. Any suggestion of an hermaphrodite nature was firmly discounted. In pre-Homeric times she was seen as the mistress of the animals, a huntress carrying bow and arrows, but by the Homeric era her earlier ferocity had waned in favour of a more timid young maiden dominated by her stepmother, Hera.

In the *Odyssey*, however, she is drawn as the virgin goddess who chases and slays wild boar and deer in company with a band of unruly nymphs. She presides over nature and over the INITIATION rituals of young girls. She is also a goddess of blood sacrifice and, paradoxically, of birth. She is important to modern PAGANS as a protector of wild animals.

Many of these elements of her nature are appropriate to her modern position as the archetypal Goddess of WICCA and she is the favoured deity of the DIANIC Craft.

ASATRU A form of modern PAGANISM modelled loosely on the religious traditions of the Norse or pre-Christian Scandinavian cultures detailed in the *Poetic Edda* of the *Codex Regius* and other ancient manuscripts, and in the *Prose Edda* of Snorri Sturluson. The term means 'loyalty to the Gods of the AESIR' and the beliefs of Asatru are focused on the activities of the gods and goddesses of the twin races of the Aesir and VANIR, chief among whom is OTHIN, or Odin, who derives from Woden (the Wagnerian Wotan) in Germanic tradition who, in turn, gives his name to Wednesday.

The Aesir are engaged in a constant war of attrition with the forces of darkness and cold and their conflict resolves itself in a cataclysmic day of destruction, Ragnarok, when the earth is cleansed by fire and flood, and a new generation of gods and humanity, sheltered from the apocalypse by the Tree of Life, YGGDRASIL, replace the corruption of the old order.

Asatru is a growing religious movement both in northern Europe and, more recently, in north America. In Iceland it is accepted as an official state religion in parallel with Christianity. In keeping with its Norse origins it is more patriarchal than many comparable Pagan cults. Its priests are *gothi* and its priestesses SEIDKONAS or VOLVAS and it has traditionally celebrated three major festivals,

Siggiblot in the spring, a Harvest Festival in late summer, and Thorriblot to mark the Winter Solstice.

The conduct of Asatru is focused strongly on principles of loyalty, honour, courage and fellowship and its concerns include the healing arts and environmental issues.

ASATRU FREE ASSEMBLY (AFA) An American organization founded in 1971 by Stephen McNallen in Texas. Essentially patriarchal in nature it is, nevertheless, open to membership by both sexes. Following Norse PAGAN traditions, it publishes a quarterly journal, *The Runestone*, and holds an annual three day open-air festival, The Althing, as well as running a number of craft guilds with an essentially skill-sharing objective.

The AFA belief is one of an underlying all-pervading divine energy or essence, expressed as Gods and Goddesses, generally hidden from us because they surpass direct understanding but, nonetheless, interdependent with us, affecting and being affected by the human race. The organization celebrates the solstices and equinoxes and offers devotion on a daily basis. It tends to remain apart from the broader Pagan movement and has, at times, been criticized for having a racist bias. In recent years its popularity has waned in the face of advances by WICCA.

ASHCROFT-NOWICKI, DOLORES A prominent modern occultist born and based in Jersey, the Director of Studies for the Servants of the Light School of Occult Science, a training order in the WESTERN MYSTERIES, in which position she is the successor to W E Butler. Hitherto she has worked with Gareth KNIGHT and his Inner Circle of WESTERN MYSTERIES, but now favours an independent role.

ASHMOLE, ELIAS (1617-1692) The English astrologer and ALCHEMIST who wrote extensively on the magic arts and who gave his name to the

Ashmolean Museum in Oxford, which was founded to contain his collection, in 1683. During the latter part of the seventeenth century his astrological advice was sought by the great and famous, including Charles II. Most of his manuscripts, and those of contemporary fellow astrologers, including Forman (1552-1611), Napier (died 1634) who was also an Honorary Fellow of the Royal College of Physicians, Lilly (1602-1681), and Booker (1603-1667), are now housed in the Bodleian Library, Oxford.

ASTRAL PLANE An ancient concept that has been popularized by modern occultists. It defines the world of the supernatural from which emanate hidden energies. The universe represents a mighty scale of vibrations of which our physical plane is merely one. Its chief modern proponent was the nineteenth century theosophist, Helena BLAVATSKY. From it derives the notion that the physical human frame possesses an astral body which survives carnal death and which can, with proper discipline, visit the astral plane for brief periods during lifetime. It is popularly perceived as being divisible into seven sub-planes representing different states of being. Among the lowest are the regions of spiritual darkness populated by individuals whose souls are debased. The grades ascend to regions of beauty transcending the earth and known as SUMMERLAND.

ASTRUM ARGENTINUM (AA) (SILVER STAR) The esoteric magical Order of the occultist, Aleister CROWLEY, founded in 1907 in response to his alleged receipt, from a spirit being named Aiwass, of the text of the *Liber AL vel Legis*, a Book of Law in the ROSICRUCIAN mould which, he claimed, would form the blueprint for the establishment of a new religion to replace Christianity.

The Order was based on rituals and grade structures modified only nominally from those of the HERMETIC ORDER OF THE GOLDEN DAWN, and it incorporated both Inner and Outer Temples. The Order published a periodical, Equinox, from the spring of 1909 until the onset of World War I. It has been suggested that Crowley used his leadership of the British OTO, the MYSTERIA MYSTICA MAXIMA, as an entry point to Astrum Argentinum and as a means of substantial fee collection for the latter. The AA was effectively disbanded in 1914, although its members turned their attention to the ritualized grades of OTO until their headquarters were raided and stripped by the Metropolitan Police in 1916. According to Francis King the raid was in retribution for Crowley's pro-German activities in the USA. There are intimations that, today, AA is quiescent rather than defunct. Its activities and membership are kept closely guarded.

ASWYNN, FREYA (born 1951) A prominent authority on Norse magical tradition, born in Holland, the ninth of fourteen children, on the ninth day of November (the ninth month of the Latin calendar). Having spent much of a disturbed childhood in children's homes, she married at nineteen. Her husband, George, died two years later. Shortly afterwards she joined the Rosicrucian group, AMORC, and became a passive member of the Theosophical Society. She was initiated into Wicca in 1980 at the home of Alex Sanders by an American Gardnerian high priest and, in 1981, formed an English coven with her future second partner. In the spring of 1983 she became interested in runes and the northern cult of Odin (Woden).

She lived in London for many years, but is now based in rurual Britain, where she is a practising VOLVA, running courses in ASATRU and giving rune lectures.

ATHAME A ceremonial tool used in WICCA ritual. A black-handled, double-edged dagger or knife employed to draw or cast, and to consecrate, the nine-foot magic CIRCLE within which a PENTAGRAM may be laid and cosmic powers concentrated. It is regarded as the most important tool of a witch and is placed on the altar during a gathering of a COVEN.

The medieval magical text known as the Key of SOLOMON includes description of a magical knife identified as an *arthana*. During the ceremony the point of the athame is used to 'cast a circle', where it is used to trace a circle in a clockwise direction to create a sacred space apart from the outside world. It is also representative of the phallus in the rite of cakes and wine, when it is dipped ritually into the chalice to symbolize the sexual and divine union of male and female.

ATHELSTAN, LAWS OF Legislation passed by the Anglo-Saxon king Athelstan between 924 and 940 AD to include the following:

We have ordained respecting witchcrafts, and lyblacs and morthdaeds; if anyone should be thereby killed, and he could not deny it, that he be liable in his life. But if he will deny it, and at the threefold ordeal shall be guilty; that he be one hundred and twenty days in prison.

The law was the first in England to prescribe the death penalty for a person found guilty of acts of WITCHCRAFT that resulted in the death of another person.

ATLANTIS BOOKSHOP A focal point and meeting place for many English PAGANS and occultists as well as for like-minded overseas visitors. Situated in Museum Street in London, the bookshop was founded in 1922 by Michael Houghton, an occultist, publisher, author and poet. The basement was converted into a temple from where Houghton ran a private magical lodge, the Order of the Hidden Masters. Houghton also founded and ran the OCCULT Neptune Press from the bookshop premises, a publishing company that survives to the present day.

In their time, many well-known personalities from the occult scene, including Aleister CROWLEY, Gerald GARDNER, John HARGRAVE, Dion FORTUNE, Alex and Maxine SANDERS and Nigel Pennick, have frequented the Atlantis Bookshop. Ownership was transferred to the Collins family in 1962 and it was run for many years by Geraldine Collins Beskin. It

has been used as a set for a number of films.

In 1989, Atlantis Bookshop was taken over by the Psychic Press and, in recent years, it has played host to the FELLOWSHIP OF ISIS Conference and the Psychic Questing Conferences. In 1995 it was purchased from the Psychic Press by a Pagan.

Today both the bookshop and the press are managed by Caroline Wise, whose administrative role is extended in an advisory capacity to the media.

ATTIS, CULT OF Prominent in Rome from 204 BC, and derived from the cult of the Phrygian goddess Kybele (Cybele) and her consort son, Attis. It was also probably known to the Minoans and Mycenaeans and closely paralleled the rites of Adonis. At the time of its introduction to Rome, the legions were engaged in a war of attrition with Hannibal and it was suggested by oracles that, if the icon of the mother goddess in Phrygia was obtained from the sacred city of Pessinus, the war would be settled in Rome's favour. The icon, a jagged black stone, was collected and installed in the Temple of Victories on the Palatine Hill. The historical record shows that Hannibal's campaign was unsuccessful.

Attis was held in the tradition of the Mesopotamian dying and rising god and, while some stories attributed the cause of his death to the tusks of a wild boar, others had him castrate himself beneath the sacred tree of the goddess Kybele where he bled to death. His corpse was transfigured into a pine tree until the time of his resurrection.

Allegedly the Greek priests of Kybele copied Attis' death in a bizarre act of self-denial. Once emasculated, these devotees, the *galli*, wore women's clothes and trappings for the rest of their lives while each year in their rites they would draw fresh blood from their arms and offer it in continuing sacrifice.

The Romans honoured Attis' death on the Day of Blood, 22 March, beginning with the introduction of a decorated pine tree to the Temple of Kybele. Shortly afterwards, dressed in white, they ran through the streets gashing themselves with sharpened swords that had been placed strategically in scabbards by the roadside. They presented themselves thus before the blood-spattered altar of the goddess where they were joined by others who, as bystanders, had been driven to a frenzy by the sight of blood and had spontaneously castrated themselves.

Three days later, there ensued the Hilaria Festival preceded by an all-night vigil with candles, the event offering clear similarities with the Christian Good Friday and Easter rites. Attis and his cult are fundamental to an understanding of the Mysteries and the death and restoration of the natural world in PAGAN religions, which observe the seasons and their spiritual significance.

AUTUMN EQUINOX One of the four Lesser SABBATS, held between 20 and 21 September. In the United States it is often called Mabon. The festival celebrates the gathering and safe storage of the harvest and marks the end of a season which began at LAMMAS. The deity at the focus of worship is the HORNED GOD, CERNUNNOS, but in some traditions the festival is also an occasion to celebrate the descent of the GODDESS into the UNDERWORLD. This concept is modelled on the myth of the Greek goddess, Persephone, who is obliged to return annually to the UNDERWORLD of Hades to serve as his queen.

AVALON The mythical Isle of the Dead, the location of which is popularly placed at GLASTONBURY in Somerset. There is no archaeological or historical foundation for this claim and it remains in the realms of romantic fiction, as does its claim to be the resting place of King Arthur.

AVEBURY HENGE The Neolithic monument constructed from sarsen stones, in about 2600 BC, in the valley of the river Kennet in Wiltshire, England. The Henge is situated a little under a mile from the Silbury mound and a little further from the

West Kennet long barrow (both lying to the south) and about one and a half miles from the 'Sanctuary' in the south east, to which it is connected by a curving avenue of sarsens. To the southwest the 'Beckhampton Avenue' curves away from Avebury, passing by another long barrow. All are contemporary late Neolithic structures and their purpose would appear to be linked. It is difficult to perceive any of the structures possessing other than religious significance.

The stones from which Avebury was constructed are as big as, or bigger than, those of STONEHENGE but, unlike the latter, are not hewn, merely dragged from where they were found on the surface of the chalk and planted erect in the ground. Originally the outer Henge consisted of about 98 stones, enclosing nearly 30 acres, within which had been built two smaller stone circles.

Regarded in medieval times as a focus of heathen malpractice, a phase of destruction began as early as the fourteenth century and continued, intermittently, until the twentieth century when, in 1937, the Scottish industrialist Alexander Keiller set about restoring what was left of the monument by clearing the accumulated debris, and excavating and repositioning some of the buried or toppled sarsens. In the interim period many of the original sarsens had been broken up and utilized for building purposes in the modern village of Avebury which lies at the centre of the main circle.

It would seem possible that the Henge and its attendant curling avenues represent a giant symbolic womb and its uterine horns. It is also plausible that the two inner circles equate with the eyes of the GODDESS. Schematic and abstracted representations of a pregnant uterus and of the staring all-seeing eyes of the deity are not uncommon in Neolithic Europe, Britain and Ireland, and there is a body of opinion which supports the theory that they demonstrate aspects of the worship of a paramount, Neolithic goddess of fertility and fecundity, the apotheosis of the living earth, whose appeal was universal. Any further speculation amid the wealth of romantic and speculative theories about the purpose of Avebury must, however, be regarded as unsubstantiated since there is no conclusive evidence of prehistoric ritual or belief.

Today Avebury and Silbury attract considerable interest from PAGANS as focuses of belief and, unlike GLASTONBURY, are of recognizable archaeological antiquity as manmade structures which can reasonably claim ritual and religious purpose in some form or other.

BADB CATHA (RAVEN OF BATTLE) As one of three aspects of the Morrigna (MORRIGAN) in Irish Celtic mythology, Badb represents a terrifying goddess of war who appears to warriors as a raven or crow, the harbinger of disaster or death, inducing panic or weakness among enemies and revelling in the blood of battle.

Badb, disguised as a crow, perches on the shoulder of the ferocious Brown Bull of Cooley in the great saga of the *Cattle Raid of Cooley* and when she confronts the Ulster hero, Cu Chulainn, Badb is first depicted with red eyebrows, wearing a red cloak and driving a chariot until she unnerves him by transforming into a crow. Badb is now of relevance to WICCA and some aspects of modern DRUIDRY.

BAGAHI RUNE Words of unknown meaning recited in the GARDNERIAN and ALEXANDRIAN INITIATION into WICCA. According to some writers it is delivered before the candidate has entered the sacred CIRCLE. The rune is first known from a thirteenth-century manuscript attributed to a French troubadour, Rutebeuf. It was speculated by one researcher to have been written in Basque. In the Gardnerian BOOK OF SHADOWS, the rune is also employed during the SABBAT of SAMHAIN.

BAMBERG, HOUSE OF An infamous German torture house built during the Inquisition by Bishop Johann Georg II, where alleged witches and heretics were subjected to the rack, the thumbscrews, the strappado, scalding, whipping and other devices to elicit confessions about themselves and their associates.

BANSHEE See BEAN SIDHE.

BANYAK An oak branch which is integral to PAGAN tradition in the Balkans. It is cut from the tree on 24 December and burned before midnight. As the banyak is carried into the house, usually by the head of the family, other members throw grains of wheat over him and his wife runs around scattering straw and clucking like a hen. The children pretend to be small chicks. Walnuts and sugar are distributed around the house to protect it during the coming year and the straw is left unswept for three days.

BAPHOMET The deity which, by tradition, was secretly worshipped by the Knights Templars, whose chivalrous order fell into disgrace on charges of heresy during the fourteenth century. The romantic image of Baphomet was embellished by the nineteenth century German antiquarian, Josef von Hammer-Purgstall, in a publication entitled *Mysterium Baphometis Revelatum* which drew the deity as a bearded, androgynous figure. A similar image appears in the form of a carving in the church of St. Merri in France. Whether Baphomet is modelled on such ancient concepts as the androgynous image of Artemis of Ephesus is unclear.

Baphomet was adopted as the tutelary deity of the OCCULT organization founded by Aleister Crowley, *Ordo Templi Orientis* (OTO), and is represented during rites by the Grand Commander following a convention adopted by Crowley as first chief of the OTO.

The name is also ascribed to the androgynous, winged, Sabbatic Goat depicted sitting astride the world in the 1896 portrait created by Eliphas Levi who used the imagery of the Devil card in the TAROT pack to elaborate a mixture of traditional and modern occult symbolism into a demonic god. Details include a flaming torch located between the horns, a star above the eyes, the breasts of a woman, a reptilian belly surmounted by snakes and goat-like hoofs. Baphomet has been the object of veneration among several other occult and magical fraternities.

BARDS, OVATES AND DRUIDS, ORDER OF
A Druidic organization founded by Ross Nichols in 1964 as a breakaway movement from the ANCIENT DRUID ORDER and which itself gave rise to the GOLDEN SECTION ORDER founded by Colin Murray. OBOD is an Arthurian Druid group whose main interests lie in Celtic mythology and EARTH MYSTERIES and whose system is not dissimilar to some of those derived from the HERMETIC ORDER OF THE GOLDEN DAWN. Their tuition takes place largely through correspondence courses.

The Bardic elders, the FILIDHS OF OISIN, train their members in spiritual poetry and sacred ecology based on the Filidhic system, which involves alternating periods of immersion in the beauties of nature with deep meditation in total darkness, from which flows a chanted poetry of a uniquely Druidic type. The ultimate aim is the achievement of a dream-like vision in which the GODDESS herself appears.

BARJESUS Also known as Elymas, the so-called sorcerer or false prophet encountered by the Christian apostles, Paul and Barnabas, at Paphos (Acts13: 6-12). According to the Biblical narrative, Barjesus was cursed by Paul for attempting to corrupt their faith.

BARRETT, FRANCIS An English intellectual, MAGICIAN and ALCHEMIST who founded a school of ritual magic and alchemy in London in 1801 based on the teachings contained in his own publication,

The Magus. His book exerted a powerful influence on later nineteenth- and early twentieth-centuries occultists.

BEAN SIDHE A woman of the fairies, popularly known in England as the Banshee, who, by legend, attached herself to a family as a spirit and warned of impending death by letting out an eerie, piercing shriek or drawn-out wail. She would also appear at the outset of battle lamenting the inevitable slaughter. In appearance, the Bean Sidhe could vary from young and beautiful to malevolent and hideous.

BEGGAR'S CURSE A non-specific form of malediction uttered by the poor and destitute upon those who refused to give alms. It was widely believed that God was more likely to avenge the destitute, if called upon to do so, than those who were better off. The form of cursing usually intended that some physical or material misfortune should come upon the victim either in the form of ill-health or a blight on domestic animals and crops. Its reputation was upheld until the nineteenth century. Some of the old curses have persisted in the modern idiom, thus the utterance 'May God Blind Thee' became 'Gor Blimey'.

BEL A Celtic pastoral deity concerned with light, solar worship and healing who, in pre-Christian times, was recognized by both the Irish and Continental European Celts and is acknowledged by modern PAGANS. Also known as Bile in Ireland and as Belenus in the Romano-Celtic period, he is accounted in the *Books of Invasions* and the *Cycles of Kings* as well as by Roman writers, including Herodian and Ausonius, and on numerous votive inscriptions.

One of the oldest of the Celtic gods so far recognized, his festival, BELTANE (Beltene), has been celebrated throughout much of the Christian era. Belenus bears many similarities with the Greek Apollo as a god of light, sun and healing and he was often worshipped during the Romano-Celtic period as Apollo Belenus. In this guise he became associated with horses, which are well attested as sun symbols in the Celtic Bronze Age.

BELENUS See BEL.

BELLARMINE WARE Pottery vessels, typically embellished with a heavily hirsute face reminiscent of those displayed on Celtic art, manufactured in the Rhineland during the sixteenth and seventeenth centuries and often associated with WITCHCRAFT (see also WITCH-BOTTLES).

BELTANE One of the four Grand SABBATS. Celebrated on May Eve between 30 April and 1 May to mark the return of spring, it stems from an ancient Celtic Druidic fire festival and is also regarded as a fertility rite to ensure the fecundity of animals and crops during the coming seasons. It coincides with the obscure Christian festival of WALPURGISNACHT and is also given the names Rood Day and Rudemas.

In Europe, the occasion has long been associated with maypole dancing, the decorated pole offering phallic imagery and tracing back to the decorated Sacred Tree of Mesopotamian religions.

In WICCA, Beltane is the rite to celebrate the sexual union or marriage of the GODDESS and the God. According to some authors, the HORNED GOD, CERNUNNOS, accepts his paternal and marital responsibilities in respect of the Goddess (who is now bearing his progeny) and begins the transition, which is completed at midsummer, from the irresponsible hunter of the greenwood to husband and provider.

BENANDANTI A fertility cult based in Friuli, in northern Italy, during the fifteenth century which conducted rites to ensure the fecundity of crops during the coming season. An unusual society, it was outlawed by the INQUISITION which linked it with the SABBAT (see BISHOP'S CANON).

BENNETT, ALLAN (1872-1923) The second in command to S L MacGregor MATHERS in the HERMETIC ORDER OF THE GOLDEN DAWN, he became the mentor of Aleister CROWLEY when the two met in 1899. His occult name was Iehi Aour. For a time he lived with Crowley in London before moving to Ceylon for health reasons (he was asthmatic) where he took up an interest in Buddhism. In 1901 he was reunited with Crowley and the two rented a bungalow at Candy in Ceylon, at which time Bennett elected to become a Buddhist monk. After he and Crowley went their separate ways Bennett settled for the rest of his life in a monastery near Rangoon in Burma.

BERKELEY, WITCH OF Described in a manuscript attributed to William of Malmesbury in about 1142 AD as a woman who practised sorcery during her lifetime until one of her favourite FAMILIARS, a jackdaw, pronounced her imminent demise. She requested that her corpse be sewn into a stag skin and buried in a stone vault. Following her death legend has it that, after three nights of diabolical happenings around the church, the door was smashed down and she was called up from the vault to be carried away on a black horse.

BESANT, ANNIE (1847-1923) The social reformer who became head of the THEOSOPHICAL SOCIETY on the death of the co-founder, Col. H S OLCOTT, in 1907. She went on to join the Co-Masons when the organization arrived in Britain from France in 1902 and became the British national delegate, overseeing the affiliation to the Grand Orient of France in 1922. On her death, her daughter, Mabel Besant-Scott, became leader of British Co-Masons. Annie Besant was a prominent member of the Rosicrucian Fellowship of Crotona, an organization which Doreen VALIENTE implies may have been used as a cover for the activities of the SOUTHERN COVEN OF BRITISH WITCHES.

BESOM A broom constructed of a sheaf of straw,

birch twigs, or other suitable material bound with strips, usually of hazel, to a wooden ash haft. It is often used as a tool of WITCHCRAFT ceremonies, including SABBATS and ESBATS, to cleanse the sacred CIRCLE. By repute, it is the instrument of levitation by which medieval witches rode to the Sabbat. In reality the broom may have been straddled by a witch for various reasons including jumping up and down to instruct crops how high to grow. It is possible that the besom 'brush' was also deliberately applied to a pitchfork tip to disguise its function as a ritual stang.

BETH, RAE See HEDGEWITCH.

BETH-LUIS-NION (**BLN**) The Tree alphabet, allegedly of Celtic origins, described by Robert GRAVES in THE WHITE GODDESS and based on the writings of Roderick O'Flaherty in *Ogygia*. The alphabet consists of five vowels and thirteen consonants, each of which, as in the modern Irish alphabet, is given the name of a tree. Each tree was given mystical associations and was used as the basis of a runic alphabet intended to convey certain (unspecified) imagery. Thus the first letter B stands for Beth, the Irish name for Birch; the second letter L is Luis, the Rowan; N stands for Nion, the Ash, and so on. It is said to be a relic of Druid oral tradition when the hand was used as a kind of esoteric signalling apparatus (not unlike the modern deaf-and-dumb sign language). Today Beth-Luis-Nion is used almost exclusively for DIVINATION purposes.

BIBLE, ATTITUDE TO WITCHCRAFT IN THE Several significant references occur in the Authorized (King James) Version of the Old Testament.

Exodus 22.18: *Thou shalt not suffer a witch to live.* The single reference point which provided justification in the eyes of the Church for its policy of advocating the death penalty for those convicted of witchcraft.

Deuteronomy 18.10ff: *There shall not be found among you any one that maketh his son or his daughter to pass through the fire, or that useth divination, or an observer of times, or an enchanter, or a witch.*

Or a charmer, or a consulter with familiar spirits, or a wizard, or a necromancer.

For all that do these things are an abomination unto the Lord: and because of these abominations the Lord thy God doth drive them out from before thee.

Isaiah 47.12ff: *Stand now with thine enchantments and with the multitude of thy sorceries, wherein thou hast laboured from thy youth; if so be thou shalt be able to profit, if so be thou mayest prevail.*

Thou art wearied in the multitude of thy counsels. Let now the astrologers, the stargazers, the monthly prognosticators, stand up and save thee from these things that shall come upon thee.

Behold they shall be as stubble; the fire shall burn them; they shall not deliver themselves from the power of the flame: there shall not be a coal to warm at, nor fire to sit before it.

Arguably these are the key verses that persuaded the Church of the efficacy of burning witches and they explain something of the different punishments meted out on the Continent (where witches were sentenced by the ecclesiastical courts) and in the British Isles (where the sentences were delivered by civil courts).

BIGGHES A name sometimes applied to the ceremonial regalia worn by the High Priestess of a WICCA COVEN and including a crown adorned with crescent moon, a NECKLACE, a bracelet and a leather garter.

BILE See BEL.

BIRTH, CEREMONY AT In most modern PAGAN traditions there is no formal rite of passage in the sense of a Christian baptism for this most important moment since Paganism rejects the concept of original sin. There is frequently a naming ceremony in which the infant or child is offered to the

GODDESS AND GOD for their blessing and is anointed. At this time the parents make a vow to raise, protect and train the child diligently. There is, however, no commitment by proxy to a particular religious movement or path. This is considered to be wholly in the hands of the individual as he or she matures.

BISHOP'S CANON The *Canon Episcopi*, issued in about 900 AD and erroneously believed to date from the fourth century, effectively introduced the concept of the SABBAT. It claims that WITCHCRAFT is a product of the imagination in which women are seduced by the Devil into believing that they ride out, spiritually, under the cover of darkness in the service of the goddess DIANA, joining together in groups to perform occult activities. (See also WILD HUNT.)

BLACK ANNIS A fabled personality of uncertain origins, who is known from British folklore as Black Annis of Leicester. She may derive from the Irish Celtic goddess, Ana, who was worshipped as a bountiful deity and after whom the twin Kerry hills, the *Paps of Anu* are named. By contrast she also possessed, with BADB CATHA and Macha, a more malevolent personality. Alternatively, her name derives from Agnes which might, according to Robert GRAVES, place her with a Danish goddess, Yngona.

Legend has it that, supported by the character of the Blue Hag in Milton's *Paradise Lost*, that Black Annis consumed children and dried their skins on the boughs of an oak tree. She also became associated with a traditional hare chase originally on May Eve but later moved to Easter Monday.

BLACKFASTING A ritual fast practised mainly in pre-Reformation times in order to cause harm to another individual by making the victim waste away. The practice relied on abstainance from meat and dairy products in a period during which the witch concentrated his or her energies on the

malevolent act. One of the more celebrated cases was that of Mabel Brigge who, in 1538, was executed having been found guilty of blackfasting in order to secure the death of Henry VIII. The practice waned in popularity thereafter but was still evident as late as the mid-seventeenth century.

BLACK MASS A parody of the Roman Catholic Mass in which the Eucharistic host, stolen from a church, is desecrated or replaced by material such as turnip stained black. Other features include the recitation of the Lord's Prayer backwards. For a Black Mass to be performed correctly, GARDNER alleges that a defrocked Catholic priest should be present to perform a valid transubstantiation. The presence of such a person would be improbable today although, in earlier times, there is evidence that clergy were actively involved in aspects of both WITCHCRAFT and diabolism.

In France the Black Mass was reported for the first time in the reign of Louis XIV. In 1680 several priests, possibly as many as fifty or sixty, were charged in the CHAMBRE ARDENTE with the sacrifice and sexual abuse of children during so-called Black Masses.

According to unsubstantiated reports, the ceremony required the priest to perform the rite over the naked body of a girl spread across an altar. At the climax, he consecrated the host over her belly and then inserted a portion into her vagina before performing sexual intercourse with her and finally washing her genital organs with water from the chalice. The holy water was, allegedly, the urine of a goat sprinkled from a black aspergillum.

In his *Historie of Witchcraft*, Reginald SCOT observes that the Eucharistic 'host' took on tremendous OCCULT significance and partaking of it became less a means of communion with the risen Christ than a magical source of benefit. The Protestant view was particularly disparaging:

... with their carnall hands they teare his humane substance breaking it into small gobbets; and with their externall teeth chew his flesh and bones, contrarie to divine

or human nature, and contrarie to the prophesie which saith: There shall not a bone of him be broken. Finallie, in the end of their sacrifice (as they say) they eate him up rawe, and swallo downe into their guts everie member and parcell of him ...

The MALLEUS MALEFICARUM cites a number of cases of witches pilfering the Eucharist for personal misuse: *When a certain witch received the Body of our Lord, she suddenly lowered her head, as is the detestable habit of woman, placing her garment near her mouth, and taking the Body of the Lord out of her mouth, wrapped it in a handkerchief, and afterwards, at the suggestion of the Devil, placed it in a pot in which there was a toad, and hid it in the ground near her house by the storehouse, together with several other things by means of which she had to work her witchcraft.*

The desire, among practitioners of witchcraft and others to misappropriate the Sacrament became so strong that in 1215 AD, the Lateran Council decreed that the Eucharistic vessels, communion bread, holy oil and water should be locked away to prevent theft and use for magical purposes.

BLASTING ROD A generic term for any kind of wand, rod or stave carried by a witch. The term has origins in the account of Moses' rod in the Book of Exodus (17.5, 6):

And the Lord said unto Moses, Go on before the people and take with thee of the elders of Israel; and thy rod wherewith thou smotest the river, take in thine hand and go. Behold I will stand before thee there upon the rock in Horeb; and thou shalt smite the rock, and there shall come water out of it, that the people may drink. And Moses did so in the sight of the elders of Israel.

This device was one of the attributes which made Moses not only a political leader but also, in the minds of many, a powerful magician. The idea of a rod that possessed magical powers therefore persisted. It has effectively been constructed of any durable wood, although the most favoured types include ash, hazel, yew and blackthorn. In practice some of these may have been used for divining, some for stroking and curative purposes, and some

of the more robustly constructed for defence. The assocation of the blackthorn rod with witches was probably largely an invention of the Church since the colour of the bark gave it suitable, if erroneous, association with dark and evil goings-on.

BLAVATSKY, HELENA PETROVNA (1831-1891) A prominent Russian spiritualist and clairvoyant who, after parting company with the Spiritualist movement and with the assistance of Colonel H S OLCOTT, founded the THEOSOPHICAL SOCIETY in New York in 1875. Its principle aim was the promotion of Hindu philosophy. Thus she orchestrated one of the two main streams of occultism in nineteenth-century Europe, the other being the HERMETICISM of MacGregor MATHERS and GOLDEN DAWN. Blavatsky claimed to have travelled extensively in the Far East and to have acquired much of her knowledge of the occult arts in Tibet from deceased ancestral masters or Mahatmas. She is credited with having done much to bring the concepts of Hindu mystical thinking before western intellectuals. Her best known work, *Isis Unveiled* (1877), provides an amalgam of various Hindu, Buddhist, Qabalistic and Gnostic concepts. In 1879, after a spate of controversial allegations including those of fraudulent practice, she moved the headquarters of the Theosophical Society to the more congenial atmosphere of Bombay. It is alleged that Blavatsky first travelled to the Great Lakes of North America to find spiritual inspiration among the Huron Indians. When they elected not to initiate her into the secrets of their religion and made their escape having stolen her boots, she altered her loyalties and went to the Himalayas for enlightenment.

BLN See BETH-LUIS-NION.

BODIN, JEAN (1529-1596) A scholar, well versed in the Classics, law and philosophy, and the author of one of the most influential theses of the sixteenth century, published in Paris in 1580, supporting the belief in the existence of witches, *De la Démonomanie des Sorciers*. Bodin based the work largely on his personal experience as a judge who had presided over many Continental witch trials. He was vociferous in denigrating those who doubted the phenomenon of witchcraft and he was one of the first to submit a legal definition of a witch: *One who knowing God's law tries to bring about some act through an agreement with the Devil.* His contemporary, Reginald SCOT, was highly critical of his views. At the end of his life he fell victim to the plague.

BOOK OF SHADOWS The handbook of modern ALEXANDRIAN and GARDNERIAN WICCA. As a text it is traceable to a manuscript, *Ye Bok of Ye Art Magical*, of Gerald GARDNER, who originally claimed that it had been copied by generations of initiates. It was later demonstrated that the compilation had taken place in the late 1940s when Gardner made a crude attempt to phrase the text in a way which appeared archaic in its style, spelling and language.

It was first pointed out by Doreen VALIENTE that some of the material which Gardner claimed to be traditional had been derived, or directly borrowed, from Aleister CROWLEY's *Book of the Law* and from other Crowleyan sources, including his *Gnostic Mass*. Today there is little doubt that the manuscript had been compiled with borrowings from Crowley and additional material trawled from a variety of sources, including Classical mythology, Celtic fertility rites, ROSICRUCIANISM, Freemasonry, Rudyard Kipling and OCCULT sources, such as the Key of Solomon (see SOLOMON, KEY OF). In no instance can it be shown that Gardner's material pre-dates that of Crowley where the two published similar material.

Recently it has been shown that the quotations which Gardner copied from the *Book of the Law* were gained indirectly, suggesting that Gardner did not possess a personal copy of the text but gleaned the material from other publications in which extracts had been published.

The Book of Shadows was put into practice by

Gardner's original Wicca COVEN and its first version was published in 1959. A considerable number of revisions were made by Doreen VALIENTE, who deleted or reworked much of Crowley's contribution including a new version of the CHARGE based on LELAND's work ARADIA. Valiente has continued to defend the notion, however, that the work contains elements which cannot be traced to any of the above-mentioned sources and which may therefore reflect genuinely traditional elements.

The book is copied by hand by new initiates in Gardnerian and Alexandrian Wicca and its contents are treated as oath-bound – that is to say, not to be printed or repeated to those not in the Craft. Nowadays, with the proliferation of self-generated Wiccan covens, Gardnerians and Alexandrians tend to share *Book of Shadows* material only with others of this lineage. Newer traditions have assembled thier own material – spells, lore, etc. – and call these books *Book of Shadows* as well.

Sometimes the personal magical diary of a witch, compiled according to individual use and taste, is also called a *Book of Shadows*, though this is more frequent in the United States than in Britain, where the term is more commonly reserved for the traditional Gardnerian text.

These manuscripts were, and still are, carefully guarded by their owners as revered and protected possessions containing their individual magical store. Gardner quotes a traditional warning which he believes is a free translation of a caveat well known to Continental witches during the main period of persecution:

Keep a book in your own hand of write. Let brothers and sisters copy what they will but never let this book our of your hand, and never keep the writings of another, for if it be found in their hand of write they will be take and tortured. Each should guard his own writings and destroy them whenever danger threatens. Learn as much as you may by heart and when danger is part rewrite your book. For this reason if any die, destroy their book if they have not een able to do so, for if it be found, 'tis clear proof against them . . .

On the morning after the Sabbat of Beltane, traditional May Day celebrations mark the marriage of the Goddess and the God at the beginning of the time of fertility and plenty . . .

. . .The Horn of Plenty is passed around so that everyone may drink from it.

During the night of Beltane courting couples go out together to collect green branches, symbolic of the return of spring.

The Page of Wands, photographed during a Beltane celebration. This is a representation of the Tarot card meaning observance, ever on the lookout for opportunity or adversity.

Whether or not as a consequence of this witch law, very little historical material has been retained, with the result that most of what is known of medieval witchcraft comes from the records of the Assize Courts and their counterparts in Europe.

BRACELIN, JACK L An intimate friend of Gerald GARDNER and the author of his biography, *Gerald Gardner, Witch*, published in 1960 during Gardner's lifetime, although, according to Doreen VALIENTE, the book was ghost written by another friend of Gardner who was associated with the Octagon Press. Bracelin was regarded as being in favour of promoting WICCA through publicity, a policy which was resisted by other more conservative witches. He and his girlfriend were exposed to adverse publicity in a hostile article accompanied by an infamous photograph of a COVEN meeting which appeared in *The People* newspaper in October 1957 and which displayed the coven members seated naked around an altar in a house in Finchley. In later years he abandoned associations with the OCCULT, became a Baptist and died in obscurity during the 1980s.

BRIDE One of the names popularly applied to the mother goddess among British WICCA COVENS (see BRIGIT).

BRIGIT A Celtic MOTHER GODDESS worshipped in pre-Christian times in Continental Europe, Scotland and Ireland, who is also known as Bride, Brigid or Banfile, the latter meaning a poetess. Celtic tradition describes her as a *wise woman, the daughter of the Dagda*. She became Christianized as St Brigit of Kildare who lived, according to a popular tradition that has never been substantiated, from 450-523 AD and founded the first female Christian community in Ireland. In Irish mythology she became the mid-wife to the Virgin Mary.

The PAGAN festival at which Brigit is celebrated is that of IMBOLC (1 February), which coincides with the beginning of lactation in ewes and is regarded, in Scottish tradition, as the date on which the goddess deposes the blue-faced hag of winter, Cailleach Bheare (Bheur).

Brigit forms the basis of many place names in Ireland and Continental Europe, and is linked etymologically with the Sanskrit *Bhrati* which means 'exalted one'.

BRITISH DRUID ORDER An OCCULT group founded in 1977 and which is oriented towards PAGAN worship with the emphasis on the GODDESS (see also COUNCIL OF BRITISH DRUID ORDERS).

BROCKEN The highest of the mountains in the Hartz range in Germany and, by repute, a traditional rendezvous for witches. Also known as the Blocksberg, it was the site of an experiment in the 1930s by the paranormal investigator, Harry Price, who is claimed to have enacted a Black Magic ritual there, though with unspectacular results.

BRODIE-INNES, JOHN WILLIAM (1848-1923) An Edinburgh lawyer who became a prominent occultist and student of WITCHCRAFT at around the turn of the century. He was first initiated into Freemasonry and developed a strong interest in theosophy, becoming elected as President of the Scottish Lodge of the THEOSOPHICAL SOCIETY. In 1891 he was initiated into the OCCULT hermetic Order, GOLDEN DAWN, rising to the position of chief of the AMEN-RA TEMPLE until he was ejected by S L MacGregor MATHERS. In May 1902, however, after Mathers himself had been removed from office, Brodie-Innes was elected as one of a triumvirate, heading the Order on an annual tenure, the other leaders being Percy Bullock and R W FELKIN. In May 1903 he attempted to force through a change in the constitution which would effectively give him sole autocratic power to govern Golden Dawn for life. The ploy was foiled largely through the efforts of a fellow member, Arthur WAITE, and it set the seal for the demise of the Order later in the same year. Brodie-Innes was succeeded by a fellow Edinburgh occultist, William Peck.

For some time Brodie-Innes adopted a conciliatory approach towards the various splinters of Golden Dawn. He became a member of STELLA MATUTINA but also joined and became chief of the ISIS-URANIA Temple of ALPHA ET OMEGA in London, a move which brought inevitable charges of duplicity against him. In 1910 he made a short-lived attempt to revitalise the Amen-Ra Temple in Edinburgh.

BROOMSTICK The device by which a witch allegedly flies through the air. Its reputation is more in the realms of children's fairy tales than reality and, if witches ever carried broomsticks to COVEN meetings, it was more because such devices possessed phallic connotations and, incidentally, provided a useful defence against nocturnal persecutors.

The accusation that a witch could fly was seldom advanced and, in the English courts, there is only one record of claim that a broomstick was applied as the machinery of levitation. This occured in a trial in 1663.

The name derives from the use of bunches of twigs originally gathered from the broom shrub *(Cytisus)* and bound to the end of a shaft. Later, more durable materials such as oak were employed (see also BESOM).

BUCKLAND, RAYMOND & ROSEMARY The Wiccans principally active in extending the Craft (see WICCA) to the United States.

Ray Buckland was initiated in England in a GARDNERIAN line in the early 1960s but then emigrated to North America where he published his BOOK OF SHADOWS. This 'going public' brought him the opprobrium of many Craft members who disapproved of the break with Wicca law. He is the author of numerous 'do-it-youself' guides to Wicca.

BUDAPEST, ZSUZSANNA An influential American NEOPAGAN, writer and active feminist, the author of the *Holy Book of Women's Mysteries.* She ran an occult shop, The Feminist Wicca, at Venice near Los Angeles and later founded a Dianic coven (see DIANIC WITCHCRAFT) in Oakland, California.

CAN-CORO'MO A talismanic human figure, carved from wood and revered as a personal, or tribal, guardian by various north European tribes, particularly in Siberia, for example, the Yukaghir. Constructed from a flat board, approximately 1 m (3.3 ft) in length, and split along part of its length to represent legs, the neck is demarcated by a notch and the mouth by a deep scar, apart from which the image bears few recognizable features. The Can-coro'mo was typically erected in a tree where it hung overlooking a mountain path.

The Can-coro'mo is one of the few modern examples from a genuine tribal society of talismanic artefacts that are significant to PAGAN beliefs.

CANDLE MAGIC The use of candles, the colours of which are of importance for their magical significance in WICCA. The presence of spirits may be denoted by the flickering of a candle flame, and the naked flame, whether of a candle or a bonfire, is believed to emanate a spiritual force. There was an old idea that a candle flame burning blue was a sign of spirit presence and the practice of gazing into candle flames has sometimes been employed as a clairvoyant technique.

CANDLEMAS A feast day in the Christian calendar marking the Purification of the Virgin Mary and the presentation of the Christ child in the Temple, coinciding with one of the four Grand SABBATS celebrated on 1 or 2 February (see IMBOLC).

CANEWDON The village in Essex where the CUNNING MAN George PICKINGILL lived and which possesses a strong reputation for WITCHCRAFT extending back to at least the sixteenth century. The first case involving Canewdon witchcraft mentioned in the Lent Assizes Records (1580) is that of Rose Pye, who was arraigned on charges of causing the death of a year-old infant. She was later acquitted.

Suggestions that Canewdon, or any other East Anglian villages, can claim a continuous lineage of witch COVENS tracing back to the sixteenth century or earlier are, however, wholly unproven and implications by investigators such as Eric Maple, one of the foremost writers on witchcraft in the east of England during the 1960s, that witchcraft was rife in Canewdon in recent decades are not borne out by more recent research.

CARDELL, CHARLES The English psychologist who headed a WICCA COVEN in Surrey and who achieved notoriety when he published, independently, an exposé of the Gardnerian BOOK OF SHADOWS under the title *Rex Nemorensis*. Cardell employed an agent, Olive Green, whose witch name was Florannis and who managed to infiltrate Gerald GARDNER's circle of friends and was thus introduced to him. Gardner, it is alleged, became infatuated with her and initiated her into Wicca. In consequence she obtained details of many ritual and initiatory procedures which she passed on to Cardell for publication. At the time a number of Gardner's associates attempted to repudiate the idea that Cardell had published authentic material. Cardell's activities were, in turn, exposed by a reporter from the *London Evening News*.

CARROLL, PETER See CHAOS MAGIC and ILLUMINATES OF THANATEROS.

CASAUBON, ISAAC A seventeenth-century intellectual to whom the debunking of the spurious pre-Christian provenance of the Hermetic books is generally attributed; he was also active in the refutation of the so-called Merlin prophecies contained in GEOFFREY OF MONMOUTH's history of Arthurian England.

CASAUBON, MERIC An eccentric member of the Anglican clergy who, in the 1650s, became involved in psychical research and who refuted the claims of astrology while accepting that certain secrets of ALCHEMY had been learned through spiritual guidance.

CATHARS The heretical sect of Christians who were persecuted during the thirteenth century in southern France. They recognized two tiers of membership: the Perfect, who had accepted a life of abstinence, celibacy and poverty, and the lay Believers. Their persecution began on a major scale in 1208 following the assassination of a papal legate in Toulouse. This was claimed by the Catholic Church to be a Catharist conspiracy and a twenty-one-year crusade was launched against them, during which the populations of entire towns were slaughtered.

A limited number survived and fled to the Balkans, where in the fifteenth century they were absorbed into the Muslim faith.

CAULDRON A device connected with water symbolism during the Late Bronze Age and Iron Age in Europe, although its precise function is confused. The vessels vary considerably in size and some are massive. The largest discovered to date is the Bra Cauldron from Jutland which holds more than 600 litres.

In Irish and Welsh traditions the cauldron symbolized plenty, and that of the god Dagda possessed magical powers of rejuvenation and inspiration.

The cauldron was also a symbol of death during the Iron Age. The writer Strabo describes the practice of the Cimbrians whereby they slit the throats of prisoners over sacred cauldrons, while other commentators described the ritual drowning of victims in such vessels. Arguably the most famous cauldron is the solid silver Gundestrup Bowl, embellished with mythical scenes, which was unearthed from a peat bog in Jutland. It should be clear that these vessels bear no cultural relationship to the Viking Era which arose many hundreds of years later.

The cauldron may also symbolize the uterus and is employed in WICCA to represent the creative aspect of the GODDESS. Also known as the Cauldron of Regeneration, a ceremony described by GARDNER, is performed at YULE during which the Cauldron, containing spirit, is placed in the centre of the circle and its contents ignited. Leaves and other ingredients are added and the Priest and Priestess stand either side of the vessel leading a chant. The other COVEN members, bearing lighted torches, form the Circle and dance around the Cauldron *deosil* or clockwise. They may also leap across the Cauldron. The rite is followed by a feast.

CAULDRON, THE One of the foremost independent journals of PAGANISM in the British Isles, founded in 1976 by Michael Howard and published quarterly. The magazine covers aspects of Pagan Old Religion, Witchcraft, Folklore and Earth Mysteries.

CERIDWEN (CERRIDWEN) An aspect or avatar of the MOTHER GODDESS worshipped in WICCA and of Welsh Celtic origin, with ARADIA probably the most familiar name associated with the Goddess among British COVENS. Aradia is usually depicted as the HAG aspect of the Goddess. Described as the consort of Tegid Foel, her children are Creirwy (daughter) and Afagddu (son). In Celtic tradition she prepares the cauldron of knowledge from which the poet-to-be, Taliesin, inadvertently drinks.

CERNE A shortened version of the name CERNUNNOS applied to the HORNED GOD and providing the origin of various English place names, including Cerne Abbas in Dorset. Here an image of an ithyphallic deity, perhaps Cerne, is carved into a hillside adjacent to the village.

CERNUNNOS A Celtic deity known by name only from a single Gaulish altar inscription. Invoked from prehistoric times until circa 1000 AD in the area of Gaul now defined as central France, Cernunnos probably evolved from the worship of stags whose tree-like antlers were the embodiment of the spirits of the forest. Cernunnos may equate with the north British stag god, Cocidius.

Cernunnos, accompanied by a boar, seems to be depicted on the Cimbrian Gundestrup Bowl found in a Jutland peat bog. However, on a stone relief from Cirencester, England, a similar deity appears to be associated with snakes (symbols of rejuvenation) some of which bear rams' horns.

The worship of Cernunnos has been revived in modern WICCA. A fertility and chthonic deity, the so-called 'Horned God', he is believed to roam the forests as a huge, phantom stag. Typically drawn as a man bearing antlers and with the hoofs of a stag, he represents not so much an animal spirit as a deity closely involved with animals and one who can transform instantly into animal shape. His attendant beast is generally the boar revered in the Celtic world for its speed. Antlers were similarly regarded as symbols of fertility and virility.

In popular medieval folklore he became adulterated into such figures as ROBIN GOODFELLOW and Puck. As a principal male deity of Wicca, Cernunnos is regarded as the consort of the EARTH MOTHER and is depicted as a hirsute man bearing antlers and hoofs. He is perceived in a variety of aspects during the year.

CHAKRA One of the spiritual energy centres of the human body over which control is exercised by WITCHES and MAGICIANS. The concept has been borrowed from eastern mysticism (probably of Buddhist origin). There are considered to be seven major chakras, beginning at the base of the spine and ascending through the sacrum, solar plexus, heart, throat, third eye and crown of the head. Each chakra is associated, as is familiar in Buddhist religious concepts, with a colour and is perceived as a spinning orb of light with the group of seven following the arrangement of the spectrum. Energy is drawn into the body through the chakras, generally that at the base of the spine being 'opened' first.

CHALLENGE The moment at the beginning of an INITIATION ceremony into a WICCA circle when the candidate is met, at the gateway, by the point of the initiator's ATHAME or ritual sword whereupon the demand is made to know if the candidate possesses the courage to pass from the world of men into that of the Lords of the Outer Spaces (the challenge may vary from COVEN to coven). If the candidate accepts the challenge and rejects fear, he or she may pass through the gate and on towards symbolic rebirth as a Wiccan.

CHAMBRE ARDENTE A special investigatory court established in 1673 in France at the behest of Louis XIV following a report by certain Paris priests that they had received confessions of murder by poisoning in consequence of marital upsets among their congregations. Subsequent police investigation uncovered a poisoning ring and the king instituted the Chambre Ardente, so named because the courtroom was lined with black drapes and candlelit. Although people from all walks of life were indicted, generally only the poor suffered execution.

The investigations and trials were terminated in 1682 by order of the king who considered the court to have become excessively zealous in its application. The Chambre Ardente was, however, never claimed to sit in judgement of WITCHCRAFT in the true sense of the term.

CHANCTONBURY RING The prehistoric earthworks, consisting of a mound and ditch, sited at the crest of a hill on the South Downs near to the village of Chanctonbury in West Sussex. In Romano-Celtic times a temple was erected there and, in the eighteenth century, the Ring was planted with a grove of beech trees (now in a state of decline).

Locally known as 'Mother Goring' the Ring is said to be haunted by a phantom horse and rider and tradition also has it that to run around the Ring seven times at midnight will call up the Devil. In past times there was a tradition of climbing the Down on May Day morning to witness the sun rise. It has been favoured as a meeting place for local witches and is still used occasionally for COVEN meetings.

CHAOS The concept of a primordial void which existed before the formation of an orderly cosmos in the universe. Chaos was perceived by the pre-Homeric Greeks as a hermaphrodite principle which engendered of itself Nyx (night) and Erebos (darkness). This pair then formed an incestuous liaison to create the first elements of the cosmos, Aether (light) and Hemera (day). In an alternative scenario, Chaos was an offspring of the Titan, Kronos.

This concept is now of relevance to the modern occult discipline of CHAOS MAGIC.

CHAOS MAGIC A comparatively new and radical occult tradition which began, in England, in the late 1970s, the principles of which are claimed to run parallel with the scientific theories of Chaos.

Although the founding father of Chaos Magic is widely regarded to be Austin Osman SPARE, the fundamental principles were first published in 1978 by one if its foremost proponents Peter J Carroll, a magician and theoretical physicist, under the titles *Liber Null* and *Psychonaut,* although without reference to the term Chaos Magic.

These publications were closely followed by that of Ray Sherwin entitled *The Book of Results.* The authors, in conjunction with the mathematician, Charles Brewster, determined that Chaos theory held the most likely explanation of how magic actually works, a radical departure from the previously held notion of Results Magic, which argued that all magical acts should aim at producing a quantifiable result. Results Magic had originated in the climate of a growing concern that most Western Magical systems focused on meditation and celebration without any affective means of evaluation.

Chaos Magic incorporates the SIGIL magic of Spare coupled with the basic format of opening and closing circles, drawn from the German Fraternatis Saturnii, and embellishes these with fictional concepts. It supports few core principles, arguing against dogmatism and in favour of contradiction, implausible as well as plausible arguments and constant flexibility of personal position. Personal experience ranks high on the agenda and stress is laid on doing rather than theorising. In apparent contradiction to the above, rigorous self-assessment and analysis are encouraged. Chaos Magic is mainly practised by individuals or independent groups (see also ILLUMINATES OF THANATEROS).

The anthropologist T M Luhrmann observes that Chaos Magic *appeals to heavy metal motorcyclists without means.* It encourages an eclectic approach to magic and argues that one of the primary tasks of the aspiring magician is to detach from the established web of notions about self, society and the world at large. It goes on to extol the merits of altered states of consciousness. Among its more recent proponents are Phil Hine and Steve Wilson, both of whom have developed results-based systems of working Chaos Magic.

In 1987 a Symposium of Chaos Magic was held in Leeds, England and Chaos Magic now enjoys a home site on the Internet. Through the efforts of at least one of its adherents, the German Ralph Tegtmeier, it also has a following in Continental Europe. The notion of Chaos science was popularized through the character of Ian Malcolm in the film *Jurassic Park* and Chaos Magic now enjoys a following in North America.

CHARGE A term of specific significance in WICCA and defined as the delivery of commands from the GODDESS when she is drawn down into the High Priestess at the beginning of a ritual. The Goddess thus delivers her instructions to the coven through the materials agency of the High Priestess (see also CHARGE OF THE GODDESS).

CHARGE OF THE GODDESS A significant element of WICCA ritual that first appeared in the *Gardnerian Book of Shadows*, having been composed by Aleister CROWLEY. With GARDNER's approval it was reworked by Doreen VALIENTE based on words contained in Leland's work ARADIA. It was first published in verse form but was later revised into the prose version by which it is known today.

Vivianne CROWLEY describes a number of Charges including the Creation Charge, the Spring Goddess Charge, the Aradia Charge, the Mother of Mystery Charge and the Autumn Goddess Charge. The most important, however, is the Charge of the Great Mother recited at Initiation, which commences with the command, delivered through the high priest or priestess as her earthly presence, *Listen to the words of the Great Mother, who was of old also called amongst men Artemis, Astarte, Dione, Melusine, Aphrodite, Ceridwen, Diana, Arianrhod, Bride and by many other names.*

The Charge proper then follows, directing the means by which the worship of the Goddess shall be conducted, followed by an insight into that which she offers her worshippers. She summons them to understand the divinity within themselves, and finally she reveals the key to the relationship between Wicca and its Gods.

CHARMS Essential elements of ritual healing by wizards, magicians or CUNNING PERSONS, either applied alone or in conjunction with medicines.

Charms were frequently corruptions of Christian prayers, the old Latin prayers being much in demand since their meaning was largely unintelligible. Often the roots of charms can be traced back over many centuries from the medieval period, either to Classical Greek and Roman religion or to the Anglo-Saxon period.

When a cunning person visited a patient, a typical approach would be to pray to the Trinity for healing dispensation and then to instruct the patient to recite Paternosters, Ave Marias and the Credo during several consecutive nights.

One of the advantages of applying charms lay in the difficulty of establishing charges against the magician who would assert that he or she had merely been relying on the efficacy of Christian prayers.

Often the prayers were debased fragments. The celebrated seventeenth-century English magician, William Lilly, offered a simple cure for toothache: the sufferer was instructed to write three times on a scrap of paper: *Jesus Christ, for mercy's sake, take away this toothache.* The charm was then to be recited aloud and the paper burned.

Alternatively the charm might be written on a piece of paper and the sufferer would then be instructed to wear it on their person. Charms were also considered efficacious when delivered to an aggressor. A pig bitten by a mad dog could be immunized against resulting infection if it swallowed appropriate charms written on the surface of an apple.

On occasions the magician resorted to pure invention of words, which were incorporated into charms, with the assertion that they were of Hebrew or similar arcane origin.

Details of many of these charms have survived in personal notebooks of the period, including such established prayers as the *White Paternoster*. Most were never designed to be published because the cunning person relied on a high level of secrecy about sources.

CHICHESTER, ARTHUR See FRATERNITY OF THE INNER LIGHT.

CHORONZON CLUB See GREAT BROTHERHOOD OF GOD.

CHURCH OF APHRODITE An American PAGAN movement which represents the earliest of the so-called reconstructionist organizations intended to revitalize ancient religions and which was founded by Gleb Botkin, a Russian émigré and fiction writer, on Long Island in 1938.

Essentially monotheistic, it invoked the Venus de Medici, envisaged sex as a divine function and developed a system of clergy. Beginning with about fifty members, Botkin held services four times a week with the stated aim of seeking and developing love, beauty and harmony while suppressing ugliness and discord.

After Botkin's death in 1969, the Church of Aphrodite was continued by a former Baptist minister, W Holman Keith. As with many of the Pagan reconstructionist movements in America, the Church of Aphrodite has lost popularity in recent years in the face of an increasing interest in WICCA.

CHURCH OF THE ETERNAL SOURCE (CES) An American PAGAN movement, constituting an amalgamation of various autonomous movements, with a focus on Egyptian gods and their associated religion, each administrated by its own priesthood. It claims to be the reconstructed religion of ancient Egypt with ideals based on the power and artistry demonstrated by the Pharaonic culture. Its founder members included Don Harrison, a commercial artist, Jim Kemble, Elaine Amiro and Harold Moss, an engineer. It has traditionally run correspondence courses for its membership, with each individual worshipping before a private shrine. Never attracting a large congregation, its popularity has waned in recent years in the face of a growing interest in WICCA.

CHURCH OF SATAN The sect founded in San Francisco by Anton Szandor LA VEY. Several branches have existed, including the obscurely named Church of the Trapezoid.

The organization has little in common with Satanism or Black Magic and, during the 1960s and '70s, largely attracted hippies. It was treated with a certain contempt by genuine occultists and black magicians, who shunned it in favour of more affluent society.

CIRCLE, WITCHES' Also known as the Circle of Being, the 2.7 m (9 ft) circumference measured and cast with the ATHAME at a meeting of a COVEN, and which generally includes an altar. A Circle correctly constructed possesses two outer rings, each 2.4 cm (6 in) apart, so that the third circle has a diameter of 3.3 m (11 ft). A PENTAGRAM may then be cast within the circle, with the object being to gather and concentrate cosmic powers and thus to provide an interface between gods and mortals. The circle passes through four cardinal points each guarded by a spirit, the Lord of the Tower, who is invoked at the outset. Of the cardinal points, north is linked with earth, east with air, south with fire and west with water.

When the circle is drawn the GODDESS and/or God is invoked and the priestess 'draws down' the moon while at the same time taking on an altered state of consciousness and becoming the earthly presence of the deity.

The Circle is formed tangibly by the device of witches joining hands, starting in the east where the priest or priestess normally stands (though invocations are normally made towards the north).

A witch may pass freely in and out of the circle, though under proper discipline. This contrasts with a magician's circle which is drawn around him in order to protect him from powers outside its circumference. At the end of the meeting it is necessary to break the circle, effectively deconsecrating the place where it was made, and the guardian spirits must be thanked. The priestess cuts the periphery of the circle with her ATHAME. Since the circle may be raised and then deconsecrated at will, it may technically be made in a place which is not kept specifically for the purpose, either indoors or outdoors.

GARDNER favours the theory that the circle derives from the pre-Celtic interest in rings which the Bronze Age cultures erected in stone, most notably in southern England at STONEHENGE and AVEBURY but also in such far-flung regions as the Isle of Arran in the Firth of Clyde.

CLAVICLE A term denoting a manuscript or printed volume detailing the esoteric rituals and symbols of transcendental MAGIC. The word derives from the Latin *clavis* meaning a key and therefore an aid to solving problems or interpreting a cipher (see also SOLOMON, KEY OF).

CLOPHILL The Bedfordshire village where a much-publicized Black Mass took place in March 1963. An eighteenth-century tomb was desecrated and the bones it contained were reassembled in an ancient, ruined church. Evidence was left of a Celtic cross beside which took place the sacrifice of a cockerel. The report led to several copy-cat incidents and provoked an attempt to reintroduce statutory laws banning WITCHCRAFT in England.

CLUTTERBUCK, DOROTHY (died 1950) The daughter of a captain in the Indian Army 14th Sikhs, her married name was Fordham and she is said to have initiated Gerald GARDNER into her New Forest COVEN. A teacher of music and elocution, she was also closely involved with the Co-Masonic ROSICRUCIAN Theatre in Christchurch, Hampshire, which she had helped to found and where she and Gardner met. Her witch name was Daffo or Dafo. Little is known of her, although she was a lady of some material means whose upbringing was among the British Raj in India. Doreen VALIENTE, who met Gerald Gardner for the first time at her house in 1952, describes her as an

elegant, graceful lady with dark, wavy hair.

It is claimed that Clutterbuck used the Rosicrucian Theatre and the Rosicrucian Fellowship of Crotona as a cover for the activities of an inner circle devoted to witchcraft and it was into this circle, the SOUTHERN COVEN OF BRITISH WITCHES, that Gardner eventually gained admittance. Gardner referred to her in various publications but, for reasons which are not clear, the story arose that she was wholly fictitious and that Gardner had 'made her up'.

It was Dorothy Clutterbuck's sword, presumably obtained during her time with the Raj, that was donated to the Druids for their ceremonials because it was claimed to fit exactly into the Hele Stone at STONEHENGE. It was also the ritual of her coven that was published, albeit as fiction, in Gardner's book *High Magic's Aid*.

CLAVICLE OF SOLOMON See SOLOMON, KEY OF.

CoBDO See COUNCIL OF BRITISH DRUID ORDERS.

COCHRANE, ROBERT (died 1966) The founder, during the early 1960s of a significant style of witchcraft, distinct from that of Gardnerian WICCA (see GARDNER, Gerald).

He claimed to be an HEREDITARY WITCH descending from a Warwickshire COVEN through which he traced his ancestry back to 1724. He professed to have been initiated at the age of five and to have become a Magister (his self-styled title for the traditional male head of a coven) at twenty-eight. He worked in various forms of employment, including narrow boats and blacksmithing and, in the latter context, named his first coven the Clan of Tubal-Cain (by tradition the world's first smith).

According to Doreen VALIENTE, who was for a time a member of his Sussex-based coven, the evidence suggests that Cochrane was no better or worse than Gardner in his panache for deviousness and fabrication. Nonetheless he abhorred the Gardnerian Craft, believing himself the custodian of a more genuine tradition and, in 1965, he was the prime architect of a period of controversy when he and a colleague, who went under the pseudonym TALIESIN (an ex-Gardnerian living in the Home Counties), submitted articles for publication in *Pentagram*, the official organ of the Witchcraft Research Association. These challenged the conservative, or Gardnerian, view of the modern Craft and suggested that 'it must undergo some violent and radical changes'. The polemics continued in subsequent issues of *Pentagram*, arguably contributing to the eventual demise of the Witchcraft Association in 1965.

Like Gardner, Cochrane became more and more authoritarian as time went on and, following an infidelity with a coven member, was divorced by his wife. He became obsessively interested in hallucinogenic drugs, including those created from *Amanita muscaria* (Fly Agaric) and *Atropa belladonna* (Deadly Nightshade). He died at the Midsummer Solstice in 1966, and is said to have committed suicide through an overdose of narcotic herbs and barbituates.

Cochrane professed a mystical approach to the Craft through which his coven celebrated SABBATS and ESBATS, and employed the traditional ritual tools while eschewing the flagellation and nudity beloved by Gardner. Members assembled in black robes and preferred to meet discreetly out of doors rather than in buildings.

Before his death, Cochrane was in contact with several covens in the United States on which is views exerted a powerful influence and which led to the so-called '1724 Tradition', from which evolved ROEBUCK. Later a significant British group known as the REGENCY was founded by several of Cochrane's friends (see also Ron 'Chalky' WHITE) and covens bearing his name persist both in the UK and the USA.

COG See COVENANT OF THE GODDESS.

CO-MASONRY A movement, derived from Freemasonry, which allows for the membership of women, strictly forbidden under the organizational rules of the latter. Co-Masonry originated in France, its first British lodge opening in London in 1902. Annie BESANT, the former leader of the THEOSOPHICAL SOCIETY, became its head and in this capacity she was responsible for its affiliation, in 1922, to the Grand Orient of France.

After her death Annie Besant was succeeded as Co-Masonic leader by her daughter, Mabel Besant-Scott. Although it has been predominantly a sorority, among its more prominent members were Charles Richard Foster SEYMOUR and his High Priestess, Christine Hartley, both of whom joined in 1941.

Co-Masons follow similar principles and ideals to Freemasons. It is a secret society organized into lodges, membership of which is through initiation and elevation by degrees, and it offers a mixture of philosophy, religion and ritual, while its members organize or help each other in material matters.

COMMUNION The part of a COVEN meeting during which consecrated cakes and wine are eaten. The practice should not be regarded as a parody on the Christian Eucharist. It is claimed to have much older, pre-Christian origins and first stemmed from Mesopotamian culture where, in Sumeria, Assyria and Babylon, there existed traditions of baking cakes in honour of the Queen of Heaven, Inana/Ishtar.

CONE OF POWER The psychic shape in which the spiritual and essentially benevolent energy source raised during the meeting of a COVEN is formed through the combined willpower of its members. The cone is raised normally by individuals joining hands and dancing around the periphery of the circle. In a limited number of covens the raising of the Cone of Power is enhanced by the enactment of sexual intercourse.

Once raised, the cone may be utilized in a general sense, or it may be directed towards a specific purpose or individual.

CORD MAGIC A form of sympathetic magic applied by means of a knotted rope. Although it is thought to have been practised since prehistoric times, one of the first historical accounts of cord magic, dating from early in the eleventh century, is that of Burchard, Bishop of Worms, who details peasants placing knotted ropes in the branches of trees overlooking pathways in order to divert harmful influences away from themselves and their livestock. The technique of knotting cords could also be used to inflict harm upon others; in particular it was thought to produce impotence in faithless husbands. Its original sense and purpose is unclear.

In modern WICCA, cord magic is used widely and cords constitute a fundamental aspect of INITIATION ceremonies in GARDNERIAN WICCA.

CORN KING In WICCA, a seasonal harvest aspect of the HORNED GOD, CERNUNNOS, also sometimes referred to as JOHN BARLEYCORN. In bygone times his role was played by a mummer with tufts of corn sticking out from his clothing. His reign is short since he comes into his own at the time of the Midsummer Solstice but at the beginning of August, at LAMMAS or Lughnasadh which celebrates the harvest, he may, in some traditions, be sacrificed, cut down by the Goddess of Death wielding her sickle.

CORPUS HERMETICUM A compilation of magical writings said, by tradition, to originate on an emerald tablet rendered by the Egyptian god Thoth who, in Greco-Roman tradition became the so-called 'Hermes Trismegistus'. In reality the Corpus was probably assembled by intellectuals during the early Christian centuries. The work was translated into Latin by the Platonist writer Ficino during the seventeenth century Florentine Renaissance and became the basis of the Hermetic Tradition.

In about 1614, any claim of pre-Christian origins was disproved by Isaac Casaubon but, for many decades afterwards, the Corpus Hermeticum was held up by its adherents as having pre-Mosaic origins. One of the most notable and staunch English Hermeticists of the seventeenth century was Robert FLUDD (1574-1637).

With a strong emphasis on astrological and alchemical lore, the teachings of the Corpus claimed that, through the power of mystical regeneration, it is possible for humankind to regain the supremacy over nature that was lost at the time of the Biblical Fall.

The Hermetic tradition is still widely recognised and adopted by modern occultists practising sympathetic intellectual magic (see also HERMETICISM).

COUNCIL OF BRITISH DRUID ORDERS (CoBDO) Founded in 1988 and active as of 1996 in response to the difficulties which had been encountered at the STONEHENGE Summer Solstice ceremony that year, CoBDO includes fifteen orders of Druids in the UK. Other British organizations include the Order of BARDS, OVATES AND DRUIDS which claims a percentage of Christian membership; the London Druid Group, founded in 1986; the GLASTONBURY Order of Druids, in which the focus is the Glastonbury religious archaeological sites; and the DRUID CLAN OF DANA, which is an offshoot from the FELLOWSHIP OF ISIS, centred in Ireland.

In 1995 CoBDO acted as a lobby group to oppose the British Criminal Justice Act imposing a restriction zone around Stonehenge monument at the time of the Summer Solstice.

COUNTER-CHARM A device by means of which a person could gain redress or relief from the malevolent effects of WITCHCRAFT. A person could guard against future attack by an assortment of magical means including herbs, such as dill, rowan or vervain or manmade objects including horseshoes. These talismans or AMULETS were conventionally hung above the threshold of a dwelling.

Countermeasures could also involve direct action against the suspected witch, including burning the thatch on her roof or physically scratching her. Such measures possessed additional dangers for the accused since, if she then enquired what was going on, or asked after a victim's health, the action only served to confirm her guilt in the eyes of the law.

COVEN A working group of witches. In modern WICCA it has more technical implications as well, referring to a bonded group of Wiccan initiates. One joins a coven by being initiated into it or, if already initiated, by being formally adopted into it. Wiccans often make comparisons between the coven and a family – loyal to and supportive of fellow members through thick and thin.

The term, coined in Scotland circa 1500 AD, is a corruption of the Latin *coventus* meaning 'an assembly'. It may also be a further corruption of the French word *convent* referring to a religious community. Despite the assertions of the author Margaret MURRAY, there is no evidence in England that the word 'coven' was associated with witchcraft prior to the 1930s or that it involved anything more than a gathering of people. Witches' SABBATS would appear to have been effectively non-existent during the sixteenth and seventeenth centuries. Witches tended to be solitary individuals and if nocturnal gatherings did occur their participants were, according to Keith Thomas, more likely to have come together in barns and outhouses to steal milk from other men's cows. Court records from Elizabethan and Stuart England offer virtually no indication of even the most tenuous links with any earlier PAGAN tradition that may have involved ritual gatherings.

In England, the nearest word that appears in the literature is *conventicle*.

GARDNER wrote that a coven should be made up of thirteen people, ideally six men, six women and a leader. According to Doreen VALIENTE, while a coven should not include more than thirteen members, it may also consist of eight individuals constituting a more experienced circle concerned principally with fertility rites. Some authors note that, although the coven proper is limited to thirteen, six couples and a priest or priestess, or less, the overall group may be larger, and in the more general sense, a coven may be a group of witches of indeterminate number, headed by their priest or priestess or both. If it includes more than the optimum number it is customary for the thirteen to make the Sacred Circle and for any others to sit or stand around the outside of the thirteen.

The word coven was largely abandoned until it returned to favour with the modern Craft.

COVENANT OF THE GODDESS (COG) A North American organization constituting a loose association of PAGAN groups, comparable to the PAGAN FEDERATION in the United Kingdom. COG was founded in northern California in 1975 at the SUMMER SOLSTICE as an attempt to forge an alliance of various WICCAN groups. In California, it was incorporated as a religious organization on 31 October 1975, and is a legally registered church. Many of the by-laws of COG were formulated by the American Pagan writer and activist, Aidan KELLY, and its charter includes a respect for the essential anarchic nature of the Craft, declining to dictate belief, policy or practice. Its principles state an intent to *increase co-operation amongst witches, and to secure for witches and covens the legal protection enjoyed by members of other religions*. This need was voiced in response to increasing harassment and persecution of coven members.

CRAFT, THE see WICCA.

CROMLECH TEMPLE An extreme esoteric magical order thought to have been founded in Scotland between 1890 and 1910 as on offshoot of GOLDEN DAWN with a Zoroastrian slant to its essentially Masonic style of initiatory rituals. It was essentially Christian in concept but also subscribed to certain principles of Gnosticism which earned it a following among disaffected Anglo-Catholic clergy in the period after World War I. Allegedly, it forged links with the Hermetic magical organization, STELLA MATUTINA, and was largely concerned with initiatory ritual while being content to leave the teaching and practice of ritual MAGIC in the hands of Golden Dawn.

CRONE See HAG.

CROWLEY, ALEISTER (1875-1947) An influential and controversial occultist during the early part of the twentieth century who, in his adult life, believed himself to be a reincarnation of the French magician, Eliphas Levi. Born Edward Alexander Crowley at Leamington Spa, England, to parents who belonged to the extreme Christian sect of the Plymouth Brethren, he was educated in the strict regime of a Brethren School and later at Malvern College, during which time he suffered from recurrent bouts of ill-health and developed an aversion to the Christian faith. He entered Trinity College, Cambridge, but failed to graduate.

In January 1900, influenced by friends he had met while mountaineering in Switzerland (Julian Baker and George Jones), he was initiated into the Second Order of Golden Dawn in the Athahoor Temple of the ISIS-URANIA lodge where he took the magical pseudonym Frater Perdurabo and developed a strong respect for S L McGregor MATHERS. His INITIATION caused outrage among the Isis-Urania chiefs, the London Adepti, who regarded him as nearly insane and suspected him of homosexuality. In the following year it was, however, the second-in-command, Allan BENNETT, who evolved as his true mentor and magical tutor,

and the two came to share a flat in London. Through Bennett, Crowley gained an understanding of the QABALAH until Bennett's deteriorating health forced him to emigrate to Ceylon. At this time, Crowley purchased a property on the edge of Loch Ness, Boleskine House, and retreated there to concentrate on mastering ABRA-MELIN. In 1900 he travelled to Mexico and, while there, coupled with mountaineering expeditions and a burgeoning sexual appetite, he pursued an interest in ceremonial magic under the tutelage of Oscar Eckenstein. On returning to Scotland in 1903 he met and married Rose Kelly, the sister of Gerald Kelly, who bore him a daughter. During her pregnancy the couple visited Cairo where Crowley's interests extended to ancient Egyptian occultism. While there he allegedly received the words of the *Book of the Law* from a spiritual source and, in consequence, took on the mantle of *The Beast 666, Prophet of a New Aeon* (see also LIBER AL VEL LEGIS). He continued with his travels, visiting China where his daughter died of typhoid and Rose became an alcoholic. During these years he wrote prolifically.

Between 1909 and 1913 he was responsible for the publication of a celebrated OCCULT magazine, *The Equinox*, a facsimile set of which was reprinted in 1992 (Mandrake Press).

While travelling he became interested in the ORDO TEMPLI ORIENTIS (OTO), being initiated into the organization in 1912. He rose to become first the head of the British branch before succeeding the German founder, Karl Kellner, as president of the international order. OTO was proscribed by the Nazis in Germany in 1937 but, during the inter-war years, Crowley spent some time in Sicily where he established the so-called Abbey of Thelema before he was deported under the orders of Mussolini who disapproved of the continuing reports of orgies conducted under its roof.

In May 1946, Crowley initiated Gerald GARDNER into the ninth degree of the Ordo Templi Orientis and, since material attributable to him appears in WICCA texts, Crowley is considered to have influenced the formulation of some of Gerald Gardner's ideas. Suggestions that he compiled some of the original Gardnerian BOOK OF SHADOWS material are unsubstantiated though difficult to ignore. It seems clear that, at the end of Crowley's life, the two men either collaborated on the compilation, or that Gardner purchased or borrowed material from Crowley.

There are claims that, in 1899, while at Cambridge University, Crowley was initiated into one of the COVENS allegedly controlled by George PICKINGILL in East Anglia. Claims also persist that Bennett was a pupil of Pickingill and a group photograph, never published, is supposed to include Pickingill, Crowley and Bennett.

Crowley drifted steadily towards black witchcraft largely as a means of appeasing his sexual and drug-taking appetites and of achieving personal power. Allegedly he wore an aphrodisiac perfume created from ambergris, musk and civet extracts which made him irresistible to women. He branded his lovers with the sign of the Great Beast and wore a medallion around his neck proclaiming himself as the *Great Beast 666* (after the mythical creature referred to in the *Book of Revelation* which had fascinated him since childhood). He also sported a seven-headed 'demon stick' which was later acquired by the Witchcraft Museum of Cecil WILLIAMSON.

Among other literary output he wrote a treatise, *Magic in Theory and Practice*, and the celebrated, if excessively violent, *Hymn to Pan*. According to Williamson, who knew him personally, Crowley admitted that most of this was material trawled from the classics and was 'a big con' composed at a time when the ritual and secrecy of Freemasonry was in particular vogue. Williamson has also made an unsupported claim that Crowley and Gardner's association was not the celebrated friendship claimed by some observers and that Crowley obliged Gardner to pay for his tuition material about which the latter made disparaging claims. At one time Crowley purchased a property at Boleskine in Scotland where he believed that he could fulfill the demands of the Abra-Melin discipline but, apparently, the exercise failed and he sold up.

He spent the last two years of his life, addicted to heroin, in a private hotel, Netherwood, at Hastings where, according to Williamson, at a meeting that took place in 1945 or 1946, Gardner attempted to make amends with Crowley and where Gardner may have purchased his OTO Charter. Williamson claims that the animosity remained unresolved and that the meeting was no more than polite.

Crowley died at the age of 72, was cremated at Brighton and his ashes sent to Karl Germer, Crowley's successor as the head of OTO, from whom they were allegedly stolen or who mislaid them after burying them in the garden of his home. Crowley's Will stated that all the heads of the OTO were to meet at a dinner in London a year after his death to pay homage to his memory. However Germer was, effectively, the only Grand Master to attend.

Crowley's biographer and literary executor is the author John Symonds.

CROWLEY, VIVIANNE A PAGAN priestess and joint co-ordinator of the WICCA Study Group, Europe's largest Wiccan teaching organizaion. She was initiated into Wicca as a teenager in the early 1970s and trained in both the Gardnerian (see GARDNER, Gerald) and ALEXANDRIAN tradition. In 1979 she founded a Wiccan group working in both traditions. In 1988 she founded the Wicca Study Group and became involved in teaching Wicca in Europe and in organizing pan-European Wiccan gatherings. Since then she has been on the committee and Council of the PAGAN FEDERATION, serving as Honorary Secretary and Interfaith Co-ordinator.

She has a doctorate in psychology and trained in transpersonal counselling with the Centre for Transpersonal Psychology in London and as a

spiritual healer with the Spiritualist Association of
Great Britain. She has a private practice as a
therapist and healer, and also works as an academic
researcher. She is the author of a number of books
on Wicca and PAGANISM, including the best-selling
Wicca: The Old Religion in the New Millennium,
Principles of Paganism and *Phoenix from the Flame:*
Living as a Pagan in the Twenty-First Century. Her
current interests are developing a modern Pagan
spirituality and building understanding between
those of different faiths.

INTERVIEW WITH

VIVIANNE CROWLEY

✳

How has the Wicca Study Group evolved since 1988?

In 1988 few people were actively teaching the Craft in a public sense and if you wanted to join a coven it was really quite difficult to find a way in. Maybe you would read a book and think, OK I'm interested, but unless you lived somewhere with an occult shop or bookshop where the people are user friendly and you could ask them if there was anything going on in the area you didn't really know where to start. Also there's quite a big jump from reading a book to deciding, all right, I want to go for this. So we thought that if there was a group teaching open classes where people could come along, they could find out a bit more about it and actually meet the people involved. They could ask themselves, OK, am I comfortable here? Are these my sort of people? If so we would either take them on for training ourselves or suggest other groups.

We started the Wicca Study Group purely as an evening course in London and, at the same time, I started teaching in Germany because, before Alex Sanders died, he had been going over

there doing various seminars and workshops. When he died there was quite a void because although there were some older witches in Germany, in fact most people were fairly young and they weren't very experienced, they wanted guidance. Back in England we did the evening course for three years but got a lot of letters from people outside London saying, could we provide something for them? So we started doing Saturday workshops. And then the Norwegians wrote to some Wiccan friends of mine saying, 'We want to become involved. How can we start a group in Norway?' So my husband and I went to Norway, where we also met and initiated some Finns. In addition we initiated some people in France so I suppose our focus has always been fairly European.

When you talk about teaching it implies that you want to set a standard, some kind of benchmark that people can follow?

In the Wicca Study Group what we are doing is teaching the basic philosophy, giving people an idea of ritual, a simple, modified Wiccan ritual, because most haven't done any ritual and don't have

The Cone of Power: energy is invoked and concentrated during a meeting by the members of a coven dancing round in a circle until the energy builds to a peak.

Two versions of casting the circle in which cosmic powers are concentrated and from within which the Goddess is invoked. The priestess 'draws down' energies and becomes the earthly presence of the Goddess.

the confidence of knowing what it's about. We talk about why we need ritual, what the basic steps are in creating a ritual, because although Wiccan traditions vary we can provide a template. It also gives people a chance to decide if they want to get involved with groups or whether they want to work alone. Others have to ask, am I that ritualistic or do I want to be a more meditative Pagan? So it's to give people a feeling of what Wicca is about rather than to train them to a standard. That's something that will come later, after initiation.

You seem to have a very hands-on approach but there is an argument that Wicca is moving more towards worship of archetypes and less towards getting things done, like trance training and spiritualism. Is that right?
I suppose if you have a dimension which says religious-spiritual on one end and magical on the other, the different traditions will put themselves at different points within that dimension and that's something which we have to get across in the public teaching, where we stand, because people can get expectations that are quite different. A lot of people are looking to learn magical techniques, a lot are interested in something that is a religion as well. Some come in wanting a Goddess-based religion and are not particularly interested in results magic. A third dimension is what I would call inner transformation, personal change, growth.

And where do you stand in the dimension?
Personally I am more interested in worshipping the gods and in the change and growth of individuals than in traditional spellcraft. I suppose that, because I am a psychologist, one of the things about Wicca that interests me is that it produces better human beings. People evolve and grow, become more creative, more integrated individuals by practising Wicca.

Is it true that nobody really knows what Gardnerian Wicca is these days?
In Britain in recent years there's been a lot of fusion between Gardnerian and Alexandrian traditions, a lot of cross-fertilization. Chris [my husband] and I are initiated in both traditions and so everybody we initiate belongs to both traditions. There are differences still but many people say they are members of both traditions.

What sort of religion were you brought up with as a child?
I wasn't taught any religion. Theoretically my mother was a High Church Anglican and my father was a Catholic. Of the two my mother was more religious but I didn't actually practise any religion until I was about nine. I practised what I would call natural religion. I used to make altars and little circles of stone. I was always making altars in the woods! And I had sacred objects I used to keep on my altars. I also used to do spells. Then,

when I was about nine, I discovered there were Catholics at my school, Italian girls, and if you were Catholic you didn't have to go to Scripture lessons. I thought this would be a big improvement in my life, I found, in fact, that I was nominally a Catholic. I asked my mother and I discovered I had been christened in a Catholic church. So I actually started going to Mass with the Catholic girls at a monastery which had rather beautiful Gregorian chants and I took up actively practising Catholicism for about five years until I was fourteen. When I was doing that I stopped practising magic. It didn't go down very well with the Catholics.

You infer that Catholicism doesn't approve of magic but there is an argument that becoming a Roman Catholic actually makes it much easier to become a Pagan. There is an awful lot of things in common. There's Mother Goddess worship, magic, emphasis on ritual rather than creed. Did that help to make the bridge towards Paganism?
It helped more than joining a very non-conformist, Protestant-type religion. But there are also some things that are very opposed to Wicca. You have to question the Catholic concept of there being only 'one way'. You have the divine feminine there to a certain extent but I find it a bit side-lined. It's there but not quite in the place you want to put it. Whereas in Britain there are a lot of ex-Catholics who are witches, in Germany, for

instance, it's been more the northern Protestant part where the Craft has grown and, if you look at the States, an awful lot of Jewish people join. There are a lot of strong Jewish women in the Craft in the States.

Can you worship the Goddess and the God without believing in their existence. In other words as the apotheosis of the Priestess and Priest?
That's not quite as I see it. I see the divine as the essential force that is present in the Universe, present around us in the world, transcendent, and our human minds, in order to understand, have to create some kind of image so the gods are, if you like, our symbols for communicating with the divine and we would say that the divine is multi-faceted.

Who were the main influences to bring you into the Craft?
What really brought me into these realms was the fact that I had started having psychic experiences as a child. I had out-of-body experiences, clairvoyant dreams and I also had a feeling that I had some kind of inner power that could make things happen, which is why I started experimenting with spellcraft. I used to round up the children to do rain dancing if they didn't want to play games! I found it very effective actually. The first serious book about witchcraft that I read would have been Margaret Murray's *Witch Cult in Western Europe*. Then I saw Alex and

Maxine on television. These two people came on the Simon Dee show and said, 'We're witches and witchcraft is a nature religion and we worship the Goddess and the God' and I thought, 'If that's what they believe then I'm one of them!' Although I had read Margaret Murray's book, I had no idea that anything like that existed and suddenly there were people saying, yes, this still exists. I suppose the problem for me with Catholicism was that a lot of my ideas about the divine actually didn't fit. I couldn't cope with the idea that Christianity was the only religious approach. I had become interested in Buddhism and I thought that hundreds of millions of Buddhists can't all be wrong. So I started thinking about why are there all these different religions, different paths, all saying that they are the right and only way. Obviously the different approaches must be equally valid in their own way so I wanted to look at the different approaches and see which one best suited me. What best suited me was Wicca.

How do you class yourself in terms of religious belief? Are you a duotheist?
Technically I'm a panentheist, where you see the divine as both immanent and transcendent.

How do you see children fitting in to the Craft? Because some are opposed to it. They say it's essentially a priesthood.

Most of my Wiccan friends who have children will bring them up not as witches but as Pagans, to do simple day-time family rituals to celebrate the seasonal festivals. Perhaps that's why Jewish women in the States feel very comfortable with Paganism and Wicca because it's very home-based, it's a very simple, natural thing. It's a very nice way of bringing children up. Witches almost invariably say to their children there are many different religions and what mummy and daddy do, the outside world mainly doesn't. So witch children have to become comparative religion experts fairly early on because the dominant religion practised in the outside world is not the one practised at home. There has been a lot of debate over what you do about school. You cannot stop children talking about things. 'What did you do over the weekend?' 'Well, mummy and daddy's coven came round and they all danced round the cauldron while I had to go to bed.' You can imagine the reaction at school. It's much easier to say, 'We practise Wicca, it's a Pagan religion, this is what we do, this is what we don't do.' It's much safer than firing people's imaginations with lurid ideas. So most Wiccan parents that I know are quite open about their religion.

Do you think that the behaviour of some of the 'Founding Fathers' of Wicca provides ammunition for your detractors? Should you make a clean sweep?

I think you have to distinguish between the messenger and the message. I think one of the reasons why everything those people taught and did hasn't been discarded is that the system works! They helped develop something which is very effective as a spiritual system and which continues to evolve.

But things have changed very radically, haven't they? You've gone from a group of dominant male priests and their female acolytes to a very women's-orientated organization.

That's not true. The men were writing books but that doesn't necessarily mean that they were the main people working together, teaching it. They were more the public voice which is the way men often operate anyway. The Craft has always been led by women but I'm quite concerned that it doesn't become too female led. I think there is a danger of it becoming a feminist women's religion, and it's much more than that. Basically the Craft is a Pagan mystery religion and it's applicable both to men and to women. In Britain more men than women were involved but now the numbers of men and women have evened up.

Is Paganism an anarchistic thing and, if so, can it survive?

I don't think Wicca is anarchistic, and I make a distinction here between Wicca and more general Paganism. There are a lot of people who are Pagans and are very anarchistic and are not the sort who join groups. Wicca has a group structure and to feel comfortable in Wicca you've got to feel comfortable with teamwork in a group situation. So people who don't feel comfortable with that will tend to drift out. People who tend to be the active organizers in the Pagan Federation tend to come from certain parts of the Pagan community, and they tend to be the more organized parts, such as the Druid groups or the Wiccan groups. Perhaps people who are more solitary tend not to want to join something that is more structured and a coven possesses a structure. Even if it's a peer-group coven it still has a structure. Most Wiccans tend to be articulate people with jobs who are part of mainstream society. They may question a lot of its values but they are not living in a tepee.

You come from an academic discipline. What do you think about the blatant historical inaccuracies that appear in certain Pagan magazines. Is it not doing the Craft a disfavour?

It is, but it's changing. There are now a lot of academics who have become Wiccans and there are academic conferences about Paganism. The body of knowledge about Paganism is going through a period of very rapid growth and there is a lot of research being done by Pagan and non-Pagan academics. We're going through a sea-change. I think a lot of people felt quite uncomfortable about it, particularly in the '80s. When academics first started saying things like, 'Well, Margaret Murray is not widely accepted in academic circles, you know', people were quite shocked. They might have seen Margaret Murray's thesis as representing the absolute truth and they had to go through the process of having a lot of ideas dismissed. Now people are very hungry for historical fact.

Do you think that as Paganism becomes more popular and more widespread, the Pagan Federation is going to have to step up its PR campaign? Because there is still this public perception of a link between the Craft and Satanism.
Well, the media response to, for example, Hallowe'en was very different this year. There is a perception that is growing in some parts of the general public that the Craft isn't about Satanism. There is a thing called Paganism. It may be whacky but it's essentially harmless. So public perception is changing and as that gradually changes so the credibility of other viewpoints is going to be dented. It already has been. People are much more aware of what is going on.

A personal question. How do you see your future when your mortal existence ends?
I do believe in life outside the body and people do reincarnate but they don't necessarily have to reincarnate. They may go into the otherworld and then move on. But I actually think religion is about living. It's about changing people now. I think we are perhaps too concerned about what happens in the afterlife. What is important is what happens to us and our planet now.

CROWTHER, ARNOLD Magician and artist, the husband of Patricia Crowther who claimed that he was responsible for making the introduction between Gerald GARDNER and Aleister CROWLEY in Hastings in 1946. One of the press photographs of the infamous 'raid' on Alex SANDERS' COVEN at Alderley Edge, Cheshire, in September 1962, shows a celebrated painting of the moon goddess by Arnold Crowther being used as a backdrop to the rites.

CROWTHER, PATRICIA A well-known English witch of GARDNERIAN lineage who published a number of books on the Craft. The wife of Arnold CROWTHER, she was the High Priestess of a Sheffield COVEN in the 1960s and was indirectly responsible for the INITIATION of Alex SANDERS through an ex-member of her coven who had gone on to found a separate group. Patricia Crowther always strongly refuted claims that she had herself initiated Sanders, although she confirmed that he had approached her on the matter. It was the testimony of Pat Crowther that was largely responsible for the exposure of the myth that Sanders was initiated as a child by his Welsh grandmother.

She claimed in her book *Lid off the Cauldron* that her husband had introduced Gerald Gardner to Aleister CROWLEY.

CRYSTAL MAGIC See SCRYING.

CUCKING STOOL The probable origin of the Ducking Stool, the term Cucking Stool derives from the word cuckold and it was so-named because, during the thirteenth century, it provided a draconian form of punishment for social deviants in a village community who were accused by their neighbours of adultery. The victim was tied to the stool and subjected to immersion in the village pond. Later, under the English Tudors, the device was applied increasingly in the punishment of 'scolds', those women who by their sharp tongues sowed discord in the community. Because of the popular notion of close links between scolding and witchcraft, there developed a logical progression to the ducking stools used to torture confessions from alleged witches in Elizabethan and Stuart times. The cucking stool was, however, never used to punish witches.

CULT OF THE HORSE MAN'S WORD See SOCIETY OF THE HORSEMEN'S WORD.

CUNNING PERSON A term which, during the medieval period, was largely synonymous with WIZARD, MAGICIAN or white witch and which distinguished someone from a maleficent witch. These were local people, often men, who engaged in healing through magic arts and who claimed to be able to counteract the magic and spells cast by witches (see also HEXENBANNER). Theirs was essentially a popular magic which operated in the face of a medical profession of limited ability, whose services were costly and whose practitioners were few and far between. Cunning men learned their arts from their mothers and fathers who handed them traditions claimed to have been in existence for centuries. Inevitably they applied themselves more to those complaints which would respond to herbal treatment and to problems which would clear up naturally in the course of time, including fevers, earache and open wounds, rather than the fatal diseases, such as smallpox or the plague. They also dispensed herbal remedies, many of which were genuinely curative, although many served as psychosomatic remedies with little other medicinal value. The skills of cunning men could also be applied to such diverse needs as finding lost property and detecting thieves.

Through the use of DIVINATION, counterspells, mirrors and other devices, the cunning man would, usually for a fee, be able to identify a felon, put a *hex* on a witch and her spells or provide the means to identify a witch against whom a charge might then be levied. Often the discovery of a culprit was achieved less by elimination than intimidation since ordinary people had a strong belief that the village wizard possessed supernatural powers.

WITCHCRAFT was a convenient defence if a cunning man's remedy for sickness did not work since the failure could be attributed to a person being 'overlooked' or 'forspoken' in which case it was arguable that the disease was not a natural one.

Astrologers such as John DEE, the court magician to Elizabeth I, were also regarded as cunning men. At the height of the WITCH-CRAZE, cunning persons were themselves at risk of being branded witches.

In modern times George PICKINGILL and Cunning Murrell are amongst the most celebrated practitioners of the art.

CUNNINGHAM, SCOTT A prominent American SOLO WITCH whose writings have had a powerful influence on other solitary practitioners. See also HEDGEWITCH.

DANCE One of the devices of PAGAN ritual adopted since prehistoric times to invoke the spirit world. In WICCA it is one of the so-called eight-fold paths, designed to raise supernatural power or to release the latent powers within the human body. One very famous Wiccan dance is the Spiral Dance. The term spiral describes the circular and upward movement of the CONE OF POWER created by the action of the dance which is conducted with alternate male and female dancers joining hands and progressing in a single or, less frequently, double ring. When a large circle is cast, the dancers may move gradually towards the centre, emphasizing the spiral nature of the ritual.

DARK GODDESS The HAG or Crone aspect or avatar of the triple goddess, associated with the UNDERWORLD, wisdom, death and transformation.

To the Celts in Ireland, for whom all three aspects took on great significance, the hag was known as Cailleach Bheare. In Ireland the quality of life was measured by the good health of humankind and animals, by success in battle and by the fecundity of herds. An analogy was drawn between the physical fitness and suitability of the Sacred King and the health of national affairs. This determined the way that the Dark Goddess was

represented. Her fruitfulness was believed to be dependent on the virility of her mortal partner who was chosen by the gods to take the Irish crown and be her mate. Thus as his physical human decay made its first appearance, or battle scars emerged, or crops failed, the beautiful goddess queen Medb or Maeve, having already transformed from Maiden to Mother, became symbolically transposed to her third aspect, the Hag, the symbol for the man to begin his lonely walk towards abdication or slaughter.

The Hag could then renew the cycle of life, often playing her casting hand for a new partner while still retaining her aged guise. In one legend a prince and his brothers have a chance meeting with this decrepit and repulsive form, whereupon she requests sexual intercourse with each man. Only one does not decline and, as their coupling commences, Cailleach Beare sheds her hideous mantle and reveals herself as the beautiful Maiden, the 'Sovereignty of Ireland' (see also HEKATE).

In British WICCA the Dark Goddess, or Queen of Death, features heavily in the Autumn Sabbats. According to some traditions she appears at the beginning of August to slay the CORN KING at the LAMMAS celebration prior to her descent into the Underworld at the AUTUMN EQUINOX.

DARRELL, SIR JOHN (died 1694) One of the most notorious English exorcists of the seventeenth century. A staunch Puritan, he effected a series of spectacular cures on possessed persons by means of fasting and prayer. However, his claims were subsequently proved fraudulent.

DASHWOOD, SIR FRANCIS Chancellor of the Exchequer between 1762 and 1763 and founder of the secret society called the Friars of St Francis of Wycombe, better known as the HELLFIRE CLUB. Having been initiated into a Masonic Lodge in Florence in 1738, he returned to England in the following year and founded the Society of Dilettanti whose membership included hard-drinking and wealthy young men. In 1751 he purchased Medmenham Abbey at Marlow in Buckinghamshire and converted it into a Gothic-style folly before establishing it as a cult headquarters for the Hellfire Club.

DEATH In WICCA and other PAGAN traditions, this rite of passage is perceived, as in most orthodox religious beliefs, as being the shedding of the physical body and the liberation of the spirit to seek a new existence, whether that constitutes an eternal one in a spirit world, or reincarnation. Death is generally considered to be an integral and necessary part of a cyclical process.

To a Pagan, the seasonal cycles of nature mirror those of human passage. Thus, at LAMMAS, the goddess MORRIGAN appears as the harbinger of death, the aspect (in company with those of war and panic) who wields the sickle that reaps the CORN KING. This heralds the decay of winter, out of whose dismemberment will spring the shoots of new life, the genesis of spring.

DEATH CURSE A magical spell which achieved some notoriety in the 1950s when it was prepared by the occultist Austin Osman SPARE, who allegedly claimed in a 1954 radio broadcast that it was possible to kill anyone using the spell. He is said to have subsequently marketed and sold the recipe in large numbers, but the whole incident may have been inflated out of proportion and perhaps was little more than a hoax. It is, in any event, not typical of Spare's style, which was generally directed towards the good of others.

DEE, JOHN (1527-1608) English astrologer and court MAGICIAN to Elizabeth I. His father held the position of rector of St. Mary's, Tenby, South Wales. Though deeply interested in ALCHEMY and NECROMANCY Dee junior was not personally involved in WITCHCRAFT; rather he was regarded as a CUNNING PERSON and built up a formidable library on diabolism and the magical arts both in England and on the Continent. He is credited with the development of the school of high ENOCHIAN MAGIC which returned to prominence in Victorian times with the HERMETIC ORDER OF THE GOLDEN DAWN. He is also alleged to have collaborated with his associate, Edward Kelly, in the development of the Enochian language.

His favoured tool of DIVINATION or SCRYING was a crystal ball and in 1659 details of his spirit-raising seances, which relied largely on the confidential but fraudulent co-operation of Edward Kelly, were published in manuscript form. Publication was, ostensibly, to persuade the public of the dangers of such techniques. Dee pursued the notion of the Philosopher's Stone, the imaginery mineral which would transform base metals into gold, and was a great advocate of the Arthurian tradition.

He was a confidant of Queen Elizabeth I and is known to have advised her on matters of astrology. At one time, however, he came under suspicion, as did many cunning persons, of practising witchcraft. During the reign of James I (see JAMES VI OF SCOTLAND) he lost his royal patronage and died obscurely in poverty at Mortlake in Surrey.

DEMETER The Greek MOTHER GODDESS whose origins may lie in the syncretization of deities of the corn and of the UNDERWORLD. In Homeric times she was associated equally with vegetation and with death. In ancient Athens the dead were titled *demeteroi*, while corn was traditionally scattered on new graves.

In an annual cycle of conflict with Hades, the god of the Underworld, Demeter leaves the temporal earth to search for her lost daughter and alter ego, Persephone, or Kore (girl). This legend accounts for the seasons of dearth and regeneration in the natural world, paralleling the Mesopotamian and Hittite-Hurrian legends of Inana and Dumuzi, Hebat and Telepinu.

The cult of Demeter was practised widely, often with a high degree of secrecy and with initiation rituals. One of the most famous cult centres is that of Eleusis, where the legends provided a stimulus for the Eleusinian Mysteries. A women's festival, the *Thesmophoria*, also took place and involved pigs being buried alive in pits or *megara*. The reported sacrifice of young virgins to Demeter has not been substantiated.

Today the myths of Demeter, and the ritual by which she is recalled to the upper world in the spring, are central to the practices of the WESTERN MYSTERIES. They are also are closely relevant to the spring BELTANE SABBAT of WICCA.

DEOSIL In WICCA tradition, this is the clockwise direction of DANCE, and the converse of widdershins. Clockwise is perceived to be the direction travelled by the sun in the northern hemisphere, and is therefore the direction of dance for good or right-hand magic.

DEVIL'S DOZEN A popular, though derogatory, term for the gathering of thirteen witches in a COVEN.

DEVIL WORSHIP, INDICTMENTS FOR Records of only three charges of deliberate Devil worship allied to WITCHCRAFT have survived and all date from the early fourteenth century. It can be assumed, therefore, that such allegations were rare. The earliest, not subsequently sustained by a Papal Commission, is that against Walter Langton, Bishop of Coventry (1301). The second, against Alice KYTELER (1324) in Ireland, was upheld and resulted in execution. The third of these charges was made collectively against the Knights Templar and, although successfully prosecuted in Europe, was not upheld in England. The Knights Templar were banned nonetheless, many in Europe were executed as heretics, their property confiscated and placed either in the care of the Order of St John of Jerusalem, who were essentially a hospitalling fraternity, or sold to fill the dwindling coffers of Edward II.

DIANA Roman moon goddess, modelled on the Greek deity Artemis, living in the forests and also recognized as a huntress, protector of animals and guardian of virginity. She enjoyed a sanctuary on the Avenine Hill in Rome and, under Roman occupation, took over the Temple of Artemis at Ephesus.

As a deity of modern PAGANS she is invoked chiefly by witches of the Dianic tradition, (see DIANIC WITCHCRAFT) who adopt ardently feminist principles and accord the horned god, CERNUNNOS, a secondary status. Diana is also perceived, however, in many non-Dianic covens as an important and favoured goddess.

DIANIC WITCHCRAFT A variant of WITCHCRAFT in which all members are female and virtually all emphasis is placed on the GODDESS, without attention to a male God. In this it contrasts strongly with its roots in mainstream WICCA, in which the God is given equal focus and male-female polarity is seen as an essential cosmic dynamic. Dianic COVENS are largely restricted to the United States and may be distinguished into two main groups. The first of these encompasses the feminist movement whose membership has established covens all over America. Some of these have rejected significant principles of mainstream Wicca and have sought to politicize witchcraft. These covens may, or may not, include a predominantly lesbian membership. In 1968, the organization WITCH (Women's International Terrorist Conspiracy from Hell) was founded with the declared aims of melding the spiritual aspects of the Craft with political activism and feminist militancy. The best known of these Dianic covens has probably been Zsuzsanna BUDAPEST's Susan B Anthony Coven, formed in Los Angeles at the Winter Solstice, 1971.

Other Dianic covens are more liberal, encouraging membership drawn from both sexes. Some of these originate from the witchcraft tradition developed in Dallas, Texas, by Morgan McFarland and Mark Roberts. McFarland's interest had developed through more conventional witchcraft covens in the American south that placed much emphasis on the WHITE GODDESS aspects of lore promoted by ROBERT GRAVES. In his Craft interests, Roberts split from McFarland and went on, in 1978, to develop another Craft movement that he called Hyperborea.

In the United States most covens start up by themselves, using Starhawk's *Spiral Dance* (see SIMOS, Miriam) or Zsuzsanna BUDAPEST's books.

DIVINATION The art of prediction based on the assumption that unseen links exist between mankind and objects in nature, including stars, crystals and stones, plants, animal organs and viscera.

Divination by CUNNING MEN was often called upon to determine the identity of a WITCH and several formulae were thought to be effective. One of the best known was that of the sieve and shears. According to a late sixteenth century manuscript in the Bodelian Library, Oxford, a pair of shears were stuck into the rim of a sieve and two persons set the tips of their forefingers on the upper part of the shears holding it, with the sieve, up from the ground. Peter and Paul were then invoked and, at the naming of the guilty person, the sieve would turn around. Once mastered, the technique of making the sieve twist around was said to be quite straightforward.

A similar principle involved a key and book, usually the Bible, wherein the key was placed at a certain point. The names of the accused were written on scraps of paper and inserted into the hollow barrel of the key one after the other. When the guilty person's name was introduced either the book would shake and fall from the hands of the holder or the key would turn. Although the technique dates from medieval times it was still in use as late as the nineteenth century.

Yet another method involved wrapping small pieces of paper bearing the names of the suspect witches in clay balls and submerging them in a pail of water. The name on the paper that first became freed from the clay would determine guilt.

At a more sophisticated level, divination by cunning men included astrology, geomancy and crystal-gazing. Geomancy involved interpreting the meaning of patterns of dots, created by the cunning man or magician during a state of trance, with reference to the twelve astrological signs. These patterns were regarded as containing cryptic messages from the soul and were seriously studied among intellectuals in pursuit of everything from buried treasure to the Philosopher's Stone.

DOWSING The old term for water divining using a rod fashioned from a forked hazel twig or other material. This was, and still remains, an activity closely associated with WITCHCRAFT. Dowsers were much sought after in country districts before the installation of services to provide piped water and their hazel twigs were cut in a precise ritual at the correct time of the waxing moon and the proper conjunction of the planets, particularly Mercury under whose dominion hazel grows. In the USA dowsers are still referred to as 'water witches'.

DRAGON ENVIRONMENTAL NETWORK An influential PAGAN group founded in London in July 1990 by Adrian Harris. Formerly the Dragon Environmental Group, it now has branches around the British Isles and also opens its doors to non-Pagans.

The basic principles of Dragon, which draws its name from the magical energy of the earth, include the belief that the earth is sacred; the development of a decentralized network of independent groups working together on local, national and international issues; a combination of practical environmental work with ECO-MAGIC; commitment to non-violent direct action, including postal campaigns, fund-raising and conservation. Their symbol is the YGGDRASIL, the World Ash Tree.

DRAWING DOWN THE MOON The WICCA

ceremony through which the High Priestess receives, through invocation, the spirit of the moon goddess and becomes her mortal incarnation. The GODDESS is invoked into her by a High Priest using the principle of polarity. As the Goddess incarnate she then delivers a CHARGE, manifesting for the COVEN members.

DREAM INTERPRETATION One of the services once regularly offered by medieval wizards. Popular manuscripts upon which their art was based included the pseudoepigraphal *Book of Daniel* and the *Judgement of Dreams* (Engl. transl 1518) from the work of the Greek physician Artemidorus of Ephesus.

DRUID CLAN OF DANA An offshoot of the FELLOWSHIP OF ISIS, centred in Ireland, which embraces a wide spectrum of Druidic principles. It is goddess based and claims to concentrate on the celebration of nature, each individual being free to interpret DRUIDRY as they choose. The Clan is structured in Groves, each with a Chief Druidess (Ar Ban Dri), Chief Druid (Ar Dri) and Bard (Ollave). The regular news magazine of the Clan is *Aisling*.

Membership is free and open to all members of the FELLOWSHIP OF ISIS.

DRUIDRY The collective name for a diverse group of organizations, most but not all of which subscribe to a form of PAGANISM based loosely on the translated oral religious traditions of the pre-Christian Celts living in continental Europe and in the regions of the British Isles to which Roman Christian influence did not extend, that is the country to the north of Hadrian's Wall and Ireland. There is an emphasis on the mystery of poetic inspiration and on healing, DIVINATION and Celtic mythology. Druids use the Ogam (Ogham) script as a system of divination and the Irish BETH-LUIS-NION tree alphabet of twenty letters described by Robert GRAVES in THE WHITE GODDESS and based

on that contained in Roderick O'Flaherty's *Ogygia.*.

Some orders of Druidry subscribe to purely charitable ends without Pagan belief, while others follow esoteric or more orthodox teachings than those normally regarded as Pagan. These include the ANCIENT ORDER OF DRUIDS (AOD); various Druid friendly societies of which the most significant internationally is the United Ancient Order of Druids; and Welsh National Eisteddfod Druids, whose main interest lies in the preservation of Welsh language and culture.

Druidry does not subscribe to a hierarchical bureaucracy but the focus of its teachings rests on a love of nature and the view that spirituality should be an integral part of daily life. Personal development takes a prominent place (see also ANCIENT DRUID ORDER and COUNCIL OF BRITISH DRUID ORDERS).

DUCKING See ORDEAL BY WATER.

DUNCAN, HELEN The medium who was indicted and imprisoned for nine months in 1944 on charges of having 'transgressed the security laws when she foretold the loss of one of His Majesty's ships before the fact was made public'. The case has been erroneously cited as the last occasion when an individual was sentenced under the 1736 Witchcraft Act, an impossibility since legislation of that year removed the crime of WITCHCRAFT from the English statute books. Mrs Duncan was prosecuted under legislation which replaced the various Witchcraft Acts and which was based on the assumption that the phenomenon of witchcraft did not exist.

EARTH MYSTERIES A discipline involving particular attention to the natural world and its phenomena, a study of PAGAN traditions and reminders that provide a route to spiritual fulfilment. The exploration of earth mysteries includes the study of the landscape, its LEY LINES, standing stones, holy wells, woodlands and other ancient places of worship and the drawing of strength from their innate spirituality. It also focuses on ancient customs, legends and lore. The discipline may involve scientific study or more intuitive analysis including, for example, the art of DOWSING.

In Britain, organized bodies include the London Earth Mysteries Circle and Northern Earth Mysteries.

ECO-MAGIC A British ecologically focused movement among some PAGANS in the UK in the 1990s, established to address a wide spectrum of environmental issues, its activities range from healing specific parts of the earth through magical means, including spells, ritual and use of talismanic devices to draw on the positive energy of LEY LINES and sacred sites, to a broader aim of transforming society as a whole. The principal organization embodying this ethos is the DRAGON ENVIRONMENTAL NETWORK.

ELEMENT BALANCING A ceremony performed by some WICCA COVENS, including that of Vivianne CROWLEY, as a precursor to first-degree INITIATION, compensating the candidate for his or her absence from the invocation of the four elements within the circle of witches at the outset of the initiation rite. It is felt that the candidate will benefit from a sense of inner balancing before the sometimes intimidating procedure of initiation.

The balancing rite offers an imagery of the featureless primeval waters into which the initiate sinks, trance-like, to rest deep within the embryonic earth awaiting its genesis. As the waters recede, the candidate struggles from its womb and begins to ascend, climbing ever higher into the air, reaching towards the warmth and vitality of the sun until engulfed by its purifying fire. Cleansed, he or she returns once more to the earth and awaits rebirth into the society of Wicca.

The imagery reflects very ancient concepts that are not limited to Celtic traditions. The primeval water from which all life emerges is fundamental to Egyptian and other ancient Near Eastern beliefs, the sun has been a source of light and vitality for most PAGAN cultures and fire is always a purifying element. Achieving the correct balance between earth, air, fire and water is considered essential for the spiritual well-being of the Wicca initiate.

ELYMAS See BARJESUS.

ENCHANTMENT A particular ability attributed to medieval WITCHES that allegedly resulted in the infatuation of one individual for another. The temporary nature of this romantic entanglement often led to husbands or wives being accused by their partner of resorting to witchcraft when the heat of passion subsided. One of the better publicized illustrations of enchantment at work is that of Henry VIII who, when he had tired of Anne Boleyn, accused her of having seduced him by devilish enchantment.

ENCHIRIDION OF POPE LEO The medieval manuscript that has been incorrectly described by various authors, including Eliphas LEVI, as a source of Black Magic ritual. By tradition, in 800 AD, Pope Leo III presented the Emperor Charlemagne, on the occasion of his coronation in Rome, with a manuscript containing a collection of CHARMS which would offer him divine protection against all known worldly perils, provided that they were recited and conducted with a precisely defined ritual. The occasion of this gift was recorded in the published edition which is said to have been first printed in Rome in 1523. That edition, if it ever existed, is lost. The earliest known editions, to which a certain amount of apocryphal material is thought to have been added, date from the seventeenth century.

ENOCHIAN MAGIC The sixteenth-century system of magic originated by the Elizabethan astrologer John DEE. This may have derived loosely from the apocryphal notion that the prophet Enoch was taken up as an eyewitness to the seven heavens, then recorded his experiences in a series of secret books which constitute *1 Enoch* and *2 Enoch*. From the latter comes the following: *And behold, my children, after I had examined the things that had been ordained on earth, I wrote them down.* It was also believed that, in company with Elijah, Enoch would appear on earth at Judgement Day, to destroy the anti-Christ. The following prediction is set out in *The Apocalypse of Elijah*: *Then will Elijah and Enoch descend. They will lay aside their worldly flesh and take on spiritual flesh. They will pursue the Son of Lawlessness and will kill him without his being able to speak.*

Enoch was thus considered to be a magician and prophet and, during the fourteenth century, there was no shortage of would-be Enochs who claimed the ability to fulfil the prophecies of the *Book of Revelation* and control the weather, inflict the plague and lay low their enemies. Apocryphal books of ritual magic were attributed to Enoch.

It is considered doubtful whether Dee's writings add up to a proper system of magic. However, he and his associate, Edward Kelly, claimed to have uncovered a secret magical language stemming from Enoch, using a crystal as an instrument of SCRYING. Other subsequent claimants insist that it is a remnant of the tongue of the fabled city of Atlantis. Kelly inscribed a series of charts, each divided into squares containing different letters of the alphabet, which bear some resemblance to those of ancient Hebrew and include consonants to which vowels must be added by the speaker. During seance sessions, letters would be pointed out through the spirit medium to reveal a message which Dee recorded.

Present-day Enochian magic has been developed out of Dee's writings and the language plays a significant role in the study and activities of some modern witches and other occultists. Probably first popularized in recent times by Aleister CROWLEY in his work *Magick in Theory and Practice*, the Enochian system provides a means of gaining entry to higher spheres of being by using the correct invocations to the angels who guard them.

EOSTRE (1) An Anglo-Saxon fertility goddess of spring and the derivation of the Christian title 'Easter'. Now part of the modern PAGAN tradition, little detail is known of her cult or personality.

EOSTRE (2) The common American name for the festival celebrated by modern WITCHES at the Vernal Equinox on 20 or 21 March. It is one of eight major annual festivals or SABBATS derived from ancient European PAGAN festivals marking changes of the seasons. British witches continue to call in the Spring Equinox.

ESBAT A WICCAN term for the COVEN meeting held at the time of the full moon. The term derives from the French *s'esbattre*, meaning to frolic. These gatherings are often devoted to spellcraft and magical work. There are thirteen Esbats during the lunar year.

According to Robert GRAVES in THE WHITE GODDESS, the lunar months are associated with trees on the basis of the BETH-LUIS-NION alphabet. Thus the first meeting, in December, is linked with birch, the second with rowan, the third with ash, the fourth with alder, the fifth with willow, the sixth with hawthorn, the seventh with oak, the eighth with holly, the ninth with hazel, the tenth with the vine, the eleventh with ivy, the twelfth with guelder rose and the thirteenth with elder. These associations are derived from the tree alphabet contained in the seventeenth century *Ogygia* by Roderick O'Flaherty. *Ogygia* is named after the magical isle where Odysseus was cast ashore for eight years in the company of a beautiful goddess, Calypso, when he offended the sea god Poseidon after taking part in the sack of Troy. The theme of *Ogygia* is that the obscure poems of the Celtic bard, TALIESIN, contained in the *Red Book of Hergest*, constitute the cover for an encrypted and highly secret alphabet known only to the ancient Druids and based on the names of trees.

Although many PAGANS subscribe to Graves' arrangement, the associations between months and trees are variable.

EXECUTIONS In continental Europe, during the WITCH-CRAZE of the sixteenth and seventeenth centuries, WITCHES were tried by ecclesiastical courts whose punishment for the crime, in extremis, was execution by burning at the stake. In England, Wales and Scotland, after the time when the civil courts began to hear cases against witches, execution was by hanging, although prior to that occasional burning did take place. The hanging method was resented by those who subscribed to the Continental view that witchcraft was an hereditary trait and that only by burning was the blood of a witch prevented from passing on its sinister elements to her offspring. The capital punishment of death by hanging for those found guilty of WITCHCRAFT was also adopted in North America where it came to notoriety during the Salem witch trials of 1692. In America, however, those who confessed to the crime of witchcraft were given a lesser sentence.

In the British Isles and Europe, capital punishment was only dispensed when the accused was found guilty of serious crimes resulting in the death or serious disability of the victim, his family or his livestock. According to C L Ewan, on the Home Assize circuit (Hertfordshire, Kent, Surrey and Sussex), between 1559 and 1736, of 513 persons accused, 200 were convicted and 109 hanged. He estimates that less than a thousand executions took place in the British Isles, while other authorities have claimed up to a quarter of a million throughout Europe and America. The most intense spate of execution in England took place in Essex and East Anglia between 1645 and 1647, through the efforts of Matthew HOPKINS, when several hundred witches were hanged. The suggestion put forward by GARDNER that an estimated nine million were tortured to death during the persecution in Europe cannot be substantiated and is likely to be highly misleading. One of the most recent academic studies (Levack 1995) estimates the figure, more realistically, at about 60,000, mostly of women aged fifty or over.

One of the benefits of execution, it was claimed, was that it brought immediate relief to the victim of a witch's curse in that the efficacy of the curse was ended.

The last executions after conviction on the charge of witchcraft took place in England in 1684 (Alice Mulholland at Exeter), in America in 1692, in Scotland in 1727, in France in 1745 and in Germany in 1775. In England trials subsequently took place as late as 1717 but all were dismissed.

FAIRIES Members of the spirit community, also including elves and goblins, who infested the medieval world, the fairies being led by their King and Queen, Oberon and MAB. Contrary to modern perceptions, during the medieval centuries fairies were perceived neither to be small nor particularly benevolent.

They conformed to no special set of characteristics but were generally feared by the general public as being aggressive or at least capricious and mischievous creatures. This was particularly true prior to the Tudor period during which, in more sophisticated circles and in the face of the immediate threat from witches, belief in fairies became passé and they were regarded more in a mythological context. Some imagined them to be emanations of mischievous ancestor spirits. Most people, however, saw them as malevolent entities to be guarded against. They were also purveyors of diseases which, once contracted, could only be cured by means of exorcism or CHARMS.

In contrast to their public image, fairies were considered by magicians to be a positive aid to their work, providing a source of supernatural power and OCCULT knowledge. The Christian establishment took the contrasting view of what it considered to be minor agents of the Devil.

By the seventeenth century, fairies had taken on the characteristics by which they are recognized today, being regarded as little people living in their own secret, woodland kingdom, venturing out to play and dance in dew-drenched fairy rings and revealing themselves to selected human observers. Occasionally they might still appear malevolent, snatching away an infant or causing a nuisance in the house. They particularly detest untidiness or personal slovenliness, but are also averse to lechery and lust The remedy was to leave out food and toiletries for their benefit, and to keep a pure, clean and tidy house. Many of these responses were frowned on by the Church, which perceived these practices to equate with diabolical propitiation.

Recent research, Pochs (1989) and Ankarloo and Hennington (1990), suggests that during the sixteenth and seventeenth centuries, in locations including Sicily, the Balkans and other parts of central Europe, belief in fairies was widespread and that it has also persisted into modern times.

Today, the most common encounter with fairies is obtained as a child through leaving a tooth beneath one's pillow at night which they will, if pleased with its owner, exchange for money. The notion amongst some modern authors on WITCHCRAFT, that the fairies represent vestiges of an army of dwarfish beings who peopled parts of the British Isles in pre-Celtic times is the product of imagination and has no foundation in historical or archaeological reality.

FAIRY QUEEN The ruler of the fairy kingdom known by various names but generally, in England, as MAB. Made famous by Shakespeare's *A Midsummer Night's Dream*, she was Titania and her consort was Oberon.

FAMILIAR Perceived to be an agent of a witch although, in reality, probably any one of an assortment of small animals kept as pets. The term was also applied to the witch when she had taken on a spirit form. The tradition of familiars is a very

TOP: *The five-fold kiss, part of the first degree of initiation into Wicca. In these pictures the kneeling man is the initiator; the woman the candidate for initiation.*
BOTTOM: *The Dark Goddess, Hecate or the Hag: the aspect of the Triple Goddess associated with the Underworld and death.*

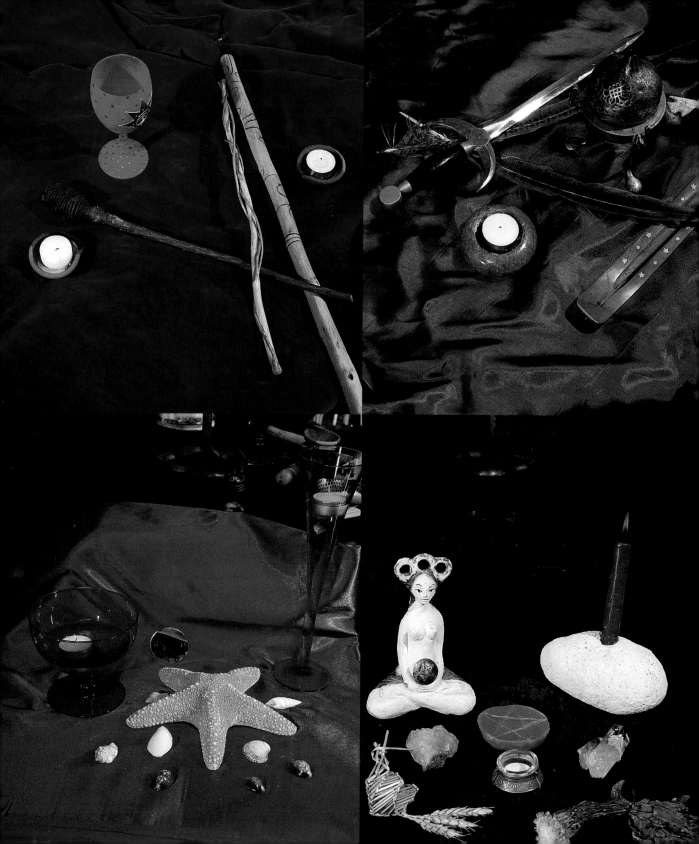

ancient one and would appear to stem from various sources.

The Old Testament contains numerous references:

Leviticus 19.31: *Regard not them that have familiar spirits, neither seek after wizards to be defiled by them.*

Leviticus 20.27: *A man also or a woman that hath a familiar spirit, or that is a wizard, shall surely be put to death.*

1 Samuel 28.3: *And Saul had put away those that had familiar spirits, and the wizards, out of the land.*

In early recorded northern traditions familiars were perceived to be among the nature spirits of folklore, including dwarfs, FAIRIES, imps, kobolds and trolls, which could be variously friendly, mischievous or harmful. Under Christian influence these became debased into minor demons in association with witches and, in the eyes of the Church, part of the machinery of the Devil. The witch was thought to have been given her familiar by the Devil at her initiation. One of the tests of discovery for a witch was to examine her for any abnormal warts, papillae or other protuberances which were regarded as nipples, the so-called Devil's teats, from which the familiars suckled. The 1604 WITCHCRAFT ACT included a clause making it a felony *to consult, covenant, entertain, feed or reward any wicked spirit, to or for any intent or purpose.*

Familiars have gone under an assortment of popular names, including Robin Goodfellow and Rumpelstiltskin, and, during the medieval period, were employed equally for beneficent or maleficent purpose. Keith Thomas cites the case of John Walsh in the Maidstone Records (1566) who confessed that, in order to discover lost goods, he employed a familiar who would appear sometimes in the shape of a pigeon, sometimes in that of a dog, sometimes in that of a man with cloven feet. The notion of witches taking on the guise of their familiars may stem from the use of animal skins and masks during ritual.

Arguably the most familiar of familiars was the black cat which some have claimed descended from the cats of the Norse Vanir goddess, Freyja. Familiars, when not residing on the hearthmat, were generally to be located in fields and woodlands.

In Wicca, the familiar is seen as a guardian spirit or spirit guide. Some modern authorities contend that, through the familiar, the boundaries between outer and inner levels of reality can be transcended, and abilities can be drawn on and developed that would otherwise be outside our senses. Others, including such commentators as Cecil WILLIAMSON, would argue that the familiar, whether in spirit or flesh, has gone for good from the lives of most working witches.

FARR, FLORENCE (1860-1917) An English actress (noted for a well-publicized affair with George Bernard Shaw) who, during the late nineteenth century, was one of the early members of Golden Dawn (see HERMETIC ORDER OF THE GOLDEN DAWN). She joined the Order in 1890, adopting the magical pseudonym Sapienta Sapienti Dona Data, and was initiated into the Second Order in 1891. She became allied with the magically-orientated members who believed in the necessity to open contact with the Secret Chiefs of the Order, was obsessed with the notion of astral travel and set up a study group of twelve members, the London Adepti. The pre-occupation with astral magic caused some unrest within Isis-Urania and this was ultimately one of the root causes of the division of Golden Dawn into ALPHA ET OMEGA and STELLA MATUTINA. Notwithstanding, in 1894 Farr became the Praemonstratrix, or female head, of the Isis-Urania Temple and, by 1900, she was the official tenant of the Vault of the Adepts at Blythe Road in Hammersmith. This was a period of conflict for the Order, largely brought about by S L MacGregor MATHERS' increasingly autocratic behaviour that resulted in his being dismissed as chief in favour of W B YEATS. Farr and her London ADEPTS had been particularly offended at the initiation of Aleister CROWLEY late in 1899, against the wishes of his Isis-Urania chiefs, by MacGregor Mathers.

Representations of the Four Elements of Wicca – fire, air, water and earth. The objects chosen will vary from coven to coven, or from individual to individual.

She became a successful writer and, in 1910, emigrated to Ceylon where she founded a College for Girls. She died, a victim of cancer, at the age of 57.

FARTING BOTTLE A flask or other container, often a BELLARMINE jug, into which a victim of a witch's curse could void the spell by passing wind. The flask was then sealed and buried in the ground. (See also WITCH-BOTTLE.)

FASCINATING The alleged practice of medieval WITCHES whereby he or she met the eyes of the victim with a special look or gaze which was empowered with a potent but invisible emanation. The victim was said to have been 'fascinated' or 'overlooked'.

It was believed that domestic animals or crops could be damaged or destroyed simply by looking at them and that infants, particularly those not yet baptised, were particularly susceptible to fascination.

Some authorities regarded the attribute as being wholly involuntary. Belief in its existence was encouraged by the incidence of ophthalmia (cataract), an eye condition which was rife in earlier centuries. It was considered that people who possessed this affliction infected others merely by looking at them and it forms the basis of the opaque stare beloved of modern horror movie makers.

The idea of maleficent glances goes back at least as far as Classical times. Keith Thomas describes the widely held notion that the glance of a menstruating woman would tarnish a mirror.

FELKIN, R W (died 1926) A prominent occultist and magician, he was one of the three chiefs of GOLDEN DAWN who were elected, in May 1902, on a year's tenure, after the sacking of MacGregor MATHERS. The others included J W Brodie-Innes and Percy Bullock. Felkin's magical name was Frater Finem Respice 7 = 4 (see under SPRENGEL, Anna for explanation of 7 = 4). It was claimed that,

for a period of time, he became the exclusive head of STELLA MATUTINA but this is contested. In 1903, at the time of the fragmentation of the original Golden Dawn, he established a new Amoun Temple in London and attempted to carry on the traditions of Golden Dawn under the name of Stella Matutina, against the more radical and mystically inclined A E WAITE, who headed the ISIS-URANIA Temple.

Felkin believed fervently in the magical brief of Golden Dawn and in the existence of the Secret Chiefs of the so-called Third Order whose higher intelligence he regarded as essential to call upon. Allegedly he received communications from them concerning new rituals and confirming the authenticity of the original cipher manuals which had effectively provided Golden Dawn with its charter. In an effort to track down these masters, he apparently tried to locate Anna Sprengel in Germany between 1906 and 1910 but succeeded only in making contact with a namesake of hers and with other German ROSICRUCIANS. In 1912 he was initiated into the German Rosicrucian Fraternity and returned to England equipped with details of several new Stella Matutina grades. At about this time he also came under the influence of an astral entity named Ara Ben Shemesh who claimed to come 'from the desert'. The same year he visited New Zealand where he founded a Stella Matutina temple. In 1912 he was obliged to return briefly to England, but took up permanent residence in New Zealand in 1916, founding several more SM temples, one of which survived until 1972. The original Amoun Temple in London was dissolved in 1919.

FELLOWSHIP OF CROTONA The quasi-Rosicrucian group founded in 1911 by George Sullivan, known as 'Brother Aurelius', with Mabel Besant-Scott, the daughter of Annie BESANT, in the New Forest, Hampshire. Sullivan also ran the Christchurch theatre, known as the 'First Rosicrucian Theatre in England', of which Dorothy FORDHAM and, later, Gerald GARDNER were members. According to Doreen VALIENTE the Fellowship of Crotona was the legal facade for the SOUTHERN COVEN OF BRITISH WITCHES which, prior to 1951, was technically illegal.

FELLOWSHIP OF ISIS A GODDESS-venerating fellowship founded in Ireland on the date of the Vernal Equinox in 1976 by the late Lawrence Durdin-Robertson, his wife Pamela and sister, Olivia (see ROBERTSON, Olivia Durdin-), and now ranking as a worldwide organization that claims a membership of more than twelve thousand distributed through more than sixty countries, it is among the largest of Goddess-venerating fellowships. The Foundation Centre, with its Temple of Isis, is at Clonegal Castle in Ireland and the Fellowship is open to both men and women. It initiates both sexes as priests and priestesses. All members have equal privileges, there is no exclusivity or hierarchy, no vows, and members are permitted to resign and rejoin at will and may practise other religious beliefs. It denies the ritual of sacrifice, even in symbolic form, and lays stress on being multi-faith and multi-cultural.

The network of the Fellowship consists of affiliated centres or Iseums, each dedicated to an individual Goddess, or Goddess and God, although all goddesses bear the magical name I.S.I.S. and each god is Osiris. The Fellowship strives for love, beauty and abundance while encouraging its members to develop psychic abilities and a compassion for all living things. Education plays a significant part in the work of the Fellowship through Lyceums of the College of Isis which carry out both the liturgy and the training of would be priests and priestesses. The College also offers correspondence courses. Its Magi Degrees (33 in total) are designed to reflect the growth charted by each individual member.

FERAFERIA A neo-Pagan religious movement founded in the United States by Frederick Adams and described by Margot ADLER as the private vision of one man of a paradisial state, never contaminated by offshoots, schisms or changes, a religion of both wildness and delicacy. The word, as derived from Latin, means 'wilderness festival'. The movement pursues celebration of Wilderness Mysteries with an emphasis on elegance and grace melding the disciplines of art, ecology, mythology and liturgy. Adams' inspiration was derived from a number of literary sources including R GRAVES, W Morris, H Thoreau, C Jung and, in particular, the work of H B Stevens, *The Recovery of Culture*, which advances the theory that the primordial period of the human race's development was that of the mythical paradise.

FILIDHS OF OISIN An Irish Druidic organization that trains its members in spiritual poetry and sacred ecology based on the Filidhic system. Training involves periods of immersion in the beauties of nature alternating with deep meditation in total darkness, from which emanates a chanted poetry. The ultimate objective is the so-called 'Aisling' dream vision in which the GODDESS appears. The tradition stems from Irish Celtic mythology and from the induction of Bardic Filidhs whose training period is said to have taken twenty years.

FITH-FATH A human doll-like image usually moulded from clay or wax and designed for use in sympathetic magic. In medieval times it was often employed in the *maleficium* by sticking pins or nails into the image. The most notorious case on record is arguably that of the Berwickshire witches who allegedly employed a wax doll while attempting to work malevolent MAGIC against King James I (see JAMES VI OF SCOTLAND). Similar devices are employed extensively in Voodooism and other branches of African magic.

In WICCA, a fith-fath is more usually employed for the purpose of distant healing.

FIVE-FOLD KISS A ritual practice of WICCA, in

which the initiator places a kiss on five parts of the candidate's body, the feet, knees, genitals, breasts and lips. This is possibly derived, by GARDNER, from Masonic ritual practice.

FLADE, DIETRICH (died 1589) An affluent rector of the University of Trier and a secular magistrate who was also, for a while, vested with the powers of Inquisitor, Flade was a moderate whose liberal views were fiercely opposed by other members of the judiciary. Eventually his rivals hatched a plan to remove him by raising a spurious charge that he had plotted to murder his archbishop. The charge was successful and he perished at the stake in Trier.

FLAGELLATION A ritual practice, extending back at least to the second millennium BC or earlier, designed partly as a sexual stimulant and partly as a symbolic form of discipline.

Flagellation is an integral part of GARDNERIAN WICCA, involving the use of a ritual instrument to scourge a candidate during first and second degrees of INITIATION when the recipient, according to Gardner's instructions, receives forty strokes. In many Gardnerian covens this has been reduced to a token measure. It is frequently applied whilst the recipient is blindfolded and in a state of bondage.

Gardner also required flagellation to be an essential component of preparation for the Great Rite, the third degree of initiation. Critics claim that he was obsessed in an unhealthy way with this form of masochism because of his predilection for physical subservience to women, a necessary pre-requisite to his achievement of personal sexual potency.

It should be noted that flagellation is not confined to Wicca and is also widely observed in other religions, including Christian and Hindu.

FLORA A Roman goddess of flowers, the consort of Zephyrus, and chiefly worshipped by young girls with offerings of fruit and flowers. Her major festivals, with strongly sexual overtones but also

identified with the dead, were celebrated in the spring months between late April and early May, and were known as *Floralia*.

A revival of the festival is now celebrated annually under the auspices of the FELLOWSHIP OF ISIS in London.

FLUDD, ROBERT (1574-1637) An English astrologer and one of the most prominent authorities on the Hermetic system. He wrote prolifically in support of HERMETICISM in spite of the fact that the intellectual credentials and provenance of HERMES TRISMEGISTUS as a pre-Christian movement had been undermined by the earlier researches of Isaac CASAUBON and other contemporaries. Most of his published work was compiled in Latin and was disseminated abroad. He took vows of chastity and claimed to enjoy the patronage of a number of leading clergy, including John Thornborough, Bishop of Worcester.

FLYING An erroneous notion that WITCHES possessed the power to levitate on broomsticks. The idea is only recorded in the proceedings of a single English witch trial although it is also known, to a limited extent, from Continental sources. In a cynical response to the more sensational claims against Jane Wenham (1712), the presiding judge, Mr Justice POWELL, commented that *there is no law against flying.*

In medieval times, popular notion had it that witches rubbed an ointment, containing fat, henbane, belladonna, mandrake and other herbs with hallucinogenic properties, on their skins to facilitate levitation. In modern WICCA, where participants perform SKYCLAD, FLYING OINTMENT is applied to protect against the cold.

FLYING OINTMENT Also sometimes known as *Unguentum Sabbati* or Witches' Salve, a concoction based on fat into which herbs with narcotic properties are introduced. Among the first recorded explanations of this is an essay which appears in the early editions of a manuscript *De Miraculis Rerum Naturalium* (roughly translated 'Magic from Natural Sources') by Giovanni Batista della Porta (Antwerp, 1560) under the heading *Lamiarum unguenta* (roughly translated 'Witches' Unguents'). This section was later deleted by Dominican monks. The Elizabethan writer, Francis Bacon, offers an extensive list of ingredients and in his *Historie of Witchcraft* Reginald SCOT, who had studied della Porta's writings, described disparagingly the sixteenth century belief that the concoction was prepared from the bowels and members of newly deceased children. Other far-fetched ingredients included bat's blood and the fat of dead infants.

Among modern authors, Margaret MURRAY (*The Witch Cult in Western Europe*) and Montague SUMMERS (*The Werewolf*) offer details of witch's unguents based on della Porta's recipes, although Summers also offers material from other sources (see also FLYING).

It is the hallucinogenic and narcotic properties of the various herbs included in the recipes, such as thornapple, henbane and deadly nighshade, all of which can be absorbed in varying degrees through the skin, that provide Flying Ointment with its apparent powers of levitation. To the witches of old it offered one of the earliest forms of 'a trip', although the consequences were highly dangerous to health.

FORDHAM, DOROTHY See CLUTTERBUCK, Dorothy.

FORNARIO, NETTA (1894-1929) An occultist of Anglo-Italian extraction who was initiated into ALPHA ET OMEGA and who died under curious circumstances which were described, by Dion FORTUNE, as psychic murder perpetrated by Moina MATHERS, the wife of S L MacGregor MATHERS. Her body was found in the vicinity of a derelict village on the Isle of Iona, naked apart from a ritual cloak and a silver neck-chain. On the ground nearby was a large steel knife. She had, apparently

cut the outline of a crucifix into the turf and died from heart failure. Allegedly she was the victim of a magical attack.

FORSPEAKING The practice by which, allegedly, a medieval witch exercised his or her OCCULT powers through pronouncement of a curse or malediction. If the curse took effect the victim was said to have been 'forspoken'.

FORTUNE, DION (1890-1946) A prominent and influential twentieth-century occultist and novelist who was born Violet Mary Firth at Llandudno in Wales and who, after her marriage, became Violet Penry-Evans. Born into a wealthy Sheffield steel-making family, she became much respected in her lifetime as a psychic and MAGICIAN. At about the age of twenty she attended a commercial school in Weston-super-Mare, a period of her life that ended in near nervous breakdown after a distressing incident in which she disagreed with the autocratic director of the school. In the period before the 1914-18 war she practised in London as a psycho-analyst and wrote minor books on the subject under the name Violet M Firth. In about 1917 she came under the influence of an occult ADEPT named Moriarty who had connections with the HERMETIC ORDER OF GOLDEN DAWN and, in 1919, having first developed an interest in Helena BLAVATSKY's THEOSOPHICAL SOCIETY, she was initiated into the Weston-super-Mare branch of the reconstituted Hermetic Order of the Golden Dawn, by that time known as ALPHA ET OMEGA. In 1920 she moved to London and moved to a lodge of the rival STELLA MATUTINA offshoot of Golden Dawn, which was headed by the wife of MacGregor MATHERS, Moina. After Moriarty died in 1921 she founded, with some of the members, a small lodge of the Theosophical Society which was intended as a recruiting ground for Alpha et Omega. However, in 1927, after increasing disillusionment with what was left of Golden Dawn and disagreement with Moina, she broke ranks with Stella Matutina and went on, with her group, to found the FRATERNITY OF THE INNER LIGHT. This was intended to bridge the gulf between PAGAN and Christian doctrines, and was firmly rooted in the Western Tradition. It was based at GLASTONBURY in Somerset and, subsequently, in London.

Dion Fortune was a trance-medium of some repute and she rapidly made contact with inner plane adepts, the secret chiefs of MAGIC who may or may not have existed in the flesh but who now offer wisdom from the spirit world. Although her Society was never represented at OCCULT conferences she became an accomplished author on the occult. One of her most respected occult works is *The Mystical Qabbalah*, which sets out Golden Dawn's version of the Christian QABALAH. Her novel *The Sea Priestess* has been hailed as one of the finest works of fiction on the subject of magic.

She married a doctor who became involved in magic, Thomas Penry Evans, in 1927, but separated from him in about 1937 and was divorced in 1945, six months before her death from myeloid leukaemia. She was buried in Glastonbury.

FOUR ELEMENTS Associated with the four watchtowers, these are aspects of ancient ritual MAGIC and of the modern WICCA circle. The points of the PENTAGRAM are associated with the five elements and the elements are controlled by elemental Kings or Rulers who, in Wicca, are described as the Mighty Ones or the Lords of the Elements. The physical elements of earth, air, fire and water correspond to the north, east, south and west quarters respectively and with the ancient notion of the four 'humours'– phlegmatic, sanguine, choleric and melancholic. According to Carl Jung, the humours further equate with four human personality functions – sensation, thinking, intuition and feeling – which combine in varying degrees to create individuality. In ALEXANDRIAN Wicca tradition, the four elements are usually named as the four winds of Greco-Roman mythology – Boreas, Euros, Notos and Zephyros. In some magical traditions the four elements are linked with non-temporal or mythical beings – gnomes, sylphs, salamanders and undines.

A fifth element, ether, is also recognized as forming fields of influence or force around physical objects. The human persona is seen to possess an etheric body which extends through and somewhat beyond its physical dimensions as an aura. In Wicca and other beliefs, a ghost is an aura or etheric body from which the physical component is missing through death.

FOUR TREASURES, ORDER OF THE See YEATS, William Butler.

FRATERNITAS SATURNII A highly secretive German magical group incorporating the basic format of opening and closing circles.

FRATERNITY OF THE INNER LIGHT The society founded in 1922 as a branch of the THEOSOPHICAL SOCIETY by Dion FORTUNE. The society formally split from the more mystically and astrally orientated STELLA MATUTINA in 1927 as an OCCULT order of MAGIC which claimed to span the PAGAN-Christian divide and which derived from principles established in Golden Dawn (see HERMETIC ORDER OF GOLDEN DAWN). It was said to be guided by spirit entities or 'Masters' residing at the Inner Plane under whose tutelage it practised white magic and believed itself in harmony with the collective soul of the British nation. It included a society within a society formed by Fortune and entitled THE GUILD OF THE MASTER JESUS.

Dion Fortune died without a successor and, although the Fraternity of the Inner Light was taken over by Arthur Chichester, it is said that she continued to run it through her trance mediums until the late 1950s, when it became known as the SOCIETY OF THE INNER LIGHT. Its membership was content to continue in the traditions which she had established until Chichester revised the entire structure.

The image of the society was then changed,

moving towards more solidly Christian principles. At least five fraternities have descended from it which have been identified, collectively, as the WESTERN MYSTERIES, so-called because they claim to subscribe to the mystery traditions of Egypt and Eleusis as well as elements of mithraism, druidry and Qabalistic magic.

FRC See FELLOWSHIP OF THE ROSY CROSS.

FUTHARK A term defining the fixed sequence of a row of runic characters, derived from the phonetic values of the first six runes (see RUNES).

GABIJA A household guardian and fire spirit, known from Lithuanian mythology, who sometimes appears as a goddess and who, historically, was attended wholly by women as the Mistress of the Holy Fire. Like most spirit guardians, her mood was capricious and it was customary to appease her by throwing salt on the fire with the words: *Sacred Gabija, be satisfied* and to leave a bowl of clean water in the hearth for her use. Her cult has survived into modern PAGAN worship.

GAIA (**GAEA**) An ancient name of Greek derivation applied to the archetypal earth mother. Her origins are pre-Hellenic and her centre of worship was in Attica. Gaia is the primal essence of the earth and is one of the creations of the primordial beings of the cosmos, Aether and Hedera. Encouraged by Eros, Gaia became the mother of Pontos (the sea) and Ouranos (the heavens) and, through subsequent incestuous liaison with Ouranos, she bore the first generation of Titans.

She is perceived as a placid and resilient goddess who had an oracle, predating that of Apollo, at Delphi. In iconography she is represented by fruit and cornucopiae.

Under Hellenic influence she became DEMETER or Da-meter, the corn mother whose daughter is the ill-fated Kore (girl), a corn spirit better known as Persephone whose fate is depicted in the Eleusinian Mysteries.

In today's PAGAN beliefs, Gaia continues to represent the apotheosis of the living earth and is, essentially, the GODDESS of WICCA.

GARDNER, GERALD BROSSEAU (1884-1964) The British founder of modern WICCA and the author of several books including the novel *High Magic's Aid* (1949) and *Witchcraft Today* (1954), the latter representing the first authoritative account of Wicca. Born in Lancashire, England, the third of four siblings, his father was a timber merchant and Justice of the Peace. However, much of his formative years were influenced by an Irish nanny, Josephine 'Com' McCombie, who possessed a dominant, bohemian personality and with whom he travelled extensively abroad in search of climates condusive to combatting a chronic asthma condition. In 1900 McCombie and the sixteen year old Gardner emigrated to Ceylon where he worked on a tea plantation before moving on, in 1908, first to Singapore and then to a rubber plantation in North Borneo. There he developed an interest in the culture and traditions of the local Dyak tribes before returning to Singapore in 1923, gaining the job of a customs inspector while expanding further his knowledge of OCCULT lore and practice. In Malaya he also developed a life-long fascination for weaponry.

He visited England in 1916 to enlist in the army but was discharged, returning to Malaya a year later. He travelled to England again in 1927 when he met and married his wife, Donna (née Rosedale), the daughter of a clergyman. In contrast with some ambivalent reactions to his personality, Donna seems to have been universally liked. By 1935 he was back in England via the Middle East where he had met the archaeologist, Flanders Petrie. In 1936 he retired to become involved in middle eastern archaeology. He spent part of the following years in

Cyprus, where he bought a temple site and had aspirations to develop a goddess cult, before being expelled by the local authorities and returning to England in 1938.

In England he developed an interest in DRUIDRY and in Rosicrucianism (see ROSICRUCIAN SOCIETY) through the Rosicrucian Theatre, at Christchurch, Hampshire, where he met Dorothy CLUTTERBUCK and through whom he was initiated into the SOUTHERN COVEN OF BRITISH WITCHES. He was also intrigued by naturism in pursuance of which he obtained a piece of land at Bricketts Wood near St Albans in the grounds of a property owned by a nudist club and from where he ran a COVEN. He found a sixteenth century timber framed cottage, alleged to have been that of a witch, that he purchased from a defunct museum at New Barnet. He had the cottage dismantled and transported to Bricketts Wood where he stocked it with various occult artifacts, partly from his own collection and partly with items obtained from the New Barnet witchcraft museum. In 1993, an investigator found part of the cottage still standing though in a poor state. It was without any of its decorations and being used as a storage hut.

The claim that Gardner was initiated into the Craft in September 1939 by Dorothy Clutterbuck has been supported to some extent by modern research. There is only hearsay evidence of Clutterbuck's coven but she is known to have been a person of means living in the Bournemouth area. The coven was said to be traditionalist but with a strong influence derived from CO-MASONIC principles. While little has come down overtly into modern ritual, it is significant that Clutterbuck's involvement with the Rosicrucians provided her with knowledge of rituals, some of which are virtually indistinguishable from those of modern Wicca. There is also an argument that the coven drew some of its inspiration and its members from the various organizations of WOODCRAFT FOLK who were active in the New Forest in the 1930s and '40s.

Gardner is said to have met Aleister CROWLEY in

1946 (the year before Crowley's death) through a mutual friend, Arnold CROWTHER, and it is claimed that Gardner was briefly a pupil of, and perhaps liaised with Crowley under whose influence he was initiated, in 1946, into the ninth degree of the *Ordo Templi Orientis*, describing himself as SCRIRE (sic) OTO 4=7. Crowley extended a charter to Gardner permitting him to organize a Lodge and to dispense the first 'Minerval' degree of OTO. The two men were perceived by outsiders to have become linked closely enough that, after Crowley's death, many lodges in the United States considered that Gardner was Crowley's appointed successor. It would seem more likely, however, that relations between Crowley and Gardner were always strained and subject to bickering, enmity and a lack of mutual respect. It is said that Gardner paid Crowley about £300 for his OTO Charter (possibly against Crowley's contribution of ritual material for Gardner's BOOK OF SHADOWS).

Gardner's biographer, Jack BRACELIN, implies that Gardner viewed Crowley as a *self-deluded charlatan who advertised himself, sometimes in the most ludicrous way and claims that Gardner followed the flamboyant instinct of the unsuccessful magician . . . wasted money like water. . .and was not too honest.* From the opposing viewpoint, in Gerald Suster's biography of Crowley, Gerald Gardner does not even merit a mention among the stream of visitors to Hastings from 1945 onwards.

Although Gardner is said to have liaised with Crowley in the preparation of his BOOK OF SHADOWS and there has been much conjecture as to whether one copied from the other, recent research suggests that much of the Crowleyan material used by Gardner was trawled 'secondhand' from magazine articles.

However, Gardner is known to have possessed copies of a limited number of Crowley's original works including *The Equinox of the Gods* which contained a reprint of Crowley's sacred text, the so-called *Book of the Law*. It is this text that Gardner appears to have used, in part, as the basis for *Ye Bok of Ye Art Magical* which he compiled in the late 1940s, claiming it to be of archaic and traditional origin and on which, in turn, he based much of the first version of the *Book of Shadows*, including the early version of the CHARGE OF THE GODDESS. The manual which evolved became an accepted source of Wiccan laws, rituals and theory but only after substantial revision in the 1950s from Doreen VALIENTE, who had become Gardner's High Priestess and who argued for the removal of much of the 'Crowleyan material'.

In terms of provenance, there is no evidence that a genuine medieval manuscript ever existed and the efforts to make Gardner's handwritten material appear arcane are, on close inspection, naive and crudely executed. In reality, much of Gardner's thesis is now known to have been drawn from the ideas of friends and other spiritualist organizations (see also FELLOWSHIP OF CROTONA and HERMETIC ORDER OF THE GOLDEN DAWN) whose intellectual teachings Gardner sought to popularize and make available to the person-in-the-street. It is also undeniable that Gardner possessed a passionate interest in overseeing the revival of an ancient and time-honoured Craft although he was probably not alone in this ambition amongst various PAGANS operating in southern England.

Gardner claimed that the NEW FOREST COVEN was a genuine survival of the Celtic craft. However his efforts at popularization of 'traditional' WITCHCRAFT brought him into conflict with some other HEREDITARY and TRADITIONAL witches who claimed he had assimilated knowledge from their COVENS and proceeded to debase their hallowed rituals, claiming them as his own. Such allegations have neither been proven nor repudiated.

Gardner's personality also brought a degree of animosity. He was not a particularly charismatic man and Cecil WILLIAMSON, who is generally critical of Gardner, describes him in the *Talking Stick* as being *very, very vain, very self-centred, very tight with money a voyeur lacking in diplomacy and a bit clumsy* . Williamson has also made repeated claims, for

example in the *Talking Stick 8, 9* that *Gardner was always economical with the truth* . Gardner implied, in a 1951 interview, that he possessed Doctorates of Philosophy (Singapore, 1934) and Literature (Toulouse), yet both universities rejected these claims as fraudulent.

Gardner also possessed an interest in DRUIDRY and befriended George Watson McGregor Reid and his son Robert, successive chiefs of the ANCIENT ORDER OF DRUIDS. For a while he was caretaker of the ceremonial sword which was used in the Midsummer Solstice ritual, having been lent by Dorothy Clutterbuck.

In 1950 Gardner took over from Cecil Williamson the Museum of Witchcraft, the WITCHES MILL, at Castletown in the Isle of Man where a unique, although often unprovenanced, collection of witch tools and weapons was displayed. It has since been relocated in Toronto. Allegedly Gardner also amplified his occult knowledge through collaboration with Williamson, in whose house he lodged for a period of time.

In his later years, Gardner spent time in both the United States (hailed as Crowley's heir) and in West Africa. He suffered a fatal heart attack in February 1964 while sailing on the SS *Prince* in the Mediterranean and his grave is in Tunis. His will is said to have caused strong public discord when the ownership of the Witches Mill museum was left to Monique WILSON, a Scottish high priestess.

For some years after his death, the Gardnerian witches were looked down upon by so-called Hereditary witches, although now the distinction has become more blurred and the hereditary concept has lost some popularity.

GARDNERIAN WICCA The 'original' branch of WICCA founded by Gerald GARDNER of which the ALEXANDRIAN tradition of Alex and Maxine SANDERS is an offshoot. Gardnerian philosophy tends to lay emphasis on folk PAGANISM while the Alexandrians are more orientated towards ritual magic. In most COVENS the two traditions have

GRIMORIUM VERUM The 'True Grimoire', subtitled *Most Approved Keys of Solomon the Hebrew Rabbi*, an OCCULT 'pocket manuscript' written in French and allegedly translated from Hebrew, purported to have been first published in Rome in 1517. Of unknown authorship, it probably dates from no earlier than the eighteenth century and is one of four known handbooks specifically devoted to the practice of Black Magic (see also GRAND GRIMOIRE).

GUILD OF THE MASTER JESUS The society established by Dion FORTUNE with the objective of meeting the needs of people who are actively engaged in the pursuit of esoteric science and with the aim of creating an atmosphere in which such souls may commune with their God. It attempts to lead consciousness up through the various stages of realization and purification to the culmination of Eucharist. The Guild rejects the claim of the orthodox Church to the authority vested in the apostolic succession of bishops but the Eucharist is celebrated as a route to contacting Jesus as initiator and Master. There is an emphasis on the practice of the higher methods of prayer exemplified by St Teresa of Avila, Francis of Assisi and others.

GUNDESTRUP BOWL A ritual cauldron, constructed of solid silver and gilded plates and discovered during peat cutting in 1891 immersed in the Raevemosen bog near the village of Gundestrup in Himmerland, Jutland. Dating from the Cimbrian period (about 2000 years ago), most expert opinion places it as being of Celtic origin made somewhere in the Danube basin and transported to Denmark as booty or a peace offering, after which its claimants may have deposited it in the bog as a gesture to a Cimbrian war god. With a capacity of 130 litres, it is engraved and embellished with mythical scenes which include a goddess with a necklace and a squatting horned god, generally assumed to be CERNUNNOS, attended by a deer and a boar (see also CAULDRONS).

HAG The dark destructive aspect of the GODDESS into whom the MAIDEN is transformed with the death of the year in autumn and who may herself evolve into the maiden reborn in springtime. In Welsh Celtic tradition, this is the aspect of the goddess known as Ceridwen while in Ireland she was also known as the Cailleach Bheare. The Hag may also equate with BLACK ANNIS of English lore (see also DARK GODDESS).

HALLOWE'EN See SAMHAIN.

HANDFASTING, CEREMONY OF In WICCAN tradition, this is the joining together of a couple in marriage. They vow to remain in partnership for as long as love lasts, after which each is permitted to leave the relationship and go their separate ways. The ceremony is taken by the High Priestess or Priest of the COVEN and usually occurs in a period when the moon is waxing. Those attending either dress in white or go SKYCLAD, and there is an exchange of rings with runic inscriptions.

HANDPART, CEREMONY OF The occasion upon which a marriage between two witches, proclaimed at HANDFASTING, may be dissolved. In practice it is hardly, if ever, enacted.

HARGRAVE, JOHN (died 1983) An English occultist, the founder of several PAGAN organizations including the KIBBO KIFT KINDRED and, later, the Social Credit Party, or Greenshirts, which, it is claimed, represented the first Green Party in Britain. In 1945 he emigrated to Canada where he established new branches of the SCP.

As a teenager, Hargrave had been influenced by the Scouting Movement and had risen to the position of Scout Commissioner for Woodcraft and Camping. At the age of 19 he compiled a classic survival manual for scouts, *Lonecraft*, but he had come to view the Movement as excessively imperialistic and militaristic, preferring to establish organizations that followed more pacifist and socialist doctrines.

HARTLEY, CHRISTINE Priestess and collaborator of Charles SEYMOUR.

HECATE See HEKATE.

HEDGEWITCH A term achieving popularity in the UK in the 1990s for a practitioner of the Craft (see WICCA) who elects to follow an independent, solitary route, does not belong to a COVEN and has not been initiated. One of the foremost proponents of the Craft of the solitary witch in England is the PAGAN author Rae Beth who injects strong feminine principles into this style of Craft, particularly with respect to healing and regeneration. In America, Sybil LEEK did much to promote the image of the Hedgewitch, though she did not use this term. One prominent solitary American witch is Scott Cunningham, though again he does not use the term 'hedgewitch'.

The 'hedge' witch is perhaps closest to the old-style village wisewoman who now practises her craft to heal and to teach others of the EARTH MYSTERIES.

Before a SABBAT celebration, the hedgewitch will cast a circle enclosing the sacred space and altar in much the same way as that created in a coven. This may be indoors or out in the open air and the altar

*The Green Man, Pagan spirit of the trees, and the
May Queen, traditional figures of May Day celebrations.*

*The Horned God, who represents both the Oak
King of summer and the Holly King of winter –
at different times of the year a pastoral deity and the
representation of austerity and death. The counterpart
of Hekate, this is the darker aspect of male sexuality.*

A Wiccan couple jumping over the broomstick which symbolized their union at the end of the handfast ceremony which effectively joins them in marriage.

A newly 'handfasted' couple. Round his neck the groom wears a pentagram, the Wiccan symbol of the Earth and its properties of material wealth, practicalities and stability.

may be a naturally occurring object, such as a tree stump or a rock. The same guardian spirits of the four quarters, familiar in other aspects of Wicca, will protect this circle. The solitary practitioner will invoke the GODDESS or God, sweep the floor anti-clockwise (widdershins) and dance clockwise (DEOSIL) around the circle before formally consecrating it, perhaps with the aid of lighted candles. A symbolic offering will be placed on the altar and the ritual is closed with a communion rite.

Rae Beth emphasizes that bathing before a ritual is important but that perfumes, deodorants, and unconsecrated jewellery should be abandoned and that ceremonial clothing, if worn, should be woven from natural fibres. She also advocates the performance of ritual SKYCLAD. The tools are essentially those of Wicca including a personal BOOK OF SHADOWS and the same eight major Sabbats are observed.

Much emphasis is laid for the hedgewitch on trance-work as the essence of MAGIC, a mental and psychical state in which the future can be divined and the spirit world contacted. Trance-work is perceived as an inner transformation, bringing the astral being to the fore. This is often exploited with the aid of an animal FAMILIAR, necessary only in spirit, with whom the hedgewitch will bond. The use of herbs also plays a strong role in the work of the solitary practitioner.

HEKATE (HECATE) A Greek goddess of the moon and of pathways who has been invoked as a patron of Medea and of other witches since Classical times. Variously described either as the daughter of Zeus and Hera, or of Perses and Asteria, she is the mother of Scylla and is specifically the goddess of pathways and crossroads travelled by night. She is depicted carrying a torch and an assortment of other attributes, and is sometimes depicted accompanied by coiled snakes and howling dogs. Traditionally, offerings have been left to her at roadside junctions. Hekate is also a goddess of the moon who became syncretized, in

Hellenic times, with Selene. In parts of Thessaly she was worshipped by OCCULT bands of moon worshippers and in some versions of the Persephone/DEMETER legend she plays a role in the seasonal return of Persephone to her mother from the arms of Hades.

HELLFIRE CLUB Opened by Sir Francis DASHWOOD in the eighteenth century and more properly known as the Friars of St Francis of Wycombe, the club listed among its members a number of distinguished personalities including Benjamin Franklin, Francis Duffield, Lord Sandwich, George Selwyn and Thomas Potter. Meetings were held at night in a grotto in the grounds of Medmenham Abbey in Buckinghamshire where members, dressed as monks or friars, ate, drank, gambled and indulged in sexual romps in a light-hearted parody of Devil worship. none were actually Satanists or witches but enjoyed a salacious reputation as hellraisers. Its last meeting took place in June 1762.

HEREDITARY CRAFT This relies on the notion of a continuous succession of individuals linking back not necessarily by direct parentage (the lineage is reported to skip generations), either to the medieval period or, in extreme, to a Celtic or Anglo-Saxon origin. It is stressed that a Hereditary witch is not initiated into the Craft but must be born into it.

HERMES TRISMEGISTOS Also known as Hermes Logos, the classical Greek derivative of the Egyptian god, Thoth (Thot), who was the tutelary deity of writing and learning and, allegedly the founder of mysticism and philosophy and the author of the *Corpus Hermeticum*. In Hermetic literature he is depicted as a sage. 'Trismegistos' means 'three times great' and is copied from the term applied to Thoth in certain epithets found in the Temple of Esna on the Nile in Upper Egypt, north of Aswan.

HERMETICISM An intellectual study of magic, chiefly of interest in Renaissance Italy but which gained a following in England, based on the translation of the Greek manuscript, *Corpus Hermeticum*, which proposed that it was possible for humankind to regain its control over the natural world, lost by Adam at the Fall. It relies on a mix of astrological and alchemical principles and lore.

The pre-Christian provenance claimed for Hermetic texts was disproved in 1614 by Isaac CASAUBON although, notwithstanding, the most prominent English hermeticist, Robert FLUDD (1574-1637), placed much store in the hermetic PYMANDER which had been translated into English in 1649 and which continued to claim origins dating to pre-Mosaic times.

HERMETIC ORDER OF THE GOLDEN DAWN
The most prominent among the many revivalist cults, this OCCULT society of magical arts was founded in 1887 by four charter members – W Wynn WESTCOTT, S L MacGregor MATHERS, W R Woodman and A F A Woodford, the first three of whom were also members of the ROSICRUCIAN Fraternity. By 1890 the Order (GD) was fully established with three Temples, ISIS-URANIA in London, Osiris at Weston-super-Mare and Horus at Bradford, each of which was administrated by three Chiefs – Imperator (Emperor), Cancellarius (Chancellor) and Praemonstrator (Administrator). The Order, which accepted initiates of both sexes, flourished in the climate of religious romance which developed both in England and on the Continent during the latter part of the nineteenth century and as a reaction to the unsettling revelations of scientists such as Charles Darwin. Its magical element was not introduced until 1892 with the inauguration of the Second Order, Roseae Rubeae et Aureae Crucis (see ROSE OF RUBY AND CROSS OF GOLD), prior to which the organization had been purely philosophical in its aims.

Golden Dawn was undoubtedly stimulated by Anna KINGSFORD's Hermetic Society from whence two of its founder members, MacGregor Mathers and Westcott, had come but, officially, it claimed descent from the Rosicrucian Order on the basis of a set of cipher manuscripts entrusted to Westcott by Woodford who had, in turn, inherited them either from a prominent nineteenth century mystic, Fred Hockley, who died in 1885, or by accident between the leaves of a secondhand book. When decoded, these manuscripts provided details of rituals and sources of occult power which appeared to be of Rosicrucian origin. They provided the five grades of the First Order, compiled by MacGregor Mathers, on which the charter of Golden Dawn was based. The Order embellished its ritual with Egyptian and Greek imagery, drawing heavily on such esoteric works as Helena BLAVATSKY's *Isis Unveiled* (1877) and it drew its membership from the educated ranks of the upper and middle classes who already had leanings towards Masonry, Hermeticism and Theosophy. It particularly attracted Freemasons and others who had difficulty with the oriental leanings of the THEOSOPHICAL SOCIETY. It demanded that its members take occult names, typically in the form of a Latin motto, and its practice was based on initiatory rituals through which the way was opened to the elite inner or Second Order, the Rose of Ruby and Cross of Gold or RR et AC, founded in 1892, the objective of which was to meld the higher and lower natures of the initiate. Golden Dawn initiates attained a series of grades within three distinct orders based, in all but the lowest grade, on the Qabalistic Tree of Life (see QABALAH), thus rising from Neophyte through Philosophus in the First Order and from Zelator Adeptus Minor to Adeptus Exemptus in the Second Order. Beyond these earthly ranks the Third Order grades extended from magister Templi to the ultimate seniority of Ipsissimus among the Secret Chiefs.

Membership included several notable personalities including W B YEATS, Bram Stoker and Aleister CROWLEY, whose association with MacGregor Mathers proved a source of feuding within the Order.

Among its activities Golden Dawn was involved in the translation and distribution of occult books and in formulating spells, curses and potions for use in magical rituals. Some of the early ideas of Gerald GARDNER may have been inspired through its teachings.

The influence of the Order was strong until the turn of the century when it was finally swamped by schisms attributed to internal jealousies and feuding within the Second Order, not least being the dissent over Crowley's membership. The established Golden Dawn Order collapsed in 1903 but its magically orientated members, led by an eminent physician, R W FELKIN, re-emerged as the STELLA MATUTINA, while a splinter group, under A E WAITE, regrouped around the ISIS-URANIA Temple, having abandoned magical work in favour of Christian mysticism. The Isis-Urania Temple (under Golden Dawn) closed in about 1900 but various factions continued to exist spasmodically until approximately the onset of World War II, when the remnants disintegrated having also lost membership in the face of Gardner's influential and popular approach to MAGIC. Out of Golden Dawn's fragments, including the remodelled Isis-Urania Temple, Stella Matutina and J W Brodie-Innes's London Temple, ALPHA ET OMEGA, there emerged a generation of new organizations. Most notably these included the SOCIETY OF THE INNER LIGHT (SIL), founded in 1927 by Dion FORTUNE (who had joined A O in 1919), from which have emerged at least five splinter fraternities. The SIL is distinct from the confusingly named FRATERNITY OF THE INNER LIGHt founded in 1922 by Moina MATHERS. These modern societies have collectively defined themselves as the WESTERN MYSTERIES.

HERMETIC SOCIETY An OCCULT organization founded in 1884 by Anna KINGSFORD. She was a clairvoyant who had been President of the London Lodge of the THEOSOPHICAL SOCIETY between 1883 and 1884, but resigned because she objected to the emphasis on eastern philosophies. The Hermetic Society was launched with the intention of promoting Western occultism built on Christian foundations and appealing to those intellectuals whose peace of mind had been severely disturbed by the revelations of Darwinism. Amongst the personalities invited to speak at Hermetic Society meetings were S L MacGregor MATHERS and W W WESTCOTT and it is arguably correct that Anna Kingsford provided the catalyst for the founding of Golden Dawn (see HERMETIC ORDER OF THE GOLDEN DAWN).

HERNE One of the aspects or avatars of the HORNED GOD, also referred to as Herne the Hunter since he is perceived as the leader of the phantom hunt in which respect he has become syncretized with the chief of the Norse pantheon, OTHIN. In mythology he is of either Celtic or Anglo-Saxon origin and is perceived as a chthonic god of the UNDERWORLD. In England he is particularly associated with Windsor Great Park in Berkshire as the British oak god. Until the eighteenth century, according to tradition, Herne roamed the Park, a preserved remnant of the ancient oak forests, as his particular domain. He equates with the Welsh deities Gwynn ap Nudd and Arawn.

HEXENBANNER The equal, in Germany, of a CUNNING PERSON who provided a local service to ward off the effects of witches' spells and who sold remedies. There are said to have been several thousand active in Germany and Austria during the medieval period and they provoked strong opposition in certain quarters. The German scholar of the occult, Johann Kruse (born 1889), was a particular critic, suggesting that the remedies of Hexenbanners might be harmful or even fatal, and that they incited hatred and violence against alleged witches.

One of the best known Hexenbanners was a man called Eberling, who equated his mission in life with that of Christ and whose particular forte lay in the diagnosis of a hex using feathers.

HIGH MAGIC'S AID The historical novel by Gerald GARDNER, published in 1949, which acts as the preface to his BOOK OF SHADOWS and which contains his earliest description of the old traditional rites on which he claimed modern WICCA ceremonial to be based. It was, he claimed, a truthful revelation about the medieval cult. However, it was derived, at least in part, from his experience with Dorothy CLUTTERBUCK's SOUTHERN COVEN OF BRITISH WITCHES. It has been argued that Gardner's fictional writing has done more to promote understanding of WITCHCRAFT than his more factual works.

HINE, PHIL See CHAOS MAGIC.

HITLER, SPELLS AGAINST During World War II, it is claimed that a CONE OF POWER was raised by British witches on at least one (probably more) occasion to direct psychic forces against Adolf Hitler and to persuade him against invasion of England. According to GARDNER a ritual at which he was present applied the words: *You cannot cross the sea; you cannot cross the sea; not able to come; not able to come.*

Gardner claimed that a COVEN had met in the New Forest. This account was supported in an article by Cecil WILLIAMSON (*Illustrated*, 27 September 1952), in which he asserted that on the night of the LAMMAS SABBAT in August 1940, a group of seventeen had gathered in the New Forest in Hampshire. Williamson's observations are, however, unreliable since, at a later date (*Talking Stick 9*, Winter 1992) he alters the story, claiming that the account of the New Forest ritual is spurious. According to Williamson's later testimony, a bizarre ritual, not attended by Gardner, was organized under the auspices of MI5, during which an effigy of Hitler was hauled to the top of a church tower and set alight to coincide with the visit of two Vatican nuncios to the Duke of Norfolk's seat at Arundel Castle. It was performed not in the New Forest but on an estate near Chuck Hatch in

Ashdown Forest. Aleister CROWLEY is said to have been present in company with his son, Amado, the local Fire Brigade, some forty Canadian soldiers and an assortment of fortune-tellers and other extras. No date is offered.

Williamson's later claim is probably to be disregarded. Conceivably two mutually exclusive rituals took place against Hitler's planned invasion but not as Williamson reported. His allegations concerning Arundel Castle are palpably inaccurate and it is implausible that the event described would have gone unreported for more than forty years.

HOBLINK A British PAGAN group established in 1989 by Gordon the Toad (a pseudonym for its founder who prefers to remain anonymous) and his associates, offering specialist support for homosexuals, lesbians and bisexuals within the Pagan traditions and OCCULT practices. It follows a diversity of Pagan and occult paths although the majority of its members have, or have had, links with WICCA. Although based in the U.K. its membership extends to Europe and North America, and it has links with comparable organizations elsewhere in the world. It publishes a quarterly newsletter.

HOCKLEY, FREDERICK (died 1885) A celebrated mystic and clairvoyant who was a member of the SOCIETAS ROSICRUCIANA IN ANGLICA. He was particularly adroit in the use of the crystal ball and the mirror for obtaining occult information and he worked closely with a fellow clairvoyant, Emma Leigh.

Hockley claimed to have recorded thirty volumes of conversations thus obtained with spirit entities and to have transcribed many unpublished manuscripts on magic and alchemy. According to one version of events, Hockley passed on the foundation rituals of Golden Dawn (see HERMETIC ORDER OF THE GOLDEN DAWN) to its founder members.

HOG See HOUSE OF THE GODDESS.

HOLT, JOHN The Lord Chief Justice of England from 1689 to 1710 who was the first prominent member of the judiciary to move away from the draconian style of witch-trial and conviction that had marked the earlier decades of the seventeenth century. He presided over an increasing number of acquittals. His successor, Mr. Justice POWELL, continued the trend of moderation.

HONORIUS, GRIMOIRE OF The influential fourteenth century manuscript, of Christian origin, describing the rituals of black magic derived from ancient texts, including the *Testament of Solomon* and the *Clavicula Solomonis* (see SOLOMON, KEY OF). The Grimoire, of which the British Museum has a sixteenth-century copy, is claimed by some authorities to have been wrongly attributed to Pope Honorius and should properly be credited to an obscure magician of that name.

HOPKINS, MATTHEW (died 1647) The Puritan witch-hunter active in Essex and the Home Counties during the English Civil War and, in England, probably responsible for more witchcraft convictions and EXECUTIONS than any other individual during the WITCH-CRAZE of the seventeenth century. He exploited worries about the war and persuaded local Puritans that a fifth column of witches was actively working for the Royalist cause in Essex. His background was as an unsuccessful lawyer but he established himself as a witch-hunter in Chelmsford between 1644 and 1645, wrote a treatise in 1647 entitled *Discoverie of Witches* and spread his activities throughout southeast England, becoming sufficiently celebrated that he employed a team of assistants and was dubbed the 'Witchfinder General'. He applied all the accepted tests of exposing a witch and investigated the continental notions of diabolical pacts as well as the more English association with beastly FAMILIARS. Any elderly woman, living alone,

who was, for whatever reason, unpopular with her neighbours, was potential fodder to Hopkins' appetite and he was paid the generous sum of a pound a head for those who were convicted following discovery and arrest.

Hopkins's chief associate was the Puritan John Stearne, who wrote *A Confirmation and Discovery of Witchcraft* (1648). Hopkins died, allegedly of consumption, having fallen from favour under growing opposition to his overbearing zeal and tactics. It was largely through adverse reaction to Hopkins' excesses that the number of convictions in the English courts subsequently waned.

HORNED GOD The male deity of WICCA, arguably a composite drawn from aspects of the Celtic CERNUNNOS and HERNE, and the Norse and Germanic OTHIN (Woden). He represents a solar and vegetation god who also, in some respects, bears characteristics of the dying and rising god of ancient near eastern traditions (Dumuzi, Tammuz, Attis, Osiris). He is the Oak King of summer, also identified with the GREEN MAN, the CORN KING and the Sun King, and the Holly King of winter, in which role he is also the Hunter and the Lord of the Underworld. At the Winter Solstice he is the Child of Promise representing the sun reborn.

In Wicca, the Horned God is thus perceived both as a strongly ithyphallic hunter and as a gentle, caring pastoral deity and, by contrast, as the dark, dying god who represents the austerities of winter.

HORNIMAN, ANNIE E F (1860-1937) A notable occultist at the turn of the century and the inheritor of her father's private ethnographic collection which became the Horniman Museum at Forest Hill in South London. A one-time student of the Slade she used her influence to persuade her father to employ S L MacGregor MATHERS for a time as museum curator and, in doing so, facilitated his marriage to Moina Bergson (see MATHERS, Moina).

Annie Horniman joined the ISIS-URANIA Temple and was made the first initiate member of the

Second Order of Golden Dawn (see HERMETIC ORDER OF THE GOLDEN DAWN) when the Vault was inaugurated in December 1891, subsequently funding several of S L MacGregor Mathers overseas studies of the occult. She was regarded as difficult and tactless, gaining the nickname 'Pussy', and she resigned her position with the Isis-Urania Temple in London at the end of 1896, disillusioned with MacGregor Mathers pecuniary demands on her and was promptly expelled from the Order. She was reinstated by YEATS when he took over as Chief but, in 1902, continuing political unrest over the existence of Secret Groups within Golden Dawn, which she strongly opposed, persuaded her to resign for good.

HOROS, MADAME (born 1854) An obscure occultist, the daughter of a German father and Spanish mother, who claimed to be Anna SPRENGEL of Golden Dawn fame (see HERMETIC ORDER OF THE GOLDEN DAWN) and for a time deluded MacGregor MATHERS to this effect. Madame Horos (her maiden name is uncertain) also claimed to have founded an American religious society, the Koreshan Unity, at the age of twelve. She was divorced twice before marrying an ex-member of the Koreshan Unity, Frank Jackson, who assumed the name Theo Horos. The pair emigrated from America and travelled in Europe until, in 1901, they moved to London and set up a bogus Golden Dawn order using many of MacGregor Mathers' rituals. Their downfall came after both were successfully prosecuted for the rape of a sixteen-year-old initiate, Daisy Adams. Theo Horos was sentenced to fifteen years, his wife to seven.

HORSESHOE Used as an AMULET or counter-charm during the period of the WITCH-CRAZE to counteract the misfortunes brought to a victim by a witch. Contemporary records indicate that most households in the West End of London during the seventeenth century kept a horseshoe for security. It was conventionally hung above the threshold.

HOUSE OF THE GODDESS (HOG) A British PAGAN centre founded in 1985 by Shan JAYRAN, centring on her activities in South London and with the object of providing contact, support, learning and celebration of Paganism. HOG has, over the years, offered open rituals and study courses, and has hosted a well-known Hallowe'en festival – in the late 1980s it was one of the very few large open Pagan gatherings. It offers a feminist approach with a strong element of psychotherapy. Contact is through a national network. Support has been provided since inception in the form of open Pagan teaching courses, postgraduate meetings and counselling. Learning is provided through a series of publications and INITIATION training.

HYDESVILLE KNOCKINGS The paranormal activities in the form of knockings and tappings claimed to have taken place during 1848 at the home of a family named Fox living at Hydesville in New York State. Their experiences became the stimulus for modern American interest in spiritualism. The ghost of a murdered pedlar generated poltergeist activity in the room where he was slain, the bedroom of the Fox daughters, Kate and Margaretta, and the girls gained a cult status on account of their psychic powers. As in many such cases, the girls were young and growing up in an impoverished environment. It is widely documented that visionaries often fall into this category.

Bernadette Soubirous was an illiterate fourteen-year-old girl living in obscurity in the Pyrenean town of Lourdes before she rocketed to international fame as St Bernadette of Lourdes and the Catholic Church places great faith in the visions of such children. Such incidents act to reinforce the belief that this faith is still creditworthy.

HYPERBOREA See DIANIC WITCHCRAFT.

IDRIES SHAH SAYID A writer on Sufi who was employed by Gerald GARDNER as a secretary in the 1950s. His most famous work is *The Sufis* (1964), which investigates the famous order of Arab mystics who still exist today. In the book he postulates that the medieval witch cult in England was of Arabian or North African origin with secret communication taking place between middle eastern mystics and their western counterparts. Some of the argument is based on the fact that the Moorish rule, and therefore influence, extended to Spain for over seven hundred years from 711 AD until 1492. Many of the Moorish sciences, including astronomy and medicine, were conveyed to Spanish intellectuals who generally fell behind in these disciplines. But the Moors were also deeply interested in MAGIC, astrology and ALCHEMY, and it seems inevitable that many of their ideas and practices concerning the OCCULT arts were copied.

Further east, the Knights Templar also opened an interface for the exchange of magical ideas and almost certainly absorbed many before they were persecuted as heretics. They worshipped the deity BAPHOMET which, according to Doreen VALIENTE, bears a strong similarity with the God of the Craft and it is significant that Gerald Gardner was a Sufi initiate.

ILLUMINATES OF THANATEROS An OCCULT order of CHAOS MAGIC, the name of which is drawn from a corruption of the Greek deities Thanatos, who with Hypnos was the offspring of Nyx and the personification of death, and Eros, the god of love whose mother was Aphrodite. It was begun as a joke when two prominent authors in the late 1970s, Ray Sherwin and Peter Carroll, published works on Chaos Magic in the name of *The Magical Pact of the Illuminates of Thanateros* jibing at small magical orders with, they claimed, pompous-sounding titles. In 1986, however, the IOT was formally inaugurated with the charter of training magicians in the system of Peter Carroll, a magician and theoretical physicist and one of the pioneers of a proposal that Chaos theory holds the most likely explanation of how MAGIC actually works.

In England the order enjoyed a popular but short-lived revival in the 1990s.

IMAGE MAGIC The technique by which a clay or wax effigy of a potential victim was sculpted and stuck with pins in the part of the body intended to be affected. Image magic can be traced back to ancient times and was practised by the Anglo-Saxons. It was prevalent throughout the Tudor and Stuart reigns in England and was occasionally the subject of witch-trials. This type of damage-by-proxy could also be effected by burying some of the victim's clothes and, on occasions, it reportedly extended to NECROMANCY, using a skull or a toxin prepared from a decomposing corpse.

IMBOLC (OIMLEC) One of the four Grand SABBATS. Celebrated between 31 January and 1 February, it coincides with both the Christian feast of CANDLEMAS and with the more ancient PAGAN festival of the god PAN. Stemming more directly from a Celtic fire festival, modern Pagans see it as the renewal of early spring, marking the cyclical transition of the GODDESS from her aspect as HAG back to that of MAIDEN. In WICCA especially the emphasis is on the Maiden aspect. She returns to the natural world from the UNDERWORLD kingdom where she has been the consort of the God of Death during the cold, dark months.

INCUBUS An essentially Continental invention, heavily castigated in the MALLEUS MALEFICARUM, of a male demon or spirit who performs acts of sexual intercourse with mortal women using semen extracted from sleeping men. The male counterpart of the SUCCUBUS. The Incubus was allegorized in Christian tradition as the embodiment of the Devil to whom witches were obliged to submit sexually.

Belief in the existence of the Incubus generated its crop of risqué reports, some of which were based on more temporal misbehaviour. Reginald SCOT, with typically dry wit, commented that *old witches were sworn to procure as many young virgins for Incubus as they could, whereby in time they grew to be excellent bawds*. Elsewhere he cites the case of a nocturnal visitation by an Incubus that: *came to a ladies bedside and made hot loove unto hir; whereat she being offended, cried out so lowd, that companie came and found him (the incubus) under hir bed in the likenesse of the holie bishop.*

INCUBUS SUCCUBUS A PAGAN rock band formed in about 1990 and comprising practising witches whom many regard as articulate spokespersons for the Craft (see WICCA) and for thousands of Pagans in Britain and Europe. They frequently perform at The Marquee (of Rolling Stones fame) in Charing Cross Road, London, and are generally supportive of Pagan endeavours. The band leaders are their lead singer Candia and her partner, lead guitarist Tony McCormack. The name of the band has recently been modified to Inkubus Sukkubus.

INITIATION, MEDIEVAL Little detail which can be verified is available from contemporary literature. Pennethorne Hughes cites a witch tract of 1705 which lists the three chief requirements of the novice:

to consent freely to the process of becoming a witch

to deny the Catholic faith
to sign a pact, verbal or otherwise, with the Devil.

It suggests that sponsorship of a novice witch was mandatory and describes a formal introduction before the COVEN during which the initiate spurned the Virgin Mary, spat on the Cross and committed other blasphemous acts before making her diabolical pact. There followed a parody of the Christian Baptism during which the initiate was given a secret name. The initiation rite was often accompanied by the sacrifice of an animal, conventionally a black hen or cockerel and the name of the initiate was entered into a Black Book or Roll kept by the Master of the coven. None of the foregoing can be reliably provenanced.

INITIATION (WICCA, FIRST DEGREE) The first of three levels of initiation and the ceremony by which an individual enters into the WICCA faith and becomes a witch. It is important to Wicca because it is a mystery religion, in much the same style as the ancient mystery cults of the Classical world, or secret societies in Africa. The chief purpose is to bring the individual to a doorway of spiritual awakening and to link the initiate into the collective mind and spirit of the COVEN, and also the collective mind of the family of Wicca, whether it be ALEXANDRIAN or GARDNERIAN.

Prior to initiation, it is assumed that the candidate seeking admission has undergone training and study for not less than a year. Initiation ceremonies vary widely from coven to coven but proceed along certain generalized lines. Vivianne CROWLEY describes the initiate being first unclothed and, in her coven, taken through a rite of ELEMENT BALANCING, which guides the candidate on a personal tour of the elemental guardians of the circle before initiation proper commences.

Initiation proceeds through sponsors, who ritually blindfold the candidate and tie him or her with three cords around the wrists, neck, knee and ankle to partly restrict movement and then secure the hands behind the back. The candidate is provided with the occult passwords *Love* and *Trust* and the circle is cast.

In some covens, at the opening of the rite, and before the initiate enters the circle, the medieval BAGAHI RUNE is recited followed by the CHARGE to invoke the deities. At this juncture a gap or doorway is created in the periphery of the circle and a broomstick is placed across the threshold to symbolize sexual union (between the rod and the brush). The initiate is challenged by the initiator who holds the ATHAME against the candidate's breast and enquires if he or she possesses the courage to step across the threshold. If the response is 'yes', the athame is laid across the broomstick and the initiate is spun into the circle with a kiss of greeting and presented to the four quarters beginning in the east and moving clockwise (DEOSIL) around to the north. The coven dances in a circle and chants after which a bell is rung and the initiator kneels before the initiate offering them a five-fold kiss on the feet, knees, genitals, breast and lips to symbolize the sacred nature of the body and to activate the CHAKRAS. There is some suggestion that, in pre-Gardnerian times, initiation involved a seven-fold or nine-fold kiss.

The initiate's ankles are loosely tied with one of the cords, and the initiate is lightly scourged before taking the oath of OCCULT allegiance to Wicca. The initiate is consecrated three times and the blindfold is removed. He or she is then presented with the eight symbolic tools of power (see WORKING TOOLS) and, finally, the initiate is led once more to the four guardian watchtowers of the circle.

INITIATION (WICCA, SECOND DEGREE)
The degree after which an initiate becomes a full priest or priestess. In ALEXANDRIAN COVENS, first degree initiates are allowed to witness the rite while in GARDNERIAN tradition, it is retained only for the audience of second and third degree witches. The rite includes the LEGEND OF THE GODDESS and, at its core, is an oath more binding than that uttered at the first degree ceremony. The initiate into the

second degree may be naked and tethered but not blindfolded, and the rite includes, in one coven, the transfer of a ring, worn on the third finger of the right hand as a personal gift from initiator to initiate. The ring also symbolizes a transference of innate powers, the so-called 'willing of the power'.

The initiate is offered wine and, as in the first stage, the initiator delivers the five-fold kiss after which the last of the bonds are removed and the initiate is presented with the eight WORKING TOOLS that he or she is now asked to put to use. They are also presented with the ritual cords and a scourge and are given the teaching of the Three Fold Law. At this juncture the Legend of the Goddess may be enacted by members of the coven.

INITIATION (WICCA, THIRD DEGREE) The
third and highest level of initiation to be completed by a witch of WICCA allows an individual to form his or her own COVEN, and to initiate other witches to second and third degree levels.

The initiation rite centres upon the SACRED MARRIAGE through which the *animus* (male spirituality) or *anima* (female spirituality) of the initiate becomes one with his or her opposite. It is performed either symbolically or as an authentic sexual coupling of priest and priestess, and is based on the ancient Mesopotamian rite dating from at least the third of fourth millennium BC, which later became translated into the Mysteries of ISIS and into the Greek *hieros gamos*).

INNER LIGHT, SOCIETY See FRATERNITY OF THE INNER LIGHT.

INNER PLANE ADEPTI See ADEPT.

INQUISITION, PAPAL The formal court of
enquiry established by the Catholic Church between 1227 and 1235, designed to enforce legal sanctions against the more serious offences (alleged) of witches and heretics. In order to combat what the Church saw as a mounting threat to its influence

from fringe sects, Pope Gregory IX established the Commission of Inquiry, known as the Inquisition, after a long period of comparative peace within the Catholic realms. It was the first official body with a specific mandate against heretics and it was established following the crusade to quash the Catharist heresy in southern France. The Inquisition did not exercise direct powers to penalise but it was empowered to detect those guilty of heresy by fair means or otherwise. It travelled a circuit and its proceedings were carried out in strict secrecy, with only the punishments being publicized at Sunday masses. Those brought before the Inquisition were never acquitted and were always at risk of being arrested again. Although Pope Innocent IV gave dispensation for the secular authorities to use torture on behalf of the Commission, for practical reasons the Inquisition often gave itself absolution to use extreme means of extracting confession. In any event, powers employed by the ecclesiastical courts after guilt had been established included the seizure of personal possessions, imprisonment, torture and EXECUTION. The Inquisition generated its own laws and manuals of enforcement and moved to make SORCERY and heresy inseparable offences.

INSTITORIS, HEINRICH (born circa 1430) The chief author of the MALLEUS MALEFICARUM. Born near Strasbourg, he became a Dominican monk and was regarded as an astute politician. In 1474 he was appointed as the official inquisitor in southern Germany. He first concentrated his efforts against heresy but later narrowed his interest to the condemnation of WITCHCRAFT and witches, a task in which he was aided by a colleague, Jakob Sprenger. He argued that the majority of witches were women because they were stupid, superstitious and sensual and that all witches, once convicted, irrespective of their sex or misdemeanour, should incur the death penalty.

His Dominican order subsequently evicted him for various misdemeanours (witnessed by Sprenger), including embezzlement, but his personal influence

on Pope Innocent VIII resulted in the publication, in 1484, of a papal bull against witchcraft (see SUMMIS DESIDERANTES AFFECTIBUS).

INVOCATION The ritualized procedure through which the spiritual presence of a deity may be called into the presence of its devotees through the medium of the SHAMAN or priest. In shamanistic and tribal religions, the shaman becomes visibly 'possessed' and may speak in strange voices, enter a trance-like state, or become violently agitated and eventually collapse into unconsciousness. This state may be drug-induced.

In WICCA, invocation involves the spiritual persona of the GODDESS or God entering into the physical body of the high priest or priestess.

IOT See ILLUMINATES OF THANTEROS.

ISIS The Mother Goddess of ancient Egypt, worshipped from about 2700 BC to 400 AD, and the object of devotion of many modern PAGANS. The offspring of Geb and Nut, she is the elder sister and wife of the god Osiris. It was she who pieced Osiris's dismembered corpse together after it had been hacked to pieces by his jealous brother Set.

In the culture of the Greeks and Romans she was greatly revered and became known by the title *Stella Maris*, Star of the Sea, represented in the heavens by the North Star. her cult is believed to have influenced the portrayal of the Christian Virgin Mary. See also FELLOWSHIP OF ISIS.

ISIS-URANIA The oldest of the Golden Dawn temples (see also HERMETIC ORDER OF THE GOLDEN DAWN) founded in London in 1888 by a group of four charter members of Golden Dawn. This initial lodge, designed to work through the five lower grades of initiation in Golden Dawn, was expanded shortly afterwards by the establishment of the AMEN-RA Temple in Edinburgh, the Horus Temple in Bradford, the Osiris Temple in Weston-super-Mare and the Ahathoor Temple in Paris.

JAMES VI OF SCOTLAND (JAMES I OF ENGLAND) King of Scotland 1567-1625, of England 1603-1625. A leading protagonist of the witch-craze in England after accession in 1603 and the author of *Demonologie* (1597), which was strongly critical of the views of such liberals as Reginald Scot. James's alienation from the Craft (see Wicca) developed after the trial of the so-called North Berwick witches between 1590 and 1592 when an elderly woman, Agnes Sampson, confessed to a diabolically-inspired plot against him, having herself been exposed by a girl, Gilly Duncan, who confessed under torture.

According to Sampson a party of witches had entered a local church on HALLOWE'EN, where they raised a storm by magical means with the intention of sinking the king's ship as he travelled to Denmark. If this failed, Sampson had intended to work further devilish arts against the king through the agency of toad's blood. Most of those implicated by Duncan were executed and James VI subsequently carried a deep personal antagonism towards WITCHCRAFT, thus ending a period of comparative tolerance in England.

JARCKE, KARL ERNST A nineteenth-century Professor of Criminal Law at the University of Berlin who made extensive studies of the records of seventeenth-century witch trials in Germany and who was the first modern scholar to promote the theory, in 1828, that WITCHCRAFT is a form of PAGANISM that has survived as a remnant of pre-Christian European beliefs.

JAYRAN, SHAN (born 1949) A prominent British PAGAN, a Craft priestess of the DIANIC tradition since 1984, establishing the *House of the Goddess* in the following year as a centre for contact, support, learning and celebration of Paganism. The author of several Pagan publications, including *Circlework* and *The Pagan Index*, she pioneered in southern England a more overt policy over conventionally occult Pagan activities. Before anyone else in London, she hosted open meetings and the concept of public ritual available to all comers (see also WEAVER).

JENNINGS, HARGRAVE A late Victorian amateur scholar known for his literary output between the 1860s and 1880s. Most notably he wrote a pseudo-history of Rosicrucianism (see ROSICRUCIANS) which became highly acclaimed among uncritical readers. He asserted that the ancient religious principles which were embodied by Rosicrucianism all possessed a resemblance to phallic symbolism.

JOAN OF ARC (1412?-1431) The French warrior maiden who persuaded Charles VII that she had a divine mission to throw the English out of north-west France during the Hundred Years War. After she raised the siege of Orleans in 1429, Charles was crowned at Rheims. She subsequently failed to secure Paris, however, and was arrested on charges of witchcraft and heresy, to be tried before a panel of ecclesiastical judges who supported the English position. She was condemned and burnt at the stake in Rouen on 30 May 1431, and eventually canonized by the Catholic Church in 1920.

JOHN BARLEYCORN A figure from folklore,

sometimes the centre of LAMMAS rites in WICCA. He is then seen as the dying, seasonal aspect of the God, who appears in late summer and early autumn.

JOHN RYLANDS LIBRARY Built as a memorial to a Manchester cotton merchant, the building is decorated with WITCHCRAFT devices including cats, mice with devilish faces, demons and dragons. It is the repository for many ancient manuscripts dealing with the occult, including a copy of the *Key* or *Clavicle of Solomon* (see SOLOMON, KEY OF) which strongly influenced the beliefs of the witch Alex SANDERS when he was a young man.

JUNIUS, JOHANNES (died 1628) A seventeenth-century German occultist and one of the more celebrated victims indicted at the Bamberg court known as the 'witch-house' on 28 June 1628. He challenged the evidence against him but an assortment of witnesses claimed to have seen him attending a SABBAT. He was subsequently tortured and made to confess to performing the MALEFICIUM, the OCCULT practice of causing injury to another person. He was executed the following month having managed to smuggle a letter out of prison to his daughter in which he confirmed that he had made his confession under threat of torture.

KALAK Among tribes of the polar regions a small version of the carved KAMAK spirit guardian given to children for their personal protection. The kalak bears a face, the 'searching face' and is threaded on a piece of string to be worn on a small child's back. If the child became sick and its soul wandered away, the 'searching face' would catch the soul and put it back. It is on these primitive blueprints that many of the modern devices of WITCHCRAFT, such as FITH-FATHS and AMULETS, are based.

KAMAK The personal spirit guardian employed by various tribes of the north European sub-arctic regions. Often these were erected on a seashore in the form of wooden posts whose spirits would attract whales and other fish. Small versions of kamaks were known as KALAKS.

KARNAYNA see CERNUNNOS.

KELLY, AIDAN A prominent modern American theorist and writer on WITCHCRAFT and the OCCULT. In the late 1970s he founded the New Reformed Orthodox Order of the Golden Dawn in America. He also began to research the origins of the modern Craft tradition although he identified the entire revival movement with GARDNER, a view which has continued to cause considerable controversy among witches laying claim to traditional and hereditary origins. Kelly's treatise went through numerous revisions, but he always asserted that Gardner had no access to an original COVEN or historical cult and that nothing in WICCA had derived from the ancient PAGAN religion of Europe. Gardner, Kelly claimed, was an under-estimated creative genius who had effectively invented a new religion while choosing to maintain the fiction of continuing an older tradition. He argued that it was Doreen VALIENTE who had contributed virtually all the Pagan theology, a position which resulted in considerable open and argumentative correspondence between the two during the 1980s. He also poured considerable scepticism on the existence of a NEW FOREST COVEN into which Gardner claimed to have been initiated. Kelly re-converted to Catholicism in 1995.

KEY OF SOLOMON See SOLOMON, KEY OF.

KIBBO KIFT KINDRED A British PAGAN organization founded by John HARGRAVE during the early 1920s which drew on an amalgam of native American shamanism (see SHAMAN) and romanticized Anglo-Saxon tradition while also adopting many of the principles of ROSICRUCIANISM. Hargrave developed the Kibbo Kift from the Scout Movement to which he had belonged as a youth and which he regarded as having become excessively imperialistic and militaristic in its aims.

Open to adult members of eighteen years or over, its aim was to restore the values of the natural world to urban dwellers. Kibbo Kift was particularly attractive to pacifists. It observed four Saxon festivals during the year and each of its members took a Craft name (see WICCA). Its Advisory Council included such notable figures as H G Wells and Julian Huxley.

Hargrave lost interest in Kibbo Kift and it sank into obscurity, although a new organization, the

WOODCRAFT FOLK, stemmed from it. The unfortunate choice of initials, KKK, did not assist its popularity and fuelled allegations that it was fascist inspired.

KINGSFORD, ANNA BONUS (1846-1888) The nineteenth-century occultist and clairvoyant who founded the HERMETIC SOCIETY in 1884. Born in Essex, she was married to an Anglican vicar, Algernon Kingsford, in 1867 but converted to Roman Catholicism in 1870. She practised as a Doctor of Medicine in London and there she joined the THEOSOPHICAL SOCIETY of Helena BLAVATSKY, rising to the post of President of the London Lodge in the years 1883 and 1884. She was, however, never enchanted with the emphasis on eastern philosophy and Hindu teaching, and constantly advocated pursuing the path of Greek and Christian occultism. Blavatsky, sensing an heretical element in her midst, effectively disbarred Kingsford from the Theosophical Society by advocating that she form the quite separate Hermetic Lodge of the Society. Thus Kingsford achieved her ambition of forging an occult group of intellectuals who would follow the ideals of Western esoteric philosophy built on Christian foundations to which were added western Qabalistic elements. Her thinking was influenced greatly by the writings of the French magus and occultist, Eliphas LEVI.

The Hermetic Society continued after her untimely death and her work came to be of considerable inspiration to Dion FORTUNE who, indirectly, through the FRATERNITY OF THE INNER LIGHT, continued as her 'successor'.

KKK See KIBBO KIFT KINDRED.

KNIGHT, GARETH An influential modern English occultist and MAGICIAN, the head of the WESTERN MYSTERIES groups in which he is an adept of the highly secretive Inner Circle to which members may be initiated after a study course. Also the founder of the Companions of Greystone, a

meeting held annually at a manor house, 'Greystones in Wiltshire' (a pseudonym for Hawkwood, near Stroud, Gloucestershire) and attended by a small select group of dedicated magicians coming from as far away as North America and Africa. It involves a two-day training course and terminates with a ritual known as the Catechism of the Grail.

Knight is an implicit believer in magical power as a revitalizing force for individuals and country alike, an authority on Qabalistic magic (see QABALAH) and he claims to have had spiritual contact with personalities from the past including the Elizabethans, John DEE and Francis Drake. His literary works include *A Practical Guide to Qabalistic Symbolism* (1965), *The Practice of Ritual Magic* (1976) and *The Rose Cross and the Goddess* (1985).

KNIGHTS TEMPLAR An immensely rich and powerful military order of the twelfth to fourteenth centuries, believed by some researchers still to exist in parts of Europe and the USA, and to use OCCULT techniques to maintain their power base. See also ROSICRUCIAN SOCIETY.

KNOCKERS Maleficent subterranean spirits recognised by miners during the early part of the British industrial era.

KYTELER, DAME ALICE A fourteenth-century lady of rank whose arraignment for ritual WITCHCRAFT is unusual in that it was the first major witch trial in Ireland and it represents one of only three to include the specific charge of deliberate Devil worship all of which took place in the early fourteenth century. Kyteler was arraigned for the murder of her various husbands and the attempted murder by poisoning of her current spouse, Sir John le Poer, with twelve associates including her maid, Petronilla de Meath, in Kilkenny, Ireland, in 1324. She was prosecuted on the evidence of some of her children and subsequently convicted though by that time she had escaped to England with Petronilla de

Meath's daughter where she vanished into obscurity and thus escaped punishment. de Meath was subsequently executed.

Having been married four times and become a wealthy widow, Kyteler had apparently alienated her elder children by bequeathing all her possessions to her youngest child. The prosecution, which was conducted by a French trained Franciscan, claimed that she had renounced Christ so as to obtain magical powers, and had subsequently sacrificed animals, specifically nine red cocks and nine peacock's eyes, to her FAMILIAR named Robert Artisson or Robin, son of Art, with whom she is alleged to have performed sexual acts. The charge was upheld by the local bishop of Ossory, Richard Ledrede, and lurid accounts of her OCCULT activities continued to be embellished for many years after her disappearance. See also DEVIL WORSHIP, INDICTMENTS FOR.

LAMMAS The WICCAN SABBAT, also known as *Lughnasadh*, now generally celebrated by many PAGANS. It marks the gathering of the harvest at the beginning of August and usually celebrates the reaping of the Lord of the Harvest, JOHN BARLEYCORN.

The concept of the dying and rising god has many precedents in antiquity. It derives most directly from the tradition of the Celtic kings in Ireland and from earlier Greco-Roman traditions in which the keeper of the grove of the goddess DIANA was ritually slaughtered at the end of his term of office. These, in turn, derived from the Phrygian cult of ATTIS when the ill-fated consort of KYBELE shed his blood in an orgy of self-sacrifice and from the Mesopotamian rite of the dying and rising god, Dumuzi, or Tammuz. The Attis rites were adopted in Rome as the Day of Blood and the Hilaria Festival and, arguably, set a precedent for the Christian Easter rites.

LANCRE, PIERRE DE A seventeenth-century French lawyer and magistrate concerned with witch trials, and who distinguishing between WITCHES who were essentially of the Christian faith but who practised natural and sympathetic MAGIC, and individuals who subscribed to PAGANISM through the worship of CERNUNNOS. In 1609, during an outburst of hysteria over WITCHCRAFT on the French Basque coast, he was commissioned to bring all sorcerers in the region to court for trial. He was openly misogynistic, possessed a fanatical dislike of Basques in general and is alleged to have set about his task with a rabid zeal, recruiting large numbers of children to assist in the task of seeking out witches for persecution

LA VEY, ANTON SZANDOR The self-styled Head of the Church of Satan in San Francisco, founded in 1966, the so-called High Priest of SATANISM and author of a popular *Satanic Bible*, published in New York in 1969. Probably influenced by Aleister CROWLEY, he formerly held various occupations, including palmistry and circus performing, and had been a police photographer. LaVey relied on his show-business background to attract a great deal of publicity and he decorated his house in a bizarre, attention-seeking style. His rituals rely on psychodrama to free the minds of his disciples and he perceives Satan to equate with the Freudian concept of libido. His performances involve naked women laid on a black altar, swords, candles, incense and incantations. The principles of the Church of Satan claim the seven deadly sins of the Christian faith to be virtues. Satan, according to La Vey, is less the opponent of God than a 'hidden force in nature'. The sect expounds the ethics of enlightened self-interest.

LAWS OF WITCHCRAFT The 161 laws of the Craft (see WICCA) compiled by Gerald GARDNER in crudely archaic language that he claimed were of ancient and inviolate origin. They did not originally constitute part of Gardner's BOOK OF SHADOWS, though he added them later. Thus some COVENS, both Gardnerian and ALEXANDRIAN, do include them in their books. Their content was, in part, blatantly sexist in tone. Specifically the Laws included the controversial advice that Priestesses should be retired from service beyond a certain age,

ABOVE AND LEFT: *Invoking the Goddess. The athame (above) is used not with any violent intent but to concentrate energy. The priestess's crossed arms (left) may represent death, or the state of waiting for the Goddess to be made manifest.*

RIGHT: *A witch blessing the harvest at Lammas.*

causing serious scepticism among Gardnerian devotees when they first appeared in the mid-1950s. The Laws emerged in the face of a set of Proposed Rules for the Craft drawn up by elders of the main Gardnerian coven to which Doreen VALIENTE belonged and which was concerned about the level of publicity that Gardner, and friends such as Jack BRACELIN, espoused. The Proposed Rules were intended to stem damaging breaches of secrecy to the tabloid press, in contravention of the Rules of Secrecy to which all initiates swear.

Gardner himself had done much to cultivate lurid publicity tales by encouraging the press, giving interviews and posing for journalists' cameras. His Laws proved controversial, effectively allowing for the deposing of priestesses beyond a certain age and their role to be little more than that of acolytes to the male hierarchy. It led to a radical split within Gardner's coven in 1957, the breakaway section being led by Doreen Valiente.

LEEK, SYBIL (died 1992) One of the most prominent British witches during the 1960s and '70s, the author of the best-selling book *Diary of a Witch* and its sequel *The Complete Art of Witchcraft*. In her time, to be a self-confessed witch was a courageous act and her books received considerable response from an enquiring public. They also led to the formation of COVENS, many of which effectively wrote their own rules without any understanding of Gardnerian principles (see GARDNER, Gerald). She was not initiated as a Wiccan but claimed to be a hereditary witch.

Born Angela Carter to a Staffordshire family of psychics, she enjoyed little orthodox schooling and, instead, was taught nature lore at home. She underwent a form of initiation at Gorge du Loup in the hills behind the French resort of Nice, for a time went to live with gypsies in the New Forest, became a reporter for Southern TV and opened an antique shop in a Hampshire village. When her association with the village generated a focus of unwanted tourist attraction she was obliged to sell up and

emigrated to America, where she settled in Houston.

It is significant that the deities invoked by Leek, the archetypes of cosmic law, are identified as DIANA and Faunus, the latter being the 'all father'. Furthermore the Dianic coven (see DIANIC WITCHCRAFT) has, for her, the broad definition introduced by Margaret MURRAY, with few feminist connotations. The distinction between Gardnerian and Dianic religion is academic and rites are conducted in unisex garments to minimize distinction between sexes.

At first Leek faced an almost universal belief in the media that WICCA and Black Magic were indistinguishable. Nonetheless, she viewed Aleister CROWLEY in a favourable light, believing him to be ahead of his time and to be a great spiritualist on whom the 'personification of evil' label was unfairly placed.

Sybil Leek is survived by a son, Julian, who continues in the Wicca faith.

LEGEND OF THE GODDESS A Gardnerian (see GARDNER, Gerald) and ALEXANDRIAN mystery play based loosely on the classical Greek myth of Persephone's descent to the UNDERWORLD where she becomes the bride of Hades. The Greek tradition was almost certainly derived from an older, near eastern, Mesopotamian tradition, extending back in time not less than five millennia, in which the Sumerian Queen of Heaven, Inana, descends to the Underworld to challenge its dark queen, Ereshkigal. In Babylonian mythology, Inana becomes Ishtar.

In Wiccan tradition, the HORNED GOD, in his winter aspect as Lord of Death, replaces Hades. This also reflects the Mesopotamian myth in which the consort of the Queen of Heaven subsequently takes her place on an annual sojourn into the Underworld. The priestess playing the part of the GODDESS is dressed in seven veils to represent the seven emblems of power which were stripped from Inana/Ishtar one by one as she passed through the

A representation of Morrigan, the Celtic Irish goddess of war, fertility and death.

seven portals of the Underworld. These, in turn, arguably form the basis for the account of the Seven Stations of the Cross in Christian tradition. She is then challenged by the Guardian of the Portal(s) whereupon she removes her veils, is bound, and led before the altar of the god. Here she is symbolically scourged before her emblems of power are returned to her in rebirth.

The WICCA COVEN may enact the mystery play in mime or using the spoken word. According to the BOOK OF SHADOWS it should be mimed to an accompanying narrative.

LELAND, CHARLES GODFREY (1824-1903) An American folklorist born in Philadelphia and Princeton educated who was, arguably, the first major influence on PAGAN thinking in modern times. A prolific author of some fifty-five books, his last and most influential work is *Aradia or the Gospel of the Witches* (1899) in the preparation of which he was strongly influenced by the writings of Jules MICHELET. Leland travelled extensively, and was in Paris at the Sorbonne during the 1848 revolution. While staying in Italy in 1866 he met a witch, MADDALENA, who became his researcher into Italian folklore and some years later, in 1886, she confided to him that she knew the location of an ancient manuscript revealing arcane details of the origins of Italian witchcraft. Although the manuscript was never produced for inspection, she sent handwritten sections of what she claimed to be the original to Leland in 1897. In reality it is unclear whether Leland faked the evidence contained in *Aradia*, whether Maddalena was herself a fraud or whether he interpreted her revelations to fit with Michelet's ideas.

It has been argued that, through Maddalena, Leland established the existence of a thread of Italian witchcraft that survived from the period of medieval persecution. However the claim remains unsubstantiated.

In 1888, Leland was elected the first President of the Gypsy-Lore Society and, in the same year, was initiated into the witchcraft movement in Italy, the *Vecchia Religione*. He died in Florence leaving a wife, Isabel.

LEMEGETON The so-called *Lesser Key of Solomon*. A medieval text or clavicle relating to the MAGIC arts of which the earliest reliable copies are seventeenth-century French and which has no earlier confirmed provenance. There are several English translations, also dating to the seventeenth century, in the Sloane Collection of the British Museum. Like its counterpart, the *Key of Solomon*, it is possibly derived from the apocryphal Hebrew Testament of Solomon and from other pseudepigraphal texts. (SEE ALSO SOLOMON, KEY OF.)

While the *Key of Solomon* is doctrinal, the *Lemegeton* is primarily concerned with listing the names and offices of demons and citing the rituals for their invocation. It is divided into four sections of which only the first part, *Goetia*, has appeared in print having been copied into the *De Praestigiis Daemonum* (1563) of the sixteenth century German demonologist Johann Weir. The *Lemegeton* covers the invocation of an assortment of spirits, both benign and malevolent, and the *Goetia* contains rituals by which to conjure seventy two demons, including LUCIFER, Ashtaroth, BEL and others.

LEPTINNES, COUNCIL OF Dating from 744 AD, the Council drew up legislation determining the association between PAGANISM and demonolatry. It detailed a list of proscribed superstitions that included making sacrificial offering to saints. This was due to the determination to rid minor PAGAN deities of their non-Christian origins in the minds of ordinary people. Previously, in 743 AD, the Synod of Rome had identified all minor spirits for whom food and drink were traditionally set out, to be demons, and outlawed the practice. The identity of these spirits was then transferred to witches who were first recognized as *bonae mulieres*, the phantom 'good women', who wandered abroad in the dead of night stealing food from houses.

LESSER BANISHING RITUAL One of the essential rituals of the OCCULT WESTERN MYSTERIES, observed by Hermeticists (see HERMETICISM), during which forces are summoned to purify the space within the MAGIC CIRCLE, to guard it against interference and to empower its magicians. The performer commences the ritual by facing east and inscribing a Qabalistic cross (see QABALAH), after which he turns to the south, west and north before returning to the east.

LEVI, ELIPHAS ZAHED (1810-1887?) A nineteenth-century Parisian occultist and ADEPT whose real name was Alphonse Louis Constant. Having spent his early childhood in poverty he was trained for the priesthood at Saint Sulpice. He reached only the level of Deacon and, in 1839, joined the sect of Ganneau which preached a curious mix of royalist and radical philosophies and, in consequence of his membership, he was imprisoned in 1847. In the 1850s he published the treatise by which he is chiefly known, the *Dogma and Ritual of High Magic*, in which he made robust assertions about the ancient credentials of the magical tradition. He was a self-styled Qabalist (see QABALAH) and it was claimed by S L MacGregor MATHERS that he was also a ROSICRUCIAN, although this claim may have been little more than a propaganda exercise. In later years his writings gained a loyal following among MAGICIANS who aspired to emulate his brand of the OCCULT. Much of his work was republished by Helena BLAVATSKY, founder of the THEOSOPHICAL SOCIETY, in her work *Isis Unveiled* (1877).

Levi was probably, more than any other author, responsible for the popularization of occultism in the twentieth century.

LEY LINES Perfect alignments which extend across the English landscape linking ancient sites of

PAGAN significance. The term 'ley' and the existence of the lines were first claimed by the Herefordshire farmer's son, Alfred Watkins in *The Old Straight Track* (1925). He proposed that they were employed by ancient man as navigation routes between isolated communities. The manmade features which mark them out may include cairns, barrows, stone circles, wells and Christian edifices built on sites of pre-Christian worship.

There exist hundreds of ley lines of which two major examples intersect at GLASTONBURY in Somerset. One, a hundred and fifty miles in length, runs from Glastonbury Abbey, through STONEHENGE in Wiltshire and on to Canterbury Cathedral in Kent and is said to have perfect accuracy. The second runs from St Michael's Mount in Cornwall, via Glastonbury Tor, to AVEBURY Circle in Wiltshire.

It is believed that ley lines may also have possessed magical significance in prehistoric times and, today, they are seen to represent paths of force emanating from the earth, the energies of which may be tapped.

According to Doreen VALIENTE many of the claims of desecration of churchyards by witches stems from the fact that meetings were deliberately held, not on Christian sites but beside the more arcane markers of ley lines.

LIBER AL VEL LEGIS The prose poem and so-called *Book of the Law* allegedly dictated to Aleister CROWLEY in three chapters by a being that announced itself as *Aiwass*, between 8 and 10 April, 1904, while Crowley was staying in a Cairo hotel and was following the psychic instructions of his wife, Rose. It is from this inspiration that Crowley's hedonistic maxim *Do what thou wilt shall be the whole of the Law* was drawn and on the strength of which he was self-proclaimed as *The Beast 666, Prophet of a New Aeon*. For a time the manuscript of the *Book of the Law* was mislaid. However it was eventually discovered in the attic of Crowley's house at Boleskine.

LIDDELL, E W 'BILL' An occultist of English origin who emigrated to New Zealand and who achieved notoriety under the name Lugh when he submitted a series of papers to the *Wiccan* between 1974 and 1977. In these he claimed to be a middle-man for a group of anonymous traditional and hereditary witches in East Anglia. These witches apparently belonged to the so-called Nine Covens of the CUNNING PERSON and Hereditary Magister, George PICKINGILL, who lived at CANEWDON in Essex.

This correspondence was subsequently collected into a single volume under the co-authorship of E W Liddell and M A Howard, *The Pickingill Papers*, published by Capall Bann in 1994. The extraordinary claims made in the correspondence are almost wholly unsubstantiated, are sometimes palpably at variance with known fact and are to be treated with considerable scepticism.

Liddell has continued to write for PAGAN journals including *The Cauldron*, but in 1996 retracted many of his claims, which are now accepted as fraudulent.

LILITH A nocturnal and spectral Hebrew demoness who derives from the Sumerian goddess of dearth and desolation, Kiskillilla, and her Akkadian/Babylonian successor, Lilitu. In Sumerian iconography she is depicted with bird-like talons replacing human feet. In Hebrew mythology Lilith is perceived as an owl goddess, the apocryphal first wife of Adam who gave birth to the Lilim, the ass-haunched 'Children of Lilith'. In the arts of black magic, Lilith is one of the foremost demonic figures to be invoked.

LITTLE, ROBERT WENTWORTH A Freemason and the founder of the SOCIETAS ROSICRUCIANA IN ANGLIA (SRIA) in 1865 (or 1886 according to some authors). Little had allegedly discovered some forgotten ROSICRUCIAN literature detailing rituals in the Freemasons Hall Record Rooms and he collaborated with fellow masons including W R

Woodman, F G Irwin and Kenneth MACKENZIE. Little was a student of the works of Eliphas LEVI and it was he who was responsible for restricting initiation into SRIA to members of Masonic lodges.

LLEW LLAW GYFFES The Welsh Celtic counterpart of the Irish deity, LUGH, who appears in the mythological texts of the *Mabinogion*. Born prematurely to the goddess Arianrhod when she was forced to submit to a test of her virginity, he was, according to tradition, fostered by his uncle, Gwydion, having been cursed and disowned by his mother.

He developed skills with the sling and the spear as well as accomplishments in music, poetry and the magic arts. He constitutes a significant character in the lore of some modern witches whose interest lies in the Welsh traditions.

LOUDON, NUNS OF Participants in a notorious conspiracy hatched in 1630 against the father confessor of the Ursuline Convent in Loudon, Urbain Grandier, by the mother superior and several nuns who claimed to have between bewitched by Grandier. He was subsequently tortured and burnt at the stake in the marketplace at Vienne in August 1634. There was a twist to the story in that, after Grandier's execution, the fever of possession among the nuns proceeded even more than before. The convent and its occupants was exorcized in 1635.

This history forms the basis of the story from which the Ken Russell film, *The Devils*, was produced.

LUCIFER The PAGAN deity who became associated with the Christian concept of Satan and Hell. Christian mythology, incorporated into the Book of Revelation 12:7, tells of a war in heaven: Michael and his angels fought against the dragon; and the dragon fought and his angels. In Isaiah (14:12) Lucifer is named as the rebellious archangel who fell from heaven: *How art thou fallen from* *heaven, O Lucifer, son of the morning! How art thou cut down to the ground, which didst weaken the nations!* This appears to be a reference to the bright morning star, further amplified in Luke 10:18): *And he said unto them, I beheld Satan as lightning fall from heaven.*

The word *lucifer* means simply *bringer of light*, but the old Italic deity became syncretized with the god PAN and was embellished with horns, hoofs, curly tail and toasting fork. According to an unprovenanced legend (see ARADIA), the goddess DIANA formed an incestuous relationship with her brother, Lucifer, and conceived a daughter Aradia, who was sent to earth as the first witch. The cult which ensued, that of the peasants or *pagani*, stood in direct conflict with the doctrine and dogma of the Christian Church.

In certain Gnostic sects, Lucifer is viewed in a less damaging light, as a divine power and the first-born son of God. Occultists may worship Lucifer as a god of dawn, associated with the Morning Star.

LUCIFERANS, THE A society of heretics formed in Austria during the early part of the fourteenth century. Allegedly it conducted subterranean orgies with virgin noviciates. Its principles allegedly included the worship of LUCIFER and the belief that there would come a day when the positions of St Michael and Lucifer were reversed in heaven and hell. Luciferans were said to meet each other with the address 'May the injured Lucifer greet you' (see also WALDENESIANS).

LUGH (1) Irish Celtic god associated with skills who was probably a late-comer to the pantheon. By repute Lugh was adept in the use of a massive spear and a sling, both of which possessed invincible magic properties. One of the epithets of Lugh is *lamfhada* meaning 'of the long arm'.

The main festival in his honour is LUGHNASADH on 1 August, which is unusual in that it was a wholly agrarian Celtic festival among people otherwise used to celebrating dates based on the earlier pastoral calendar. He may have superseded a pastoral god named Trograin since an alternative name for the 1 August festival was *Bron Trograin*, the 'Rage of Trograin'.

It was believed that Lugh possessed the power of shape-changing and one of the possible translations of his name is 'lynx'.

Lugh seems to have been adopted as a deity in various places in Romano-Celtic Britain and Europe hence place names such as Luguvalium [Carlisle] and Lugudunum [Lyons]. In WICCA the name persists only through the festival of Lughnasadh.

LUGH (2) See LIDDELL, E W.

LUGHNASADH An alternative name, commonly used in the United States, for the SABBAT festival of LAMMAS. It derives from the Celtic god LUGH and is pronounced *loo-nassa*.

LUPERCALIA The Classical Roman festival held annually on 15 February in honour of the god Faunus, the old Italic deity responsible for the fertility of herds and the well-being of shepherds. The priests or *luperci* paraded naked around the Palatine Hill, their foreheads marked with the blood of a sacrificial goat, whipping the women that they met with the animal's hide, a ritual which allegedly improved fertility. The Lupercalia survived until long after many of the other rites of PAGANISM had been abandoned and was only proscribed, amid great opposition, in 1118 under Pope Gelasius. The flagellation aspect was carried through into medieval occultism and was almost certainly the inspiration for Gerald GARDNER's incorporation of flagellation in the rites of WICCA.

MAB The Queen of the FAIRIES in English tradition and made popular, if distorted, in Shakespeare's *A Midsummer Night's Dream* as Titania.

The name has no obvious basis in Classical mythology other than a loose resemblance to the race of Greek primordial deities, the Titans. The name Mab may derive from the Irish goddess queen Medb, or Maeve, but it is worthy of note that Mab is also the midwife of the fairies and *mab* in the Welsh language means baby.

MABINOGION More properly the Four Branches of the Mabinogi included in the thirteenth-century *Red Book of Hergest*. The main repository in verse of Welsh Celtic oral tradition, dating from the late eleventh century, it is strong on mythology but reveals limited factual or objective information about Celtic religion. Only one of its mythological figures Mabon (Divine Youth), the son of Modron, is known (in his Romano-Celtic form Maponus) from inscriptions and place names.

The best-known modern edition is arguably that of Lady Charlotte Guest (1848). GRAVES identifies two possible meanings for the term *mabinogion*, 'juvenile romances' or, less widely accepted, 'tales of the son of a virgin mother'.

McFARLAND, MORGAN See DIANIC WITCHCRAFT.

MACKENZIE, KENNETH R H An English Freemason and one of the nineteenth-century founder members of the SOCIETAS ROSICRUCIANA IN ANGLIA (SRIA) who, in 1865, returned to England from Austria where he had worked as an English tutor to Count Apponyi and from whom, allegedly, he received initiation into the brotherhood of Austrian Rosicrucians. He was given permission to open Rosicrucian lodges in England and collaborated, with this aim in mind, with a fellow Freemason, Robert Wentworth LITTLE. In 1877 he published the Rosicrucian grading structure in a more general work entitled the *Royal Masonic Cyclopaedia*. He claimed the list of grades to be his own original development but it is believed, according to R A Gilbert, to have been copied from a German text dated 1871.

MADDALENA The Italian Tuscan gypsy who acted as a collector for the American folklorist, Charles LELAND, while he was living in Florence during the latter part of his life. He is said to have met her in 1866 and to have been impressed by her knowledge of arcane Italian lore and legend. In 1886 she informed him of the existence of a medieval manuscript, the so-called ARADIA, or the Gospel of the Witches detailing the old Italic Pagan religion, *La Vecchia Religione*. At no time did she provide Leland with sight of an original document but, in 1897, she sent him what she claimed to be a facsimile in her own hand. It is therefore not possible to establish whether the claimed medieval manuscript ever existed.

MAGIC The art of producing marvellous results by compelling the aid of spirits, or by using the secret forces of nature, such as the powers supposed to reside in certain objects defined in Chambers Dictionary as *givers of life; enchantment; sorcery; the art of producing illusions by legerdemain; a secret or* *mysterious power over the imagination or will*; by Aleister CROWLEY as *The science and art of causing change to occur in conformity with will*; and by Dion FORTUNE as *The science and art of causing changes in consciousness to occur in conformity with will.*

MAGIC CIRCLE (CEREMONIAL MAGIC) A device to prevent adverse or malignant influences intruding on the work of MAGICIANS, not to be confused with a witch's circle. In the ritual of consecration an exorcist, clothed in black robes and wearing shoes of russet leather, each marked with a cross, stands at the centre of the proposed circle. Taking a magical wand, preferably a fresh hazel stick of about 1 m (3 ft) in length, he must point it at arm's length towards all four winds three times, turning the hazel around at every wind and reciting the words from Reginald SCOT's *Discoverie of Witchcraft: Book XV, Appendix 1:*

I who am the servant of the Highest, do by virtue of his Holy name, Immanuel, sanctifie unto myself the circumference of nine feet around me, from the East, from the West, from the North, from the South; which ground I take for my proper defence from all malignant spirits, that they may have no power over my soul or body nor come beyond these limitations, but answer truely being summoned, without daring to transgress their bounds.

MAGICAL ALMADEL The mirror used by occultists for SCRYING and DIVINATION.

MAGICIAN A person practising the arts of MAGIC, the term deriving from the Greek *mageia*, the Latin *magia* and, in later times, the French *magique*. The Greek *magos* is applied in a different context and defines the astrologers who accompanied the Persian army of Xerxes in their invasion of Greece. Magicians did not generally invoke deities during ritual or practices but were equated, during the medieval period, with WIZARDS or white witches.

MAIDEN A young girl chosen as the nominal representative of the GODDESS at large COVEN meetings. In the past she was selected on the basis of her looks and was frequently the daughter of the High Priestess. The Maiden worked in the capacity of a figurehead but was usually destined to become an initiate in the coven, eventually taking her mother's place. Similarity of appearances would often strengthen the physical manifestation of the aged Goddess becoming rejuvenated.

The Maiden is the youthful aspect of the TRIPLE GODDESS, who is transposed first into the Mother and eventually the HAG or Crone before the cycle is renewed.

MALLEUS MALEFICARUM (1486) (*The Hammer against Witchcraft*). One of the most influential early printed books, compiled by the German inquisitor Heinrich INSTITORIS with the collaboration of a fellow Dominican, Jakob Sprenger. The latter subsequently turned against Institoris. The treatise was endorsed by Pope Innocent VIII and prefaced by his papal bull of 1484 (see SUMMIS DESIDERANTES AFFECTIBUS). It listed the essential features of witchcraft as they were envisaged by the Catholic Church, namely renunciation of the faith and becoming a disciple in the service of evil. This included sexual pacts with the Devil and the initiation of unbaptized children. It identified the majority of witches as women and also catalogued the ability of witches to levitate, change shape, defile the Eucharist and prepare magical potions and ointments.

The *Malleus Maleficarum* was published in no fewer than fourteen editions by 1520, although it did not appear in English translation until recent times. According to Montague SUMMERS (1928) the authors were Heinrich Kramer and James Sprenger.

MALEFICIUM The Latin legal term for the damage allegedly brought by a witch against his or her victim, perhaps involving physical injury or damage to property and, in extreme cases, the death of an individual and/or their domestic animals. In the Continental courts the charge of *maleficium* also included interfering with sexual relations between couples and tampering with the weather.

The fear of *maleficium* in the public mind accounted for many of the accusations and trials although, in the courts, the charge was frequently turned into one of diabolism in the hands of a skilled prosecution, in part because maleficium was harder to prove.

MANSON, CHARLES (born 1934) The American hippie occultist and founder of a genuine and malevolent Satanist movement in America during the 1960s. As leader, Manson styled himself: 'Devil, Satan'. Manson's cult followed principles of violence, including torture and murder, and he came to public notoriety through the infamous serial killings at the home of one of the victims, Sharon Tate, in 1969. Born illegitimate and remaining effectively illiterate, Manson assembled his beliefs from visits to the cinema and from magazines. They included the bizarre notion that the personalities of Christ and the Devil, personifying good and evil, could be united within him and through his influence.

He collected around him a group of followers who lived in communes on deserted properties near Los Angeles. There he preached a hatred of conventional society values, indulged in drug-crazed sexual orgies and, eventually, resorted to mass murder. In this he was influenced, it has been claimed, by the cult movie *Rosemary's Baby*. With his acolytes Susan Atkins, Leslie van Houten and Patricia Krenwinkel, he was sentenced to execution in the gas chamber. The sentences were commuted and all are currently incarcerated.

Manson's cult bears no similarity to, and has no association with, NEOPAGANISM in America.

MANTRA A thought form, MAGIC formula or mystic syllable(s) common to several religions including Hinduism, Jainism and Buddhism. It consists of a sequence, with or without intelligible sense, and is considered to be a shortened form of a *dharani*, or mystical, verse. A *mantra* may be voiced aloud as a *kanthika*, literally 'throated', or as an *ajapa*, non-uttered. It is a device of meditation which relies on the focusing of the mind upon a repeated word or phrase that is chanted at a slow and constant speed. In Indian religions the recitation of the *mantra* is assisted by the *mantracakra* or prayer-wheel and the most sacred *mantra* is that of the syllable OM.

The application of the *mantra* has become popular with several twentieth-century cults, including that of Hari Krishna. It is also used by modern PAGANS and MAGICIANS whose interest includes eastern mysticism and who rely on the mantra and other devices for meditation.

MATHER, COTTON (1663-1728) One of the most outspoken seventeenth-century American critics of WITCHCRAFT in New England. An intellectual theologian who worked as a Puritan minister in Boston, Massachusetts, Mather wrote prolifically on history, science and theology including several treatises on the subject of witchcraft including *Memorable Providences Relating to Witchcraft and Possessions* (1689) and *Wonders of the Invisible World* (1693) in which he upheld the belief in witchcraft. The publications were instrumental in the conduct of the famous witch trials in the village of SALEM.

MATHERS, MOINA (1865-1928) The wife of S L MacGregor MATHERS who, after his death in 1918, headed a breakaway section of GOLDEN DAWN, the ALPHA ET OMEGA Order, in partnership with J W BRODIE-INNES. Her name is frequently corrupted in literature to Mina. According to Francis King it was through the exhortations of Dion FORTUNE, who had been initiated into AO as a neophyte in 1919, that the FRATERNITY OF THE INNER LIGHT was founded in 1922 as an 'outer court' for the more esoteric activities which also derived from the traditions of Golden Dawn. Later Moina became strongly critical of Dion Fortune for 'betraying the inner secrets of the Order'.

MATHERS, SAMUEL LIDDELL MACGREGOR
(1854-1918) Educated at Bedford Grammar School
and later living in Bournemouth, he was one of the
most influential of the modern revivalist magicians
and occultists in addition to professing a strong
interest in military history. In 1877 he joined the
Masons and became initiated as a ROSICRUCIAN.

In 1887 he became one of the four founder
members of the HERMETIC ORDER OF THE GOLDEN
DAWN for which he was delegated to devise the
rituals, based on the cipher manuscripts that had
come into the possession of W W WESTCOTT, but to
which he added an Egyptian element. He was
widely regarded as one of the so-called Secret
Chiefs of the Order. Mathers became a protégé of
Annie HORNIMAN and used her as a source of
funds. In 1890 to facilitate his marriage to her
friend, Moina Bergson (see MATHERS, Moina), he
was given the post of curator at the Horniman
Museum until he was dismissed the following year
when Annie Horniman became disillusioned with
his constant drain on her financial resources. In
1891 he had used some of her funds to visit Paris
where he obtained the ritual details from a high
ADEPT for the establishment of the Second Order of
GD. He set up permanent residence in Paris in 1894
with Moina who was still being supported
financially by Horniman until she finally lost
patience with MacGregor Mathers' lack of gratitude
and severed all finances in 1896.

After various resignations from the high offices
of Golden Dawn, Mathers became its supreme
Chief, becoming steadily more autocratic and pre-
occupied with the darker aspects of MAGIC, partly
under the influence of Aleister CROWLEY, until he
was forced from office in 1900.

Obsessed by ancient Egyptian tradition, Mathers
formulated the *Rites of Isis* and was regarded as one
of the main contenders, with Aleister Crowley, for
the role of chief magician in Europe. He adopted
various pseudonyms, including S'Rhioghail Mo
Dhream and Deo Duce Comite Ferro.

He was responsible for important translations
into English of several medieval magical texts
including the *Key of* SOLOMON, the *Lemegeton* or
Lesser Key of Solomon and the Sacred Magic of
Abramelin the Mage.

In later years he became increasingly eccentric
and paranoid. He died of influenza and was
succeeded by Moina who went under the magical
pseudonym of Vestigia Nulla Retrorsum.

MATRES The Roman form of the Celtic TRIPLE
GODDESS worshipped in WICCA. Evidence for the
popularity of this triad of aspects of the MOTHER
GODDESS is evident from the extent to which icons
have been preserved. The Matres were worshipped
across Continental Europe but particularly in
Rhineland, until Christianization in about 400 AD.
They are also known as *Matronae* and *Deae Matres*.

The Matres were perhaps employed mainly as
household guardians, protecting against disease and
famine. In the British Isles one of the most
important sculptures of these goddesses, dating to
the fourth century, was unearthed from the walls of
London in a section adjacent to the river Thames.
Several unnamed Matres are to found in the
Corinium Museum at Cirencester, Gloucestershire.

In Europe, one of the best preserved sculptures
is that of the *Matres Aufaniae* found at Cologne and
dedicated by the Roman quaestor, Quettius
Severus. Many were specific to regions, hence the
Treverae around modern Trier, or the *Nemauscae* at
Nimes.

The sculptures of the Matres are typically
embellished with such attributes as baskets of fruit,
cornucopiae, loaves, sheaves of grain and other
symbols of prosperity and fertility. They may also
carry or suckle children.

In Wicca, the Celtic triple imagery has been
taken to represent the three aspects of the GODDESS
– MAIDEN, MOTHER and HAG.

MATTHEWS, CAITLIN A prominent figure in
modern PAGANISM and an authority on Celtic
traditions. As a priestess she is ecumenical in

outlook while offering shamanistic counselling and soul retrieval. She also provides a reconsecration service for women. Her partner and fellow PAGAN is John Matthews.

MEYER, ANTON A German authority whose views on modern WITCHCRAFT conflicted with those of the author Margaret MURRAY in that he perceived the supreme deity to be female, the earth goddess, rather than the male figure of the HORNED GOD, CERNUNNOS.

MICHELET, JULES (1798-1874) A respected French historian who wrote a 17 volume work entitled *Histoire de France.* He was also an occultist who proposed, in a treatise of 1862, LA SORCIÈRE, that WITCHCRAFT arose among the lowest and less well-to-do levels of society during the middle ages as a form of democratic resistance to the Church establishment whose members were primarily drawn from the feudal ruling classes. Michelet claimed, furthermore, that medieval witchcraft represented the surviving remnants of a pre-Christian north European fertility cult whose adherents celebrated the SABBAT by means of a BLACK MASS which culminated in ritualized sexual intercourse between the priestess and the Devil. His arguments offered a challenge to those of his contemporary, Franz-Joseph Mone who had published his views in 1839, essentially claiming that witchcraft had originated as a PAGAN cult worshipping Dionysos and HEKATE in the Greco-Roman world. The ideas of Michelet have influenced the thinking of traditionalists in the modern Pagan revival.

MIDWEST PAGAN COUNCIL A modern American organization of NEOPAGANS.

MILTON KEYNES The town in Buckinghamshire, England, constructed along PAGAN geomagnetic lines with its central highway, the Midsummer Boulevard, aligned to the sunrise on the longest day of the year. The roundabouts, of which there are many, are modelled on ancient harvest hills and a substantial number of roads are named after sacred Celtic sites. Plans were made, but abandoned, to construct a replica of STONEHENGE within the urban limits.

More recently, witches at Milton Keynes made legal history through the purchase of land specifically for the purpose of holding SABBATS.

MOÏRA A French OCCULT publication that is widely respected as a general PAGAN information centre for France.

MONE, FRANZ-JOSEF A nineteenth-century Director of Archives in Baden, Germany, and author of a treatise published in 1839 reflecting the nineteenth-century romanticism which claimed that WITCHCRAFT had originated in the lower strata of Greco-Roman society, involved the worship of Dionysos and HEKATE and had been adopted subsequently by the Celtic tribes occupying the regions around the northern Black Sea coasts. Mone argued that witchcraft was perceived by the European medieval aristocracy as a strategic tool to undermine the social order.

MONTALBAN, MADELINE See NORTH, Dolores.

MOONRAKER'S RAKE A device used by some witches, taking the form of a 1.8 m (6 ft) wooden pole, one inch in diameter, topped with a large iron shoe from a carthorse. According to one of its devotees, Cecil WILLIAMSON, the tradition of the moonraker began in Dorset where smuggling was *de rigueur* in bygone times and where the rake was used in the concealment and retrieval of smuggled French brandy. Today it is valued in the making of moon/pond magic to manoeuvre another significant tool, a large round copper hand wash basin, on the surface of a pond where the ritual is enacted.

MORRIGAN The Celtic Irish goddess of war, fertility and death who, by tradition, mates with Dagda at SAMHAIN to ensure the future prosperity of the land. The name translates, literally, as 'Great Queen'. As Maeve or Medb of Connacht she was ritually wedded to the mortal king whose antecedent was Ailill.

Like the Welsh goddess, RHIANNON, she is closely associated with horses and also epitomizes the sacred nature of the earth, in which capacity she is also known by the title 'Sovereignty of Ireland'.

She assumes a separate form as a triad, not dissimilar to the Romano-Celtic MATRES, and is known as the Morrigna. In her shape-shifting capacity she can not only transform from MAIDEN to HAG but also into other zoomorphic aspects, including deer, ravens and crows (see also BADB CATHA and NEMAIN).

MOSES ROD A device based on the Biblical Rod of Moses that medieval MAGICIANS endeavoured to re-create. In popular tradition Moses, like other heroes of the Old Testament, was regarded by atheists and the like as a magician since Adam's cosmic knowledge, although lost to him personally in the Fall, had been preserved through Noah and certain of his successors. In some of the medieval mystery plays he was depicted as a SORCERER. Moses' innate powers had been expanded and strengthened through his time in Egypt and it was believed that the supernatural capacity ascribed to Moses had been effected by means of his divining rod.

MOTHER GODDESS The generic term for female deities who represent the fertility and fecundity of the earth and its progeny. They have probably been recognised since prehistoric times when fat, pregnant images of womanhood were carved by the Palaeolithic hunters. Among the earliest known by name are Inana (Sumerian), Ishtar (Akkadian), DEMETER (Phrygian), ISIS (Egyptian) and Circe (Roman). Such goddesses are also referred to,

particularly in Christian literature, where they are seen in a derogatory light, as the Queen of Heaven. The concept of the Mother Goddess in WICCA is known, simply, as The GODDESS.

The consort of the Mother Goddess in ancient mythology is the SACRED KING, the dying and rising god, who reflects through his abdication or slaughter, the death of life in winter and, in his restoration, the coming of spring and genesis.

MURRAY, COLIN Founder of the GOLDEN SECTION ORDER OF DRUIDS.

MURRAY, MARGARET ALICE (1863-1963) Born in Calcutta, Murray became a prominent Egyptologist and is the author of *Witch-cult in Western Europe* (1921) as well as other books on the OCCULT. The proponent of the folklorist or Murrayite tradition concerning the interpretation of European witchcraft, Murray was a pioneer in the study of a subject which had, hitherto, been virtually devoid of academic research. Although her basic thesis is now largely discredited, she made a significant contribution to the study of the WITCHCRAFT phenomenon.

Influenced by the views of Sir James Frazer, she argued witchcraft to be a survival from an ancient fertility religion whose devotees had worshipped the horned god, Dianus (Dionysos).

Modern commentators tend to reject the Murrayite tradition as untenable on the grounds that, while evidence is lacking for the specific Dionysian religion to which she refers, the elements of her proposal clearly include a miscellany of cultic beliefs and practices gathered from all over Asia Minor and Europe. It is also argued that no evidence exists for organized PAGAN cults surviving the substantial time gaps between conversion to Christianity during the Anglo-Saxon period and the European middle ages, and between the end of the WITCH-CRAZE in the seventeenth century and the emergence of modern PAGANISM in the late nineteenth century. It is also to be noted, in contradiction to some of Murray's ideas that, when the main evidence for the existence of witchcraft begins to emerge in the fourteenth century, the phenomenon is described less as a Pagan fertility religion than as an aspect of Christian heresy.

The opinion of Keith Thomas in *Religion and the Decline of Magic*, and that of other modern academic researchers, is that Murray's conclusions were largely groundless and her research was fundamentally flawed in that, rather than accepting the implications revealed by the more thorough and systematic recording of witch trials by C L Ewen in *Witch Hunting and Witch Trials* (1929) she relied on contemporary accounts of some of the more famous witch trials. Most of her evidence comes from the writings of continental demonologists and, selectively, from confessions extracted in England by Matthew HOPKINS. Ewen's research was not initially available to Murray but, after publication, she chose to ignore it.

Her argument that the evidence gained from the Matthew Hopkins records, pointing to all witches operating in 'COVENS' of thirteen members, was unproven and demonstrated only that, in England, 'coven' was a descriptive word for an 'association'. Evidence was chosen on a highly selective basis and then was often conjectural. The following is a not uncharacteristic extract: *At the meeting of the North Berwick witches (1590) to consult on the means to encompass the king's death, nine witches stood in one company, and the rest, to the number of thirty persons in another company; in other words there were thirty nine persons, or three Covens present.*

MURRELL, CUNNING See CUNNING PERSON.

MUSEUM OF MAGIC AND WITCHCRAFT See WITCHES' MILL MUSEUM (ISLE OF MAN).

MUSEUM OF WITCHCRAFT Formerly at Box Bush House at Bourton-on-the-Water in Gloucestershire where it was opened in the early 1950s by Cecil WILLIAMSON. The museum was subsequently moved to Boscastle in north Cornwall (see WITCHES' HOUSE MUSEUM). The museum is not to be confused with the similarly named Museum of Magic and Witchcraft.

MYSTERIA MYSTICA MAXIMA The British subsidiary of the OTO headed by Aleister CROWLEY (see also ORDO TEMPLI ORIENTIS).

NECKLACE The property of a female witch of
WICCA, sometimes made from amber beads or from
alternating amber and jet beads. Because amber is
of organic, rather than strictly geological, origin it is
regarded by witches as a *goddess stone* that
symbolizes the life force, while jet symbolizes death.

In the Mediterranean region, female figurines
with fertility connotations and dating to at least
3000 BC have been found wearing necklaces and,
in northern Europe, similar sculptures, presumed to
represent fertility goddesses, are known from the
Bronze Age.

The use of a necklace with magical powers
probably stems from Norse tradition. The *Brisinga
men* mentioned in the *Poetic Edda* is a necklace and
is probably identical to the *Brosinga mene* mentioned
in the *Beowulf Saga*.

According to another early source, the *Sorla
battr*, the necklace was fashioned by four dwarfs and
was worn by the fertility and vegetation goddess,
Freyja, as her most treasured possession. Some
authorities, including the writer of the Icelandic
Haustlong, have suggested that the *Brisinga men* was a
girdle. However, the word *men* is generally applied
to a woman's ornament worn around the neck.
Brisinga means 'bright' or 'shining', although
whether this refers to the nature of the ornament or

to a family name is unclear. It seems clear, though,
that it was made from amber and is described as
'coming from the sea'.

NECROMANCY An ancient form of SORCERY
enlisting the aid of the dead or parts of a corpse.
One of the earliest detailed accounts appears in *The
Golden Ass* by APULEIUS in the story of Thelyphron,
the itinerant student who becomes inadvertently
involved with necromancy while guarding a corpse
to earn money on his travels. Robert Graves, in
1950, writes of:

*The necromancer, yielding to his (the dead man's
uncle) entreaties, touched the corpse's mouth three times
with a certain small herb and laid another on its breast.
Then he turned to the east, with a silent prayer to the
sacred disc of the rising sun. The whole market-place
gasped expectantly at the sight of these solemn
preparations, and stood prepared for a miracle . . .
presently the breast of the corpse began to heave, blood
began to pour again through its veins, breath returned to
its nostrils.*

During the medieval period necromancy may
have been closely allied with astrology and, from
the evidence of Court Records and old magical
formulae, it appears to have been practised
occasionally as late as the sixteenth and seventeenth
centuries when either the ghost of a dead person
was involved or materials from a graveyard,
including earth, skulls and whole corpses. It has
been claimed that the latter was utilized as the basis
for toxic potions. Some authorities believed that
witches possessed the power to raise the bodies of
dead persons for the purpose of necromancy.

The third WITCHCRAFT ACT (1604) in England
included a clause making it a felony to take up a
dead body in whole or part for magical purposes.

NEMAIN (PANIC) One of the more aggressive
aspects of the Irish Celtic goddess triad, the
Morrigna (see MORRIGAN). The consort of the war
god, Neit, she is perceived to fly over the battlefield
as a raven or crow, inspiring bloodlust. She may

equate with Macha, the consort of Nuada. Nemain forms an integral part of the Celtic lore that is relevant to many Druids and witches who pursue a traditional path.

NEOPAGANISM The term generally applied in the United States to modern PAGANISM, including WITCHCRAFT and other OCCULT disciplines that adopt a reverence for the natural world and the mother earth. The term is less commonly used in the British Isles or Europe. It reflects the view of the majority of practising PAGANS, who now recognize that there has been a revival of the Craft (see WICCA), the so-called Old Religion, possessing no direct links with previous forms of WITCHCRAFT but whose roots go back to the pre-Christian tribal religions of the West. Some traditionalists continue to recognize the principle of a survival of ancient ideas handed down through family inheritance from medieval times or earlier (see MICHELET, Jules) and some claim to be 'genetic' witches.

More or less all practising Pagans subscribe to the idea that each person possesses some degree of psychic powers. However, psychic powers are thought to be developed to a greater degree among particular individuals.

In the United States neoPaganism encompasses a broadly New Age philosophy and has attracted more women than men. As many as fifteen per cent of COVENS conform to strongly feminist and/or lesbian values (see DIANIC WITCHCRAFT). The Craft is reckoned to include between 50,000 and 100,000 members in the USA.

NEW AGE PHILOSOPHIES A broad cultural ideology which subscribes to a plethora of interests, including the OCCULT arts, meditation, ecological protection, astrology, TAROT and holistic medicine. New Age devotees look forward to an idealistic and utopian Age of AQUARIUS in which there is social equality, a somewhat anarchic lifestyle with little structured organization and where science and technology are devoted wholly to the public good.

The Age of Aquarius is supposed to commence sometime early in the next millennium.

NEW FOREST COVEN The allegedly genuine survival of a traditionalist COVEN, the SOUTHERN COVEN OF BRITISH WITCHES, based in Hampshire, into which Gerald GARDNER was initiated in September 1939 prior to the outbreak of World War II. While the existence of a surviving coven was asserted by Gardner, the claim was also supported by Aleister CROWLEY's close associate, Louis Wilkinson. The coven was led at the time by Dorothy CLUTTERBUCK and was the same group that allegedly raised a CONE OF POWER, some time between May and August of 1940, against Adolf Hitler's threatened invasion of England. According to Wilkinson the coven was made up of middle class people and local villagers, and enshrined a genuine tradition.

The author, Francis King, makes the colourful if improbable claim that, on the occasion when the cone of power was raised to counter the German invasion threat, that the coven engaged in human sacrifice. In order to add potency to the rite a frail and elderly volunteer offered to leave off his protective FLYING OINTMENT and thus to expire from exposure. It was, King claims, an extremely cold May night and in total three members of the coven died of pneumonia in direct consequence of the night's activities.

NORN A term which derives from the Old Norse *norn* meaning 'she who whispers' and which defines one of three mystic beings in Nordic and Germanic mythology who control fate, or *orlog*, in its three aspects, what has been, what is now, and what is yet to come. The Norns live near the well of Urd, the spring of destiny, which wells up between the roots of the YGGDRASIL, the world ash tree, in the realm of Asgard, which they water daily. They are Urdr (fate), the eldest, who determines the past, Verdandi (being) whose concern is the present and Skuld (necessity) to whom is entrusted the future. In Norse tradition the Norns are closely connected with the birth of children and the determination of the fate of an individual from the moment he or she is born. There is scant mention in the texts to the weaving of the thread of fate by the Norns, a concept promoted disproportionately by Richard Wagner.

There are some indications that, in antiquity, there were many Norns but that they became syncretized into the more familiar triad.

In Anglo-Saxon lore they become the Sisters of Wyrd. In the modern cults of ASATRU and the ODINIC RITE they are part of the essential revival of the Norse and Germanic religions.

NORTH, DOLORES (died 1982) A London-based PAGAN, also known to Gerald GARDNER as the 'Witch of St. Giles', although the pen name under which she wrote to occult periodicals was Madeline MONTALBAN. She developed a system of inner ceremonial/angelic MAGIC which she called 'Hermetics', and was reputed to give psychic tips to financial speculators in exchange for a share of any profits. She was allegedly retained as a psychic adviser to the Mountbatten family during World War II and was a friend of Gardner. She was also responsible for generating the typescript of Gardner's novel *High Magic's Aid*.

There are unsubstantiated claims that she was involved with Gardner's NEW FOREST COVEN largely stemming from the book by Kenneth GRANT, *Nightside of Eden*, which refers to a 'Mrs. South' who may have been one and the same with Dolores North. In fact, she was known to be anti-WITCH, which tends to belie this claim.

NORTON, ROSALEEN 'ROIE' (1917-1979) The Australian WITCH and OCCULT artist who achieved considerable notoriety for her avant-garde paintings and behaviour during the 1950s and '60s. A colourful and at times highly controversial figure, she was instrumental in the establishment of practising WITCHCRAFT in Australia.

She was born into an orthodox Church of England family which, in 1925, emigrated to Sydney, Australia, from her birthplace at Dunedin, New Zealand. As a child she was precocious, tended to be reclusive and, from an early age, found an interest in art and animals. She also developed striking looks, having a long face, dark hair and arched eyebrows.

As a teenager during the 1930s she progressed towards occult art, through which she displayed the ghoulish and bisexual overtones that reflected her own developing preferences. Having left college she worked, spasmodically, as a writer and illustrator on various journals and in other jobs, while her nonsecular attention became focused on the god PAN. In 1935 she was married, briefly, to one Beresford but, in about 1944, while working as an illustrator for the fringe magazine *Pertinent*, she met and married the poet, Gavin Greenlees, thirteen years her junior. They settled in the Kings Cross area of Sydney and lived together until his death in 1983.

From 1940 she experimented with self-induced hypnotic trance under the influence of which she claimed to have created much of her more esoteric art. In 1949 some of her works were confiscated by the police in Melbourne on grounds of decadence and obscenity but the charges were dismissed. Her art continued, however, to attract controversy and court appearances. By the 1960s she was deeply interested in witchcraft, allegedly building up a substantial COVEN, and became known popularly as the 'Witch of Kings Cross', amid lurid tabloid reports of black magic in the Sydney suburbs.

Remarkably, there is no evidence that she was ever initiated or trained – she seems to have been entirely self-taught and self-motivated, with no known personal contact with other witches to inspire or teach her.

She died a victim of abdominal cancer, a virtual recluse, living alone in a small, gloomy basement room. To the last she maintained fervent belief in her PAGAN principles.

OATH (OF WICCA) The binding oath of secrecy and loyalty that each and every initiate takes prior to entry into a WICCA COVEN, as defined by British terminology i.e. Gardnerian (see GARDNER, Gerald), ALEXANDRIAN and their derivatives. The words are secret but, according to Vivianne CROWLEY, they reflect the climate of persecution during the WITCH-CRAZE of the sixteenth and seventeenth centuries when to reveal the activities of witches could readily result in their imprisonment or death. The oath therefore binds those who take it to protect certain intimate details of the Craft (see WICCA).

OBOD See BARDS, OVATES AND DRUIDS, ORDER OF.

OCCULT Something which is hidden, secret or esoteric and which may be beyond the range of the physical senses. It is therefore in the realms of the magical, mysterious or supernatural. From it arise various doctrines and disciplines, including theosophy.

ODIN See OTHIN.

ODINISM See ASATRU.

ODINIC RITE, THE A charitable heathen organization based in London and devoted to the cult of Odinism. It also focuses strongly on north European and English heathen traditions and runework.

OGAM (OGHAM) A series of symbols which allegedly constitute the earliest form of goidelic writing in Celtic Ireland, based on the Roman alphabet but ascribed to Ogma, one of the major warrior deities of the Irish pantheon, and a son of the Dagda. There is no substantive archaeological proof of the claim.

The alphabet, described in detail by Robert GRAVES in THE WHITE GODDESS, includes twenty letters consisting of fifteen consonants and five vowels, each constructed in the form of intersecting lines above, below, or cutting through a base line which, according to some authorities, reflect the fingers of one hand placed against the palm of the other to effect a form of unspoken sign language. The only examples of Ogam that have survived, dating from the fourth and fifth centuries BC, were inscribed on stone but there is suggestion in the literature that Ogam was more frequently applied to the bark of hazel or aspen wands. It has also been titled the Tree Alphabet since each letter has been given the name of a tree in its BETH-LUIS-NION variation.

OIMLEC See IMBOLC.

OLCOTT, COLONEL H S (1832-1907) The co-founder with Helena Petrovna BLAVATSKY of the THEOSOPHICAL SOCIETY in New York in 1875. On Blavatsky's death he became the sole leader of the Society and was succeeded by the social reformer, Annie BESANT.

ORDEAL BY WATER Described in the Charters of the Anglo-Saxon king, Athelstan (r. 929-935 AD), this is a form of torture applied to suspected witches (see also ATHELSTAN, LAWS OF).

The Tarot archetype of the hermit, seen here as an aspect of Othin. Othin, leader of the Aesir gods in Norse mythology, is now the focus of worship for followers of Asatru.

In a practice known as 'swimming' the indicted person was prepared, in the presence of a local minister, by prayer and fasting, then tied. The binding differed according to the sex of the individual. If the accused was male, the right thumb was secured to the right big toe and the left thumb to the left big toe. For a woman suspected of being a WITCH the binding was crossways – the left thumb to the right big toe and the right thumb to the left big toe. He or she was then thrown into a pond or lake. If the person sank, it was considered to be a sign of innocence; if they floated it was a sign of guilt. 'Swimming' was often conducted by 'kangaroo courts' of villagers, by-passing the machinery of the courts and several alleged witches died in the process. The death was then treated by the courts as murder. Many women survived the ordeal and few suffered further consequences of floating unless they were particularly disliked by the local populace.

ORDO TEMPLI ORIENTIS (OTO) A German society in the Templar tradition founded in some obscurity in about 1904 by the occultist and high grade Freemason, Karl Kellner, who claimed that his doctrinal sources were largely oriental although the product was also seen to have elements of European Tantrism, an advanced shamanic technique deriving from Tibetan Buddhism. The Buddhist Tantra school aims at ecstatic union of the individual soul with the world soul through the use of mystic formulas. In the west, Tantra alternates faith and scepticism until it reaches beyond the ordinary limits of both and arrives, it is argued, at the basis of all magical working. Never widely recognized among magical and esoteric societies, OTO is alleged to have originated in various organizations the oldest of which, the Order of KNIGHTS TEMPLAR, dates from the twelfth century. More probably it represents a splinter group of Hermeticists (see HERMETICISM) and MAGICIANS in the eighteenth and nineteenth centuries.

According to a magazine article published in 1912, it possessed the Key to all Masonic and Hermetic secrets, including strong emphasis on sexual magic, the lore of nature, Freemasonry and all systems of religion.

It was structured with nine active grades on which was superimposed a tenth, purely administrative grade. Grades one to six were awarded by ritual INITIATION, while the remainder were achieved wholly by instruction and were largely concerned with sexual magic. It is organized not into Lodges but Oases.

Aleister CROWLEY was a member of the OTO, having been initiated into the ninth degree in 1912, becoming first the British president of a subsidiary order, the MYSTERIA MYSTICA MAXIMA. In 1922 he took over the international leadership having succeeded Kellner's successor, Theodor Ruess. and compiled a set of rituals said, questionably, to have been heavily influenced by those of George PICKINGILL, including ceremonial garters and a dagger immersed in a chalice representing a symbolic rite of sexual intercourse. Crowley was responsible for a revised formulation of the ninth degree which focused on heterosexual magic.

In 1916, the Metropolitan Police raided the London headquarters of the OTO and removed much of its content, allegedly in reprisal for Crowley's pro-German stance while living in the USA. In Germany, the activities of OTO came to a halt in 1937 when all occult organizations were effectively proscribed by the Nazis.

Crowley was succeeded as head of OTO by Karl Germer who subsequently emigrated to the United States. A modified British version of OTO, known as the New Isis Lodge OTO, was initiated by a former Crowley disciple, Kenneth GRANT who, in 1955, was expelled from the official OTO by Karl Germer on the grounds that the New Isis Lodge had effectively distanced itself. Germer was succeeded as head of the official OTO, on his death in the 1960s, by a Swiss named Metzger. The present head of OTO lives in America but approximately three Oases are known to exist in the U.K.

The Mother aspect of the Triple Goddess, the phase of maturity and fecundity. She carries a pentagram, symbol of life.

ORLOG The Old Norse term for destiny or fate in the northern tradition. In Norse mythology, orlog is controlled and shaped by the Norns and affects both gods and the human race alike. Ragnarok, the day of doom, is perhaps the most profound aspect of orlog. It may be described as the primal cosmic law. Orlog forms an essential part of the revivalist religion of ASATRU.

OTHIN (**ODIN**) The Norse and Icelandic god who is the focus of worship among followers of ASATRU or Odinists. Othin means 'All father' and, as head of the AESIR sky gods, he is the principal god of victory in battle and the god of the dead. The centre of the Othin cult was at Uppsala in Sweden and the main period of worship in bygone times was between about 700 AD or earlier, through the Viking era, until about 1100 AD or later. His synonyms include Sigtyr, god of victory; Val-father, father of the slain; Hanga-god, god of the hanged; Farma-god, god of cargoes; and Hapta-god, god of prisoners. He is thought to have evolved from a syncretization of the Germanic war gods Wodan and Tiwaz.

Othin lives in Valhalla, the Hall of the Noble Slain in Asgard (according to Snorri Sturluson situated in Sjaelland which is now part of Denmark). Here he rules over an army of warrior spirits, the Valkyries, and peoples his fortress with chosen heroes, slain in battle on earth, who will defend the realm of the gods against the Frost Giants on the day of doom, Ragnarok. Othin passes out magical weapons to certain of his earthly heroes, including Sigmund the Volsung.

In personality, Othin is considered untrustworthy, despite his eminence, a breaker of oaths. He rides an eight-legged horse, Sleipnir, born in consequence of a mating between the fire god, Loki, and a stallion who belonged to the Frost Giant builder of Valhalla. Othin is also capable of shape-changing, an indication of his derivation from an older, shamanistic religion. He is to be regarded as a SHAMAN, in constant pursuit of occult knowledge through communication with the dead. He wanders the earth disguised as a traveller.

His symbol is the raven and his weapon is a spear carved with his RUNES or treaties. When thrown, this spear may influence the course of mortal battle. He is also symbolized by the *valknut*, a knotted rope which represents the power to bind or unbind the minds of his followers. Once Othin pierced himself with his own spear and hung himself from the World Tree, YGGDRASIL, in his desire for knowledge. He also gave his right eye to the god Mimir as payment for permission to drink from the Well of Knowledge which rises from a spring beneath the roots of the Tree.

According to the writer, Adam of Bremen, a special festival of the gods was held each year in Uppsala when men and beasts were sacrificed and hung in trees as offerings. Followers of Othin were also burnt on funeral pyres. He was the patron of the fanatic warrior cult, the Berserks.

OTO See ORDO TEMPLI ORIENTIS.

PAGAN An individual or member of a group who accepts the principles of, or who practices, PAGANISM. The word derives from a Latin root meaning *one who lives in the country*, a rural dweller. However in the derogatory sense of a rustic, it probably took on connotations of one practising a non-orthodox religion because Christianity, as it spread, took hold more strongly in urban areas while the remote country districts were among the last to accept conversion. In present-day convention, followers of all religious faiths other than Judaic, Christian and Islamic (those acknowledging the monotheistic principle of a single male god in the heavens) are defined as Pagans.

PAGAN DAWN The magazine of the PAGAN FEDERATION, published quarterly to coincide with the Fire Festivals and formerly known as *The Wiccan* whose founding editor was John SCORE in 1968. The first edition of *Pagan Dawn* was published at SAMHAIN 1994.

PAGAN FEDERATION The organization founded in 1971 (as the PAGAN FRONT) with the objective of providing information and countering misconceptions about PAGANISM. Its aims include the promotion of contact between Pagan groups and genuine seekers of the Old Ways; the promotion of contact and dialogue between the various branches of European Paganism and other Pagan organizations worldwide; and the provision of practical and effective information on Paganism to members of the public, the media, public bodies and the Administration. The Federation works for the rights of Pagans to worship freely and without censure according to Article 18 of the UNIVERSAL DECLARATION OF HUMAN RIGHTS, which states:

Everyone has the right to freedom of thought, conscience and religion; this right includes freedom to change his religion or belief, and freedom, either alone or in community with others and in public or private, to manifest his religion or belief in teaching, practice, worship and observance.

The Pagan Federation publishes a quarterly journal, *Pagan Dawn*, and arranges both members-only and public events, while also maintaining correspondence with the wider Pagan community. It holds an annual conference, and membership is open to all who agree with the principles and ethics of the organization (see also PRINCIPLES OF PAGANISM), and is based in London.

PAGAN FRONT The organization founded by John SCORE in May 1971, the inaugural meeting of which was chaired by Doreen VALIENTE. Its publication, *The Wiccan* (now *Pagan Dawn*), was first published in 1968 and was the effective foundation stone of the organization. In later years its name was changed to the present title of the PAGAN FEDERATION.

PAGANISM The belief in a religion other than that of Judaism, Christianity or Islam. In Christian terms this equates with lack of religion or heathenism. Pagan religions tend to be lumped together collectively by Christian polemicists, although they actually vary greatly in beliefs and practices.

Paganism in Europe did not die out concurrently under the advance of the Christian apostolic

missions. In England, according to the historian
Bede, the south-east of the country was firmly in the
grip of Paganism as late as the seventh century AD.
In 640 AD, the Kentish king, Earconbert, was the
first to issue an edict ordering the destruction of
idols in his kingdom. At that time idolatry was
practised by many faiths and was extensively
adopted in Roman Catholicism. It does not
constitute a significant aspect of modern European
or North American Paganism. In other parts of
Europe, however, particularly in Scandinavia,
Paganism survived until late in the thirteenth
century.

Wherever Christianity succeeded Paganism
there was rarely a clean-sweep conversion and
many PAGAN traditions and festivals were retained
and modified in compromises which suited both
rank and file individuals and Christian ideals. Thus
the Christian festivals of both Christmas and Easter
are deeply rooted in the rites of the old Pagan
calendar (see also SATURNALIA).

Modern Paganism is represented by a diversity
of groups and individuals linked by a common
belief in certain traditions, including the old nature
and fertility cults of the Celts and Norsemen,
magical and alchemical traditions, Mystery
traditions and others. It is generally characterized
by a lack of hierarchy or bureaucracy, although
some organizations are becoming increasingly
hierarchical in their construction.

Most modern American Pagans describe
themselves as NEOPAGANS.

PAGAN WAY Known in Britain as the PAGAN
MOVEMENT, this organization constituted the first
truly open PAGAN movement to function in the
States and in Britain during the early 1970s. It was
founded in Britain by Tony Kelly, the author of
Pagan Musings, a leaflet putting forth a Pagan idealist
vision and a rallying call to Pagan spirituality. From
there it expanded to America and was linked with a
magazine also published in the early 1970s entitled
Waxing Moon, edited by T Giles and Ed Fitch. It was

re-titled *Crystal Well* when it changed its format and
publication moved to California.

PAN The Greco-Roman god of shepherds who was
seen as the personification of undisciplined nature
and who, above all, epitomizes the image of
PAGANISM. He is the son of Hermes and, as one of
the company of Satyrs, is depicted with the horns
and feet of a goat. Many of the connotations
associated with Pan are strongly phallic. He plays a
set of pipes, his interest in which derives from his
infatuation with the nymph Syrinx, whom the
goddess GAIA changed into a clump of reeds to
preserve her from Pan's lustful advances.

Among his other traits is the sudden frightening
of travellers, hence the word *panic*. There is some
argument that the imagery of the Christian Devil is
based on that of Pan.

PANIC See NEMAIN.

PAN-PACIFIC PAGAN ALLIANCE A PAGAN
networking and information organization for
Australia and New Zealand, a sister group to the
PAGAN FEDERATION, founded in about 1990 by Julia
Phillips, a British émigrée in Australia. It is now
large and successful and publishes the magazine
Pagan Times.

PANTHEISM A religious concept accepted by
many PAGANS which identifies the gods to be
immanent with the Universe as a whole. In other
words, the divine is present in all matter. The
concept derives from the ancient principles of
ANIMISM and implies that there is no spiritual
distinction between humanity and its environment.

PARACELSUS The philosopher and alchemist
born in Switzerland at Einsiedeln in 1493, whose
full name was Phillipus Aureolus Theophrastus
Bombastus von Hohenheim.

Variously regarded as an eccentric and as a
dangerous heretic, Paracelsus was at the heart of the

neo-Platonic revival in northern Europe. He attempted to unite the mysticism of nature with Christian dogma and argued for the existence of a hierarchical ladder of creation ascending from base matter to God. He defended the need to demolish barriers between ritual practised in and out of church and described MAGIC as an art which reveals its highest power and strength through faith. He observed: *There are holy men in God who serve the beatific life; they are called saints. But there are also holy men in God who serve the forces of nature and they are called magi. God shows his miracles through his holy men, both those of the beatific life and through those of nature; what others are incapable of doing they can do, because it has been conferred on them as a special gift.*

Paracelsus argued the entire cosmos in terms of a single entity, the *Diva Matrix* or divine womb of the earth mother. In consequence of his views about the femaleness of the cosmos, he was labelled by the Church as a 'woman worshipper' and he probably did much to stimulate interest, among women in the medieval period, in the notion of religious alternatives by which femaleness and female sexuality were neither abhorred nor subjugated.

PATHWORKING A technique through which psychic forces are generated, drawn together and released through the power of collective imagination. It is facilitated by the narration of an imaginary journey, typically involving a descent, an encounter, a subsequent dialogue or activity and a return to the point of departure. The fantasy is rendered by the narrator to a group who are instructed to relax, with their eyes closed, and to project themselves into the imagery. During the pathworking, the narrator will allow a period of silence for the participants to develop their own personal excursion into the realm of fantasy.

PATTERSON, GEORGE Founder of the self-styled Georgian branch of WITCHCRAFT in California. Patterson, who established the Georgian branch in Bakersfield, claimed to be an eclectic revivalist and once informed Margot ADLER: *You don't become a Pagan. You are a Pagan. Most Craft teachings are really un-brainwashing – attempts to let you think for yourself so you can be free to live your own life in your own way without hang-ups.* The Georgians established a number of COVENS in the States during the 1970s and published a regular newsletter.

PENTACLE A magical and symbolic device associated with the Wiccan (see WICCA) altar and constructed in the form of a disc, usually of metal or wood, which represents the earth and its properties of material wealth, practicalities and stability. In bygone times they were also made of beeswax. This offered the advantage that, if discovery was imminent, the device, with its magical signs, could be rapidly returned to the innocent state of a lump of anonymous wax.

PENTAGRAM The foremost religious symbol in WICCA, the pentagram is a five-pointed star-shaped geometric device inscribed by WITCHES for various purposes, including INVOCATION. It is also a symbolic representation both of the journey though INITIATION and of the different aspects of personality. The pentagram may be inscribed with the ritual sword, or ATHAME, in a series of five strokes. It is then sealed with a sixth and final stroke which retraces the path of the first.

When the pentagram points upwards, it is a symbol of life but, when reversed, it becomes the symbol of the HORNED GOD as the Lord of Death, the spirit descending to the inner depths. It also has Christian associations with diabolism. In the second degree of Wicca initiation the pentagram also points downwards since, at this stage, a witch must confront his or her inner self..

The Pentagram is also a formal position adopted by the priestess when her arms are extended, a posture that symbolizes birth and is the reverse of the arms-folded position that symbolizes death.

The Pentagram is also the name of a defunct OCCULT magazine which collapsed in the late 1960s.

PICKINGILL, GEORGE (1816-1909) One of the most publicized of the modern East Anglian CUNNING MEN, he is said to have been born to Susannah Pickingill (née Cudner) in Hockley, Essex. By repute, although unsubstantiated, he became the leader of the witches in the village of Canewdon as well as being head of a number of COVENS into several of which both Aleister CROWLEY (in 1899) and, subsequently, Gerald GARDNER are rumoured to have been initiated. An alternative scenario suggests that Gardner's connection rested only in vaguely defined links between his NEW FOREST COVEN and those of Pickingill. Gardner himself never claimed to have been initiated into Pickingill's covens and there is no corroborative evidence of such a connection.

The folklore writer, Eric Maple, who derived most of his information secondhand from an elderly parishioner, Lillian Garner, said to be the last of the local 'white witches', described Pickingill as a tall, unkempt reclusive figure with long fingernails and intense eyes who carried a blackthorn walking stick. Pickingill himself claimed a title of Hereditary Magister or 'witch master' and allegedly syncretized rites culled from other OCCULT organizations, including the Freemasons and ROSICRUCIANS (for which he recruited a writer and researcher named Hargrave JENNINGS), with some of the more traditional concepts of WITCHCRAFT including the coven structure. This was done within a framework of three degrees of INITIATION.

A reputation grew around him in the local area and beyond, which marked him as both a beneficent and maleficent WIZARD of capricious mood feared by local people. During his lifetime he is alleged to have received visitors seeking knowledge of the occult arts from far and wide, a claim that is, again, unsubstantiated and improbable.

After his death in an infirmary, to which he had been confined for some time, he was buried in the old part of the CANEWDON churchyard. The parish records contain an entry for the burial of George Pettingale (a family synonym of Pickingill), aged 103, on 14 April 1909. This discrepancy in age is probably an inadvertent error by the recorder. Lurid stories surrounding his demise persist, and include lightning flashes from a clear sky that destroyed his cottage and shadows of the Cross falling upon him as he strolled the village on the day before his death.

A considerable amount of unproven or erroneous lore has been published in respect of Pickingill and much of the ethos surrounding him is of questionable provenance. In particular, the so-called *Pickingill Papers* of E W LIDDELL and amplified articles in *The Wiccan*, under the name Lugh in the early 1970s, are controversial and short on substantive evidence. The writer Charles Lefebure further embellished the aura surrounding Pickingill, describing him as the Devil incarnate descended from a line of hereditary witches whose ancestry traced back to Arthurian times. Pickingill was also described as having held nocturnal Satanic orgies in the parish churchyard.

In truth, Pickingill was probably little more than a local farm labourer who possessed a dominant, perhaps psychic, personality and who practised the cunning arts of wizardry. He was also frequently inebriated and elected to build an intimidatory reputation around himself in order to obtain material advantage over a susceptible village community.

Canewdon has attracted a degree of sensationalism since Pickingill's day and, from time to time, a headless wraith drifts through the churchyard and a pin studded sheep's heart or doll is left strategically placed to maintain the popular interest.

POENITENTIALE THEODORI The ecclesiastical legislation compiled at Canterbury by Archbishop Theodore (died 690 AD) that includes the first English laws proscribing PAGAN activities, including sacrifice to devils, and celebration of feasts in heathen temples.

POPES IN WITCHCRAFT The basic ritual of the Catholic Church opened the way to accusations of WITCHCRAFT and several pontiffs throughout the history of the Church of Rome are recorded as having practised witchcraft or SORCERY. A list of them, in common circulation in Protestant England during the sixteenth century, alleged that a full eighteen Popes, representing an unbroken line from Sylvester II to Gregory VII had been accused of being conjurers, sorcerers or enchanters and, during the Renaissance, several Popes openly adopted beliefs fringing on Neoplatonism and HERMETICISM. Popes were by no means the only clerics against whom the charge was directed and, in England, such eminent figures in the Tudor period as Cardinal Thomas Wolsey and John Morton, Bishop of Ely, were rumoured to practise sorcery and diabolism.

According to the Elizabethan lawyer, William Lambarde, the Pope was the 'Witch of the World' and Daniel Defoe claimed that Popery was *one entire system of anti-Christian magic.* Catholic miracles and indulgences were also firmly attributed to witchcraft.

POWELL, MR JUSTICE The eighteenth century successor to Sir John Holt as Lord Chief Justice of England who presided over the trial of Jane Wenham at Hertford in 1712. She was the last person to be condemned on the charge of WITCHCRAFT but was reprieved from execution by Powell. She was said to have lived under the stigma of being a labelled a witch for sixteen years, during which time she had been thoroughly ostracised by her neighbours. When the more sensational testimony was given that Jane Wenham travelled aloft on a broomstick, Justice Powell is said to have uttered the famous rejoinder: *there is no law against flying.*

PRICKING OF WITCHES The practice of applying a sharp object on various parts of the body of an alleged witch during the period of the WITCH-CRAZE. If any area was found to be insensitive to pain, a spot protected by the Devil, the accused was convicted. The efficacy of the system of torture lay either in surreptitiously reversing the instrument and pressing the blunt end against the skin or inflicting so much pain that areas of the body eventually became numbed.

PRINCIPLES OF PAGANISM The three fundamental rules of conduct laid down by the PAGAN FEDERATION. Revised and ratified by the Council of the Federation in 1995, these include:

Love and kinship with nature. Reverence for the life force and its ever-renewing cycles of life and death.

The Pagan Ethic: *If it harm none, Do what thou wilt.* This is a positive morality, expressing the belief in individual responsibility for discovering one's own true nature and developing it fully, in harmony with the outer world and community.

Honouring the totality of Divine Reality, which transcends gender, without suppressing either the female or male aspect of Deity.

PROGRESSIVE WICCA A movement within WICCA in Britain which claims to adopt a more eclectic approach by spanning traditions. COVENS embracing Progressive Wicca place emphasis on networking, proximity to nature, personal growth and co-operative development. Strict adherence to a BOOK OF SHADOWS is rejected and the movement grows and changes with each new witch. It reflects less a tradition than an attitude and its membership is drawn from Gardnerian (see GARDNER, Gerald), ALEXANDRIAN, TRADITIONAL CRAFT, WELSH TRADITIONAL WITCHCRAFT, HEREDITARY CRAFT and others. Its roots originate in England in the early and middle 1980s and it has spread to Europe, America and Canada. The name, Progressive Wicca, was, however, effectively launched only in 1989 through discussion between Ariadne Rainbird (Cylch y Gwyllt a'r Rhydd) and others, including The Company of Witches and Silver Rose.

Among the principal aims of Progressive Wicca is care for the environment and it follows a preference for outdoor working. Outside of these commonalties, however, covens within the network operate very differently from each other. They subscribe to an initiatory tradition but without fixed rituals.

Progressive Wicca is not an organization as such because of its considerable diversity but rather reflects an attitude towards the Craft. A Progressive Witchcraft Foundation has been set up through the Cylch y Gwyllt a'r Rhydd coven to provide information and training. Other training courses also exist and details are available through the magazine of Progressive Wicca, *Dragons Brew*.

PSYCHIC QUESTING A technique developed in the late 1970s and '80s by Andrew Collins, who notes: *Psychic Questing is not a religion, it is a set of techniques enabling the human mind to interact and communicate with the hidden energies and intelligence existing beyond the normal reaches of space-time. Such abilities were once understood by our distant ancestors, those builders of great stone and earthen monuments that stand as a stark reminder of our own ignorance of the subtleties of nature.*

Collins worked for several years as a psychic investigator and was impressed by the accuracy of the information given by 'spine guides' through certain mediums. He took mediumistic abilities out of the seance room and into the landscape, applying them to sacred and historical sites, believing that through working with dreams, meditation techniques and contact with the 'spirit guardians' of different sites, various results would be achieved e.g. recovery of an artefact.

He has since applied magical techniques drawn from many systems, claiming that Psychic Questing draws information from the sacred site itself rather than imposing irrelevant rituals; it relies on being in tune with natural rhythms of earth, sun and moon.

PUCK See ROBIN GOODFELLOW.

PYMANDER The work allegedly composed several hundred years before the time of Moses, that formed the basis of the Hermetic creed (see HERMETICISM). The seventeenth-century hermeticist John Everard rendered an English translation in 1649. This he did in spite of the fact that earlier in the century Isaac CASAUBON had convincingly discredited any notion that the Hermetic books were pre-Christian in origin.

forming a complex pattern somewhat like a child's Cat's Cradle. The paths, identified with TAROT cards, lead downward and are separated into stages or *sephiroth*. This map of the descent of spirit into matter is often referred to as the Tree of Life. The sephiroths reflect aspects of the human psyche from physical nature, Yesod, to the abstract spirit at the crown, Kether, above which lies limitless light. The paths may be used as the framework for modern PATHWORKING.

QABALAH (**KABBALAH**) An essential element of the Jewish mystery tradition that was adopted by Christian European occultists interested in pursuing HERMETICISM during the fifteenth century. It returned to vogue during the romantic revival of the nineteenth century, when it became the basis for the rites of Golden Dawn. (see HERMETIC ORDER OF THE GOLDEN DAWN It is now widely employed among the modern WESTERN MYSTERY orders and taught in ALEXANDRIAN COVENS of WICCA.

The principal text of the Qabalah is the Zohar, which claims to preserve the mystical teachings of Rabbi Simeon bar Yochai. This was committed to manuscript form and circulated in Spain by Moses de Leon during the thirteenth century, although with a dubious provenance.

The essential message of the Qabalah is that the creation of the world was achieved through a series of emanations, the ten *sefirot*, dispensed by the Ein Sof (Godhead). These provide the essence, not only of divine manifestations, but of all reality in which a flow of energy sustains both mankind and nature. Of the many extant textbooks and manuscripts on the Jewish Qabalah, those of Isaac Luria (1534-1572) are amongst the most important.

In its modern usage, the Qabalah consists of twenty-two branched and connecting pathways

RAVEN A carrion-feeding bird which has long been associated with PAGAN religion and MAGIC, particularly as creatures of otherworld symbolism. In Irish mythology ravens are associated with the war goddesses BADB and MORRIGAN who are able to transform into ravens or crows to become harbingers of disaster in battle. Similar concepts exist amongst modern nomadic tribes in Siberia. The Druids used the entrails of ravens and crows in augury.

In Germanic and Norse tradition they are the birds of Woden and OTHIN in which context they are associated with foretelling battle and slaughter. They are also seen in a different and probably more ancient light as symbols, sent out to cover vast distances, of the thought and memory of the SHAMAN.

RAVEN OF BATTLE See BADB CAITHA.

RDNA See REFORMED DRUIDS OF NORTH AMERICA.

RED ROSE AND CROSS OF GOLD, ORDER OF The second, inner order of Golden Dawn (see HERMETIC ORDER OF THE GOLDEN DAWN), founded in 1892 by S L MacGregor MATHERS based on the legend of the discovery of the tomb of Christian ROSENKREUZ and including a so-called 'Vault of the Adepts'.

REFORMED DRUIDS OF NORTH AMERICA Founded at Carleton College in 1963 as a protest against the college's enforcement of regular attendance at Christian services, its practices at first bore strong similarity with alternative Christian celebrations but slowly took on an increasingly PAGAN flavour. The policy of the College was revoked in 1964 the RDNA grew in strength.

Dogma is largely rejected whilst the organization asserts the need for unity between the human race and nature. The eight seasonal SABBATS are observed and rites are performed as much as possible in the open air with the priests dressed in white robes.

REGARDIE, FRANCIS ISRAEL (born 1907) An English-born but Americanized occultist who, in 1928 on a visit to Paris, became the unpaid secretary and companion of Aleister CROWLEY. The association continued until 1932 when the two parted company. Regardie was with Crowley during the period of the latter's marriage to a Nicaraguan High Priestess of Voodoo, Maria Teresa de Miramar, an era which also saw the publication of *Magick: In Theory and Practice* (1929) and Crowley's expulsion from France to England. Through Crowley's influence, Regardie also managed to obtain entry to British soil.

Crowley's influence is apparent in Regardie's most notable published works, his guide to practical occultism: *The Tree of Life* (1932) and its companion volume *The Garden of Pomegranates*.

He became an initiate of STELLA MATUTINA in 1934 and rose through its grades but left the Order having become disillusioned with what he saw as a state of decay and demoralization. He gained a notoriety when he elected to publish the OCCULT teachings of GOLDEN DAWN, thus breaking his vows of secrecy and ensuring the effective demise of both

Stella Matutina and ALPHA ET OMEGA, the splinter organizations that had arisen from Golden Dawn.

REGENCY, THE A British witchcraft group founded in the 1960s by friends and associates of Robert COCHRANE (see also Ron 'Chalky' WHITE) and which took its inspiration from Cochrane's beliefs in the ancient mystic elements of the Craft (see WICCA) and which proclaimed itself to be a 'religious society with a central belief in a Goddess as mother and creatrix of all things'. The doctrine supported the view of a stable feminine principle allied to the Gods and that many of the principles of PAGANISM held a permanent relevance for humanity.

The Regency was a non-hierarchical organization celebrated at the time for its innovation particularly towards outdoor seasonal festivals which were open to anyone whilst still maintaining the more OCCULT rites of the CIRCLE.

REX NEMORENSIS (KING OF THE WOOD) The title given to the old Italic god, Dianus, the consort of DIANA. The same title was also taken by the priests of Diana who were ritually slaughtered in their sacred oak groves at the end of their periods of office.

Rex Nemorensis is the title of an infamous expose attributed to Charles CARDELL.

RHIANNON (GREAT QUEEN) The Welsh Celtic goddess who features in the Mabinogi of Pwyll, Prince of Dyfed. Associated with fertility, with ravens and with horses, particularly mares, she also has strong associations with SORCERY and the UNDERWORLD. The daughter of Hefaidd Hen and the consort of Pwyll, she rides a white mare and may be synonymous with the Romano-British goddess Rigantona. She equates, in part with the Romano-Gallic horse goddess, Epona. It should be noted that the links, in Celtic tradition, between fertility and horses are extensive.

RITUAL SHAFTS (CELTIC) Also known as offering pits and funerary wells, these excavations, dating from as early as the late second millennium BC may be as much as 200 feet deep and were probably perceived as entrances to the UNDERWORLD. Most of those in Britain date from the late pre-Roman and Romano-Celtic periods. When examined they are often found to contain votive offerings and to have, at the bottom, a wooden stake set upright in the ground and accompanied by remains of flesh and blood. Whether this always reflects human or animal sacrifice to an Underworld god is unclear.

RITUAL WEAPONS See WORKING TOOLS.

ROBERTS, MARK See DIANIC WITCHCRAFT.

ROBERTSON, OLIVIA DURDIN- (born 1917) Co-founder with her brother, Lawrence ('Denny') Durdin-Robertson, and his wife, Pamela, of the FELLOWSHIP OF ISIS at Clonegal Castle in the Republic of Ireland where she and Denny had lived since childhood. She claims that at the age of eleven she was already involved in spiritualistic matters aiding the transition of recently deceased from one world to the next and was developing psychic and visionary powers.

During the years of World War II she abandoned some of her pacifist principles and worked for the Red Cross in England but returned to Ireland after the cessation of hostilities to become a successful novelist. She was converted to the worship of the GODDESS in about 1956 following in the footsteps of her brother who had, until sometime during the 1950s, been a vicar of the Anglican Church but, through his THEOSOPHICAL studies, had become convinced of the paramount existence of the Divine Mother.

Between 1963 and 1974, Olivia trained in London as a medium and healer. There she pursued a strong interest in the religion of the Egyptian goddess, ISIS, and in 1975 this translated into the publication of her theosophical work, *The Call of Isis.* Olivia, Denny and Pamela, herself an accomplished mystic, founded the Fellowship at the Vernal Equinox in the following year, creating a worship and study centre with an Isis temple as its religious core.

In 1990 she was instrumental in bringing about the first Fellowship of Isis World Convention in London whilst her brother founded the chivalrous Noble Order of Tara, followed in 1992 by the DRUID CLAN OF DANA. She still works actively in the promotion of the Fellowship of Isis.

OLIVIA DURDIN-ROBERTSON

※

How would you classify yourself spiritually?
I believe in God and am working on the feminine aspect of God to bring balance to patriarchy and to the male God who has prevailed for 2000 years. I see myself as a Pagan, but I also see myself as belonging to all the major world religions to an extent. I can correlate with them. My brother, who was a clergyman, selected the name Isis because she has 10,000 names. In a sense both of us were mystics and received spiritual and visionary revelation direct – so, off the top of our heads, we were guided.

Do you, therefore, regard yourself as a polytheist?
Yes. I believe in the one God, but I also believe in the three, the God and two more, the God and Goddess emanating, and then the great seven archetypal deities, and then a pantheon, and finally animism because I believe in the Holy Spirit or divine spark in all beings and even in atoms. So I believe in the lot.

But there is a famous quotation from The Golden Ass *where Apuleius has Isis say that from her comes every god and goddess, so*

doesn't that make you a monotheist?
All deities say that, because all deities come from source, including all time and space. Kali says the same thing, so does Christ. Anyone who represents deity will always *be* the one because we all emanate from the one, and if you had a mystical experience, you would be the one!

It has been said that Pagans are an assemblage of alienated intelligentsia and natural anarchists. Do you have to be one of the intelligentsia to be a Pagan?
No, you don't! But I must say that my brother was an MA, and I've got a degree in the history of European painting. I do think if you're going to be an occult scientist, you need a grounding in science and you need to get accurate mythology before you start laying down the law. A lot of zany ideas go around that are half-baked. People read a book and come out with all these funny ideas. I think you do need a grounding in academia.

And what about anarchy?
You don't really need to be an anarchist. The very essence of some deities is law and order. Kali is obviously an anarchist,

she blows everything up, but then you get a Goddess who is very strict on law and order.

Why Isis, in a country [Ireland] which is not only strongly Catholic by tradition but whose Pagan traditions are, I would have thought, very far removed from Isis?

It's worked beautifully, especially with Catholicism. I received an experience of the Goddess in the form of white light, the white light of truth, and the name given to me was Isis. That power manifests in Ireland as the Virgin Mary, who has all the titles she took over from Isis – Satis Sapientis, the seat of wisdom; Stella Maris, the star of the sea; Regina Coeli, the queen of heaven. Isis is Maria. She is another incarnation of the divine Goddess.

So how do you distinguish Isis from Maria Virgine?

There's no distinction. They are manifestations of the same being and the likeness gets more and more. You see Our Lady of Guadeloupe appearing with twelve stars around her head, the Zodiac. She's also arrayed with the sun crown, the crown of Hathor.

Is it possible for you to worship Isis without actually believing in her existence as an entity?

Ah! This is the total difference of why we disappoint people who belong to occult Orders because we are *religion*, the religion of the Goddess. We have never

disguised that. Many occultists think that we have their idea that there is this stuff called cosmic essence which sounds like the electricity supply board. We totally believe in the deities. with the occultists you have the theosophical idea that you work your way up the ladder and ultimately become the Magus, the Master. Most occultists are very 'late nineteenth century'. They don't believe in the goddess but they love the word Jung. They believe in archetypes. They consider that there are no such things as gods and goddesses. They're thought forms that we create. They talk about such things as the Virgin Mary at Fatima as being created by local magicians! My God, how conceited can you get! They are very humanist in that they think the ultimate reality is man and you're a master and man's next step is to be a god. Hitler got hold of that idea with the Nazis. I do think that all occultists have this odd fascism going on, thinking that they *are* the gods and goddesses. If you have a godless Christianity, if you get rid of deity, you're just left with all these awful gurus. When we began the Fellowship of Isis, we had these people joining and, to be honest, they were claiming me to be the successor to all sorts of people like Dion Fortune. Well, I was no successor to anybody. I got my stuff direct, but to them it was *no good* because it was direct. For them it was all this old-fashioned stuff of a secret, ancient wisdom which was conveyed by taking your Enochian tablets three times a days, and therefore no direct revelation could be accepted by them.

It is arguable that the Pagan movement was revived in the twentieth century by three individuals: Gerald Gardner, Alex Sanders and Aleister Crowley. They were very strong, dominant personalities who 'hit the headlines'. Those people have gone, but are there any charismatic headline-hitters taking their place, or is this no longer the role you see for leaders of Paganism?

I think a lot of those people were very patriarchal. We had Druid ceremonies and they had girls or maidens waiting on them, groupie-looking girls of about seventeen, handing them their beer. The guru thing is going to die out, but there are women who love to serve a master. What I objected to in Wicca was that it was a fertility religion, so that when a woman had the menopause she was out, but the old bloke, if he could still function, could have *young girls*. I was talking to a witch who said, 'I'm nothing now, I'm empty because I've had a hysterectomy.' What I admire about Margot Adler, Starhawk, all these people, was that the American women, and Doreen Valiente, took this witchcraft and lifted it above that, first with the feminist movement and later with the green movement, and they are *great* movements with millions of people. By linking with the feminists and the greens they have lifted it above being a circle of kinky old blokes who like young girls with no clothes on.

History would seem to suggest that organizations and governments do not exist for very long without a hierarchical infrastructure and yet the emphasis in Pagan groups is on autonomy, on government by consensus, on anarchy. Can organizations like Fellowship of Isis survive without a hierarchy?

I feel the New Age is built, not on an evolutionary ladder where you end up, usually by seniority, as the Master or the Adept, but is more like a spiral going either in or out. It's formed by groups who have common consensus and a mystical experience, more like Quakers, of direct revelation with the deities. It's a very personal thing. One lady wanted to be Supreme Oracle of the Fellowship of Isis and I said, 'Well, we're getting oracular claims every day from members. How are we to say who is the top person?' I think Protestantism was the first beginnings of that spiralling movement.

Golden Dawn went into endless factions because they *were* hierarchical. They all wanted to be top guy, but we don't have a top person. I'm administrator, yes, and Caroline will administrate after me. We do the work. You've got to have a centralized 'computer' with all the names, but each priestess is co-equal. In the membership nobody has spiritual authority over another. If we were running Golden

Dawn like that Crowley could have been in it with MacGregor Mathers and W B Yeats. They would all be on an equality.

We're multi-religious, multi-faith, multi-cultural, multi-racial. We don't stick to the Celtic [tradition], therefore there's no point in people fighting with each other. If you don't like the way one person runs her Iseum, then start your own. Don't fight over it. We don't have fragmentation because we start off fragmented! We're like a lot of intertwining circles, like the Olympic symbol.

Can you see a future in which Paganism is linked with politics? This seems to be the trend in the States?
Very much so, because, if you notice, the woman influence, and that is very much the Goddess influence, has made a great difference to the laws about rape and particularly child abuse. The whole of Ireland is utterly shattered by the recent revelations of child abuse. It was going on and they didn't dare speak out against the priests who were doing this and the men seemed to have got away with incest, everything, because they had the money. Men have had a double standard of morality and we are smashing through those prejudices, but it is very horrific what is coming out about male practices. We are now in eighty-five countries, including Finland, and they say that child abuse is just the norm in Finland, always was. The heart is religion and your heart is moved by seeing children ill-used. The heart involves one in fighting against war, bringing peace and harmony, but above all in saving our earth. If we are gong to destroy all life by contaminated air, if we are going to destroy all grass, if we are destroying the whole climate with poisonous clouds and so on, then the Green Movement is the most important. But it's only been brought about by women.

Can women who pursue this spiritual career also follow a responsibility towards the family unit which, in America particularly, is in such a state of dissolution?
Well, the Fellowship of Isis has the family. Priests and nuns of the Catholic tradition are meant to be celibate because the Virgin Mary *was* a virgin. She had no husband. But the twins souls idea of Isis and Osiris now inspires people as it never did before. The more advanced races now wish to choose their partners and are interested in the twin soul idea, as companion, not just mother of children. They want partners and Isis and Osiris provide that to absolute perfection. They are the ideal husband and wife...and they have *sex*!

Do you think that you, as the Fellowship of Isis, have a definable identity and, if so, what is it?
We have a very powerful identity because of the supernatural element. The Green Movement is important, but look at the

Olivia Durdin-Robertson

A witch (left) and druid combine forces to direct and magnify energy, using hand-made runic wands which represent fire.

The pentacle, traditional magical device used on the Wiccan altar, with symbolic inscriptions.

Invocation using the pentagram.

UFO tradition. There's 40,000 Americans who believe they've been abducted and genetically interfered with by some etheric beings they call Ufonauts. The etheric world is mostly just beyond our scientific instruments but in some cases not and the veil is thinning because people are allowed to develop in the way of following the etheric. The Fellowship of Isis, in a sense because of the Egyptian element, is in a unique position to create a bridge between the supernatural and the natural worlds. In other words, we can offer mediumship, we can offer communion between people and the spirit world. I don't know of any other spiritual organization, apart from the Spiritualists, who can do that. We can offer communion with the next world. We can teach people how to do it themselves.

Well, that's what the Fellowship of Isis is doing today, so where is it going? You have a successor-in-waiting. What's your message to her for the next generation of Isians? Communion with the Goddess! There are beings more advanced than us who are drawing near the earth. They've allowed us time to cock snooks at them and play at sciences and at patriarchy, but now women have a very good role in harmonizing our relationship with the gods and goddesses, and that is our role, I feel, because we sense that we can act as public relations officers, as a priesthood, between the deities, God if you like, and human beings, by offering ourselves in the ancient way of the priesthood. We can act as mediators across the threshold between heaven and earth.

ROBIN GOODFELLOW One of the best known FAIRIES or FAMILIARS during the medieval period in England, he equated with Puck. He was originally classed as a hob-goblin or personal guardian who performed certain household chores but became assimilated into the ranks of fairies during the Elizabethan era.

ROEBUCK A well-known COVEN which operates in Los Angeles, being run by a couple who were initiates of one Joe Wilson. Wilson passed on to them material he had gained from British sources, most notably from followers of the Robert COCHRANE 'school', known in the United States as the '1734 tradition', who subscribed to 'traditionalist' doctrines. Legend has it that Wilson performed a ritual to conjure up the shade of Cochrane at SAMHAIN in 1975.

ROSE OF RUBY AND CROSS OF GOLD The elite Second, and highly secretive, Order of Golden Dawn (see HERMETIC ORDER OF THE GOLDEN DAWN) with rituals based on the alleged discovery of the tomb of Christian ROSENKREUZ. This Second Order comprised a controlling corpus, the so-called 'Vault of the Adepts' whose members were known only by secret mottoes and were believed to possess superhuman abilities. According to W Wynn WESTCOTT, one of the charter members of Golden Dawn, the rituals were obtained from a Belgian ADEPT, Dr Thiessen of Liege who went under the magical name of Frater Lux Tenebres.

ROSENKREUTZ, CHRISTIAN (Christian Rosycross, 1378?–1484?) The character, almost certainly mythical, depicted in anonymous early seventeenth-century pamphlets published at Kassel, Germany and founding the Fraternity with a quorum of friends who, collectively, framed the magical charter and language of Rosicrucianism (see ROSICRUCIAN SOCIETY) and set the seal on its OCCULT nature. According to *Fama Fraternitas* the tomb of Rosenkreutz was subsequently rediscovered in circumstances which appear to provide a clear allegory on the story of the Christian Resurrection, including the revelation of an uncorrupted cadaver.

Irrespective of the credentials, or lack of them, in its origins, membership of the Rosicrucian Fraternity rapidly took on a kudos because of its mystique and since its members were believed to possess supernatural powers. It remained, however, ultimately secretive and thus interest amongst the seventeenth century public rapidly waned. Interest was revived in the early decades of the twentieth century when Rosicrucianism formed one of the building blocks of occult organizations including the HERMETIC ORDER OF THE GOLDEN DAWN.

ROSE-CROIX OF HEREDOM The Masonic degree also known as the Rose-Croix Eighteenth Degree, claimed by some historians to derive from ancient principles of Rosicrucianism, a claim vigorously denied by more conservative Freemasons, particularly those who stem from the Christian clergy. Much of the trapping of the Masonic Rose-Croix degree appears similar to that described for Rosicrucianism including a fundamental doctrine of initiation and spiritual rebirth.

The Rose-Croix degree is believed to have been worked in England, as an independent Masonic discipline under Sir Thomas Dunckerley, from about the end of the eighteenth century.

ROSICRUCIAN SOCIETY Also known as the Societas Rosicruciana in Anglia (SRIA). An OCCULT organization founded in England by Robert Wentworth Little with the assistance of fellow Freemasons, W R Woodman, F G Irwin and Kenneth MACKENZIE. According to some authors inauguration took place in 1886 but the alternative date of 1865 is proposed by both Francis King (1970) and R A Gilbert (1983). The SRIA claimed association with the Fraternity of the Rosy Cross, a German society, the roots of which are alleged to trace back to Christian ROSENKREUZ. This claim was supported through the collection by Mackenzie, during a stay in Austria, of certain details of the medieval German grades and rituals. These were claimed to be authentic contemporary documents though, in reality, most were almost certainly copied from a German text dated no earlier than 1781.

Rosicrucianism achieved the height of its popularity in England in the Puritan years of the Interregnum when many of its texts were translated and published, though it was being attacked for 'turning divinity into fantasy' as early as the beginning of the seventeenth century.

During the nineteenth century Rosicrucianism attracted many within Freemasonry, an essential prerequisite for membership, and a number of these Masonic Rosicrucians became interested in, and were initiated into WICCA. Amongst the most influential in England was Hargrave JENNINGS. The English Rosicrucians also published a short-lived magazine, *The Rosicrucian*. In the twentieth century, Dorothy CLUTTERBUCK, Gerald GARDNER's initiator, is said to have met him through a local Rosicrucian society centred on the theatre in Christchurch, Hampshire which was opened in June 1938. Allegedly, there were also links between a number of Rosicrucians and such notable WIZARDS as the Essex CUNNING PERSON George PICKINGILL.

An inventive claim (E W LIDDELL, 1994) suggests that the rituals of SRIA were compiled in 1865 as a result of collaboration between Pickingill, Hargrave Jennings and W H Hughan and that Pickingill 'materially influenced the founding of SRIA and Golden Dawn'. It is implausible that Pickingill, a farm labourer, possessed the required intellect for such a task and Hughan was admitted to the Scottish Rosicrucian Society only in 1866 whilst Hargrave Jennings did not join the English Society until 1870. Neither man was involved in the foundation of SRIA.

The Society has followed loose principles of Gnosticism applying a quasi-Christian doctrine to those of other theosophies, ALCHEMY, reincarnation and esoterism. It relies on the fundamental alchemist's notion that purity of life is a pre-requisite to scientific progress. Implications that it presents an interpretation of Christianity are strongly refuted by Christian and non-Christian scholars alike.

Many of the grades subsequently employed in the HERMETIC ORDER OF THE GOLDEN DAWN mirror those of SRIA but suggestions that one organization was based upon the other are unsubstantiated since their respective rituals bear little similarity.

SRIA members were, at times, criticised for being overly materialistic and pre-occupied with worldly pleasures. Membership was, however, restricted to Master Masons who professed devout belief in the Christian doctrine and membership of SRIA turned out to be a pre-requisite for entry into several other OCCULT societies which arose around the turn of the century.

The Society also supported the concepts of clairvoyance and had, amongst their ranks, the eminent occultist Frederick HOCKLEY. W W WESTCOTT, one of the founders of Golden Dawn, was also a prominent member and for a time W R Woodman was its Supreme Magus.

The present headquarters of the Society are in California where it preaches 'reason' and promises 'success'.

ROYAL TOUCH A method of mystical healing considered efficacious during the Tudor and Stuart reigns in England. Prominent surgeons of the day testified that they had witnessed substantial numbers of cures administered in this way, through the laying-on of the monarch's hand.

There is no evidence supporting the claims of efficacy and most cures resulted only after a period of time, nonetheless the cures attracted great conviction amongst the public, driven by the belief in the divine nature of the king and by what seemed preferable to the more conventional surgeon's remedies which were frequently painful.

The afflictions allegedly cured came under the generic title of the 'King's Evil' and included various eye complaints, scrofula and tuberculosis. Scrofula was an intermittent disease, a factor which lent readily to the appearance of being magically cured, and some forms of tuberculosis possessed the characteristic of healing spontaneously.

RR ET AC See ROSE OF RUBY AND CROSS OF GOLD.

RUNES The symbols or characters of archaic origin which appear in inscriptions from Nordic and Germanic cultural areas and are traditional to north European peoples where they have been used as the basis for systems of DIVINATION. Runic symbols are considered by some authorities to be an offshoot from the same north Italic root that gave rise to Greek and Latin and would originally have taken the form of sound SIGILS. They comprise twenty four symbols collectively known as the elder FUTHARK, from which were derived Anglo-Frisian and Anglo-Saxon variations. The futhark is divided into groups of eight known as *aettir*.

They were first employed by Germanic and Scandinavian peoples in the second century AD and were continuously employed until the Viking era during which the god Othin is reputed to have cpnveyed Runic lore to the human race. In the eighth century AD the 24-rune futhark was reduced to sixteen runes although today the original 24-rune *futhark* is employed in ASATRU as an essential tool of magic and divination.

RYLANDS LIBRARY see JOHN RYLANDS LIBRARY.

SABBAT One of eight principal festivals in the calendar of WICCA or modern witchcraft including the four Grand SABBATS – CANDLEMAS, BELTANE, LAMMAS and SAMHAIN – and the four Lesser Sabbats – Spring Equinox, SUMMER SOLSTICE, AUTUMN EQUINOX and WINTER SOLSTICE (YULE). These are typically celebrated out of doors to mark the passing of the seasons and the gift of life that each brings. In seasonal rituals, the priestess becomes the physical incarnation of the GODDESS through a rite, the DRAWING DOWN OF THE MOON. Once invoked and present she delivers a CHARGE (see also CHARGE OF THE GODDESS).

The origin of the name *sabbat* is unclear. It may derive from the Jewish holy day or *sabbath*. Alternatively it may possess more arcane origins. Doreen VALIENTE suggests that it may derive from the alternative title, *Sabadius*, given to the Greek god Dionysos.

At the time of Christian conversion the members of the Sabbat were perceived by the clergy to be wild, part-human, part-animal, men and women (see WILD HUNT, THE). Christian commentary during the witch-hunting period of the fifteenth and sixteenth centuries depicted the Sabbat as an orgiastic nocturnal meeting, although the spirit beings had, by that time, evolved in their mortal guise into witches, travelling through the forests on broomsticks to meet and dine off the corpses of children in a parody of the Eucharist, after which they engaged in bizarre sexual rites.

In Nordic and Germanic traditions the leader of the Sabbat was Frigg (Frija), the consort of OTHIN (Wotan). In other traditions the leader was a male figure such as HERNE or Bertholt.

During sabbat meetings the witches allegedly applied magical ointments to facilitate shape-changing and levitation. There is, however, very little reliable documentation of Sabbats in England and Wales. Most reports of them from past centuries (and even in the early part of the twentieth century) are luridly embellished, based on hearsay and must be treated with considerable caution. Today, tabloid newspaper articles invariably attempt to link WITCHCRAFT and its sabbats with Satanism.

SACRED FOOD The cakes and wine that are blessed by the high priest and priestess of a WICCAN COVEN in preparation for the ensuing feast and as the final act before the closing of the CIRCLE. The priest holds the cup (symbolically female) which is blessed by the priestess through the instrument of the ATHAME (symbolically male) which is dipped into the cup, the rite being an allegory on sexual impregnation. The cakes are likewise blessed with the athame.

The Feast thus enacted has religious connotations, but there is no suggestion that the food and drink symbolize the flesh and blood of the deity in carnal form. In earlier times the use of mead or ale rather than wine was probably more conventional, and also had echoes of feasts described in medieval accounts of witches' SABBATS.

SACRED KING See DARK GODDESS.

SACRED MARRIAGE An ancient rite of regenesis, central to many PAGAN faiths and at the core of the third degree of INITIATION in WICCA. It is first accounted in Sumerian cuneiform texts inscribed in the third millennium BC but probably dates from a much earlier period of prehistory.

In Sumerian belief, the essence of the Sacred Marriage was the union between god and goddess, symbolizing the male and female elements of nature who, through their divine intercourse in the spring of the year, brought new life to the world. The earliest deities to whom the rite is attributed were the Sumerian goddess of life, Inana, and her dying-and-rising consort Dumuzi. In Babylonian tradition the pair became Ishtar and Tammuz. Throughout Mesopotamia, the festival was held in April or May at the time of harvest when the effects of drought could also be at their most severe. Inana was the womb of the earth tilled by the peasant farmer and it was necessary to fertilize the womb with the godly semen that came from the skies in the form of rain. At the climax of the festival, a bed made of cedar and rushes was prepared in a bower and the high priestess of the goddess was received by the king in sexual partnership among great paraphernalia and in public view.

There is strong argument that the words of the Biblical *Song of Solomon* allegorize the Sacred Marriage in such verses as: *My beloved put his hand by the hole of the door, and my bowels were moved for him. I rose up to open to my beloved; and my hands dropped with myrrh and my fingers with sweet smelling myrrh, upon the handles of the lock.*

Visual analogy of open and closed rooms, and locked and unlocked doors, was frequently called on by contemporary poets to convey the condition of a hymen. The link is, however, strongly rejected by the Jewish and Christian establishments to whom such practice would be anathema.

An old Sumerian hymn captures more overtly the magical essence of the rite:
As for me, my vulva. For me the piled-high hillock,
Me, the maid, who will plough it for me?
My vulva, the watered ground – for me,
Me, the Queen, who will station the ox there?
To which is framed the rapturous response:
O Lordly Lady, the king will plough it for you,

Dumuzi the king will plough it for you.

In Wicca, the symbolic device associated with the Sacred Marriage is the upward pointing PENTAGRAM, the symbol of life, crowned with a small triangle. The essence of the rite reflects the union of goddess and god, and the tracing of the final line of the pentagram back to the goddess from whence it began at the time of the first degree of INITIATION.

SALEM, WITCH TRIALS OF The trials that took place in the village of Salem, Massachusetts, in 1692 and that represent the most well-documented proceedings of their kind in America. The events stemmed from the OCCULT activity of a group of Salem children who experimented with DIVINATION to establish the identity of their future husbands and shortly afterwards began to exhibit bizarre symptoms, including convulsions, which may have been self-induced. Nonetheless, the father of one, a local minister called Samuel Parris, considered that the behaviour raised the spectre of diabolical possession. Under intense examination the girls implicated three women, one a West Indian slave, on charges of bewitching them. The slave girl confessed freely, admitting to being in league with a black devil. Later, in the face of continuing and spreading hysteria, several other women were implicated.

Ironically, the lives of those Salem residents who confessed to the crime of WITCHCRAFT were spared while many of those who denied guilt were executed. The hangings, which were carried out between 10 June and 22 September 1692 claimed the lives of nineteen Salem residents.

In consequence of this irrational slaughter, often on the flimsiest of evidence, gained under intense pressure and intimidation, a tide of public revulsion arose against the Salem trials and they were not continued beyond the initial indictments.

SALISBURY, COUNTESS OF Allegedly a WITCH whose inadvertent *faux pas* provided the origin for the Order of the Garter. According to the contemporary observers, Polydore Vergil and Selden, an account supported by modern research, the incident took place while the Countess was dancing with Edward III at a ball held at Calais to celebrate the fall of the town in 1348. The young Countess dropped her blue garter but the King, who was at the time infatuated with her, gallantly retrieved it and placed it on his own leg with the now immortalized remark *Honi soit qui mal y pense*. Subsequently, the Garter became symbolic in the foundation of the Order of the Garter, which was made exclusive to twenty-six knights, twelve with the King and twelve with the Prince of Wales. The attractive but slightly risque story of the garter appealed to Victorian England and Christmas cards featuring the 'Blushing Countess' became a vogue.

The historian Margaret Galway has placed the Countess as Joan of Kent, a celebrated beauty of her time who was destined to wed the Black Prince. Gerald GARDNER claims that the blue garter identified the Countess as a priestess and the king was saving her from indictment. He bases this on the fact that the third consecration sign marked on a witch's tools is a double S and that the SS insignia also appears on the Order of the Garter. He also suggests that the exclusivity of the Order of the Garter to twenty-six members provided for two COVENS of thirteen apiece. However these embellishments of the story possess tenuous substance. The blue sash or garter has strong Christian connotations as the colour worn by the Virgin Mary and it seems evident that Edward intended to use the device to ally himself firmly with the principles of brotherhood and chivalry.

SAMHAIN (HALLOWE'EN) The most significant of the four Grand SABBAT festivals, celebrated on 31 October and marking the ancient Celtic and Druidic New Year, the start of the WHEEL OF THE YEAR. The objective of the rite was twofold: to celebrate the slaughter of livestock for the winter months and to invoke the gods to restore the power of the waning sun at the onset of winter.

Since it was also a time when the elderly members of the tribe were most likely to succumb, Samhain represented a rite at which the barriers between the temporal and spiritual worlds were at their weakest and communication with deceased ancestors was most feasible.

In Anglo-Saxon tradition Samhain was called 'need-fire' and was marked by the lighting of bonfires which were thought to impart heat and strength to the sun by means of imitative magic. The name Hallowe'en arose through Christian influence since All Hallows (All Saints) Day falls on 1 November and therefore 31 October is All Hallows Eve. The rite became debased, in the Christian calendar, to an occasion on which children hollow out pumpkins and play pranks on adults in the form of 'trick or treat'. The bonfire tradition was retained in Britain, although it moved to 5 November in celebration of Guy Fawkes Day.

In modern WICCA, Samhain (pronounced *Sow-in*) is also known as the Festival of the Dead when the HORNED GOD is invoked in his aspect as the Dark Lord of the UNDERWORLD and the mysteries of death are contemplated. It is also the occasion when the temporal and spiritual realms come into close alignment and the dead may part the veil and cross the threshold between the two worlds.

The object of hollowing out pumpkins and illuminating them with candles as Jack O'Lanterns, is to provide a light to guide the spirits of the dead to where a portion of the festival meal is left out for them.

SANDERS, ALEX (1926-1988) Born in Manchester, England, to Harold and Hannah Sanders, he was an influential modern PAGAN and founder of the so-called ALEXANDRIAN branch of WICCA whose beliefs are, arguably, based on those of GARDNER, although Sanders claimed distinct origins for his branch of the Craft.

Sanders believed himself to stem from a long line of witches tracing back to Owen Glendower.

According to his biographer, June Johns, Sanders always claimed that his Welsh grandmother, Mary Bibby, initiated him into the Craft as a seven-year old child and he himself was still making this claim until shortly before his death. Others close to him suggest that he was either self-initiated or, more probably, that his INITIATION was carried out in a Gardnerian COVEN in Manchester in about 1962 by a priestess called Pat Kopanski. Kopanski was an ex-maiden of the Sheffield coven run by Patricia CROWTHER, who in turn was one of Gardner's high priestesses. Some of the material that Sanders quoted as having been given to him by his grandmother was palpably Gardnerian in origin and had been adapted by Doreen VALIENTE in the 1950s. This supports a theory that Sanders was given a copy of the BOOK OF SHADOWS on a visit to Gardner in the Isle of Man. It does not, however, prove or disprove his initiation claims.

Sanders discovered an aptitude for clairvoyance, took on the OCCULT name Verbius and, according to Johns, continued in his training through his grandmother until her death in 1941. He was, at times, scathing of Gardnerian Wicca but appears, nonetheless, to have been strongly influenced by Gerald Gardner and his own *Book of Shadows* is largely Gardnerian in derivation.

He worked for a time in the JOHN RYLANDS LIBRARY in Manchester where he dismantled and removed a copy of the *Key of Solomon* (see SOLOMON, KEY OF) piecemeal before being discovered. Swayed by a growing sexual appetite and an awareness that he could use his knowledge of the Craft to obtain power over women, he turned to Satanism for a time, but then reverted back to practising more benign aspects of WITCHCRAFT, mingling elements of Qabalistic (see QABALA) and Egyptian lore. After the death of his sister, Joan, he became closely involved with the ABRA-MELIN system of Hebrew magic.

In 1965 he was approached by an un-named individual who asked him to be proclaimed 'King of the Witches' and although at first he declined he

was eventually persuaded. According to Maxine SANDERS, twelve witch queens who had come from places as far away as Scotland were present at the coronation which took place at Chorlton-cum-Hardy near Stretford in what is now Greater Manchester. In the same year he HANDFASTED, on one of several ceremonial instances, with the nineteen-year-old Maxine Morris. In 1967 they moved to London, legally marrying in 1968 and subsequently had two children, Maya and Victor. They were separated and divorced in 1973, Maxine remaining in London, Alex moving to Bexhill on Sea, where he remarried and divorced again rapidly amid rumours of bisexuality.

During his time, and in spite of his bizarre showmanship, Sanders did much to put a respectable public face on the Craft and, despite their divorce, he was much-loved to the end by Maxine. He died of lung cancer, alone and more or less destitute, in a Hastings hospital on 30 April 1988. It is said by those close to him that he had intended a last publicity stunt for Beltane and that he carried it off in his usual showman's style.

SANDERS, MAXINE (born 1946) The daughter of Victor and Doris Morris, she was convent educated at St Joseph's, Manchester, as part of a strict Catholic upbringing. As a young child she was introduced to Alex SANDERS through her mother who had befriended him in the hospital where she worked as a nurse. Later, at the age of fourteen, she met him again through her mother's membership of an Indonesian cult, Subud. In 1962 when she was sixteen and a student at secretarial college, she became initiated into the COVEN of a priestess known as Sylvia. Alex Sanders was also a member. Maxine's father had suffered a sudden and fatal heart attack shortly before and her mother was ailing rapidly. At about this time she also abandoned her secretarial studies. Amid a volley of critical and exaggerated publicity resulting from sensationalised press exposure of her OCCULT activities with Sander's own coven at Alderley Edge (unaware that she was being photographed, nude, by an employee of a local tabloid, *The Comet*) she was subsequently disowned by the rest of her family and was subjected to considerable, at times violent, local vilification. When her mother died from cancer she was forced to recant and suffered, she claims, considerable police harassment because of her occult activities and because of the innocent association that she and Alex had with the site of the Moors Murders at Saddleworth. They had occasionally arranged coven meetings at the remote area where, unknown to them, Myra Hindley and Ian Brady were engaging in their horrific child killings.

In 1965, shortly after the death of her mother, she entered into one of several HANDFASTING ceremonies with Alex, having already been initiated into the Third Grade of Wicca (see INITIATION) and, in 1968, was also legally married to him in a civil ceremony. By that time she and Alex had moved to London, where most of their Craft associates and friends were living. They thus entered a more convenient climate in which to practice their beliefs and rituals.

In 1973 she obtained a divorce from Alex, choosing to remain at the family home in London with their two children. In 1975 she was interviewed by the tabloid newspaper the *News of the World*, resulting in a series of articles in which she revealed a disillusionment and, in certain respects, disgust with aspects of her life. However she has since retracted some details of the interview, which she claims were exaggerated by her in order to get her own back on the press. When Alex died in 1988, she orchestrated, through a high priestess named Victoria, and with the help of Nigel Bourne and Seldiye Bates, a Qabalistic (see QABALAH) funeral at Hastings Crematorium.

In recent years she has become occupied with teaching aspects of the Craft and with pursuing her own personal and private style of faith. She has also remarried and has written an autobiography.

INTERVIEW WITH

maxine sanders

✳

Your childhood was framed by a strict Catholic upbringing, you were convent educated. At fifteen you changed tracks and adopted Paganism. You were a Third Grade Wiccan. A lot of water has passed under the bridge since then. What are you now? Who are you now?

I'm a priestess of the Craft. I'm not a witch queen. I'm not actually practising with a coven at the moment but my love is witchcraft in the way that I've been trained and in the way that I've learned. I haven't just stuck with the way I was in 1960 or whatever. I've grown, I've had to study, I'm interested in the occult, I suppose I am an occultist. Something that interests me at the moment is Buddhism and I'm studying it and enjoying it. It gives me a way. I'm seeking spiritual advancement, whether it takes the form of Witchcraft or Buddhism or Catholicism, and I haven't got any boundaries on what I can do or what I can't do.

Do you also see yourself in terms of magicianship?

I work magic but it never occurred to me to call myself a magician.

And what about the psychic, clairvoyant part?

I've always been psychic, even as a child, it's always been a part of my nature. So witchcraft hasn't brought that out. I don't think I got involved with witchcraft because of some great vocational interest. I think that it was circumstance and probably fate.

Were you involved with the Liberal Catholic Church, which I think has closer cultural links with the old Theosophical Society than Roman Catholicism?

It was my daughter actually. Alex and I decided that we would bring the children up in the Christian religion because it's supposed to be a Christian land and we didn't want to impose our beliefs on them, or cause difficulties for them. The Catholic Church refused them, the Church of England accepted them. When Maya was about thirteen she was going to a Convent School and she investigated Roman Catholicism and found it not suitable, she went through the Temple library and found books on the Science of the Sacraments and wanted to know about the Liberal Catholic Church, so we went and had a look. She quite enjoyed it, she wanted to become a member and, of course, I got interested and thoroughly enjoyed it too. It didn't stop me working the Craft.

Why were you concerned that your children were free not to adopt the Craft?
Because I don't think the Craft is for children. I really don't think that it is. I've had too many experiences now where even adults can be disturbed by dabbling in witchcraft. I think that children should have the safety and security of the country's religious thought-form and, on the whole at that time, in '67 or '68, England was a Christian country. I don't think you can call it a Christian country now. If my daughter came to me with her children and said, Well, I want my children to be involved with witchcraft, I would still say no. But there's nothing to stop them studying folklore.

If it's not for children, who do you think it is for?
You have to remember that the Craft is a priesthood, one that works as any other priesthood. They work their rituals, they are dedicated to spiritual advancement and perfection, but they also take on the mantle of the priesthood which gives them a responsibility to have an ever-caring nature towards the general public, and when approached by the public they should be there to give their priestly advice or whatever is needed.

What was your reasoning for becoming a witch? Do you know what your reasoning was, because you were very young at the time?
I think there are several reasons that contribute to my becoming involved with witchcraft. I had a dreadful, dreadful childhood and, on meeting witches, I found them to be open, loving, caring people who didn't frown at my gifts, didn't frown because I spoke about travelling out of my body, didn't frown at my ability to travel into the future. It just felt like home. I think that there was an inadequacy that had been put on me by my father, the craft offered a sense of security.

What inadequacies did your father put on you?
He was an extremely abusive man, very violent, and I'd been subjected to all sorts of violence for most of my childhood.

So joining the Craft was not some sort of teenage whimsical fad?
I was never, never a whimsical teenager (*laughter*). I'm probably far younger today than I was when I was a child or in my 'teens. I had too many responsibilities as a child, too many hardships, to enjoy childhood. And I regret it, I'm quite envious of children nowadays because I look at them and think, what a wonderful childhood. I didn't have that.

Was there, to any degree, a desire to shock and to rebel in a period when provincial English society was very easily shocked by such revelations? Alderley Edge is pretty twee and middle class. It must have been something of a bombshell up there.

It really didn't occur to me. It hadn't occurred to Alex. I know, in hindsight, that he was a natural showman. He wanted to shock, he wanted to rebel. It was said that it was the 'work', that he wanted the Craft to be acceptable, which I think it is to-day, but he did it in a very shocking way. He brought it out because he was a showman and in retur? the Craft, to a certain degree, used him and rejected him. They had a love-hate relationship with him and his work succeeded. But, personally, I didn't like it. The first time I knew about any publicity I was standing on the altar stone at Alderley Edge thinking, this is a strange kind of clairvoyance with these flashing lights, a couple of days later a little newspaper called *The Comet* had this picture of me on the front page saying, 'Ex Convent Girl working Naked Witchcraft Rites on Alderley Edge' and it just snowballed from there.

Did that in a sense close doors on you? Did it give you a feeling that there was nowhere else to go but with Alex? Or was it more that you were positive anyway?

I was more like a leaf than a positive tree. I went with it. I enjoyed it, not necessarily the publicity. I didn't enjoy that but I loved the Craft and I loved the people in the Craft. I remember Alex sitting at the sewing machine all night, once, sewing up thirteen robes because he always insisted that if the cameras were going to be there he wanted the Craft to be represented well. He didn't want anything shoddy and nasty to go forward, with people in unironed robes and that sort of thing.

There seems to be a bit of a paradox in some ways because on the one hand you are very quietly spoken, you say that you are to some extent reclusive, and yet in other ways you appear to have courted publicity. Did any of this showmanship rub off on you?

Yes. Because when the publicity was happening, the early publicity, you would work with it and you would think, yes, they're going to get the atmosphere of the Craft, they're really going to see the beauty of it. Then, of course, the 'Sundays' would come out and it would be shock-horror and I felt hurt by that.

I didn't just get letters, I got bags of them. The postman used to be quite annoyed. And I was cursed by Christians quit? regularly? I can't blame them because they actually thought I was doing very wicked things. And I wasn't doing very wicked things at all. I was accused of being involved with blood sacrifices and I hadn't been. I took on a cause and I was going to fight for it tooth and nail.

There is a good argument that the ritual of Roman Catholicism and the ritual of Paganism are not too far apart. Mother goddess worship, magic, emphasis on ritual rather than creed. Was the convent education, in a sense, an easier place from which to move over to Paganism rather than the barrier one might imagine?

I think a lot of Catholics end up in ritualistic cults because Catholicism lets itself down through politics and that was the thing that turned me against the Church – no, not against the Church, I can't be against the Church because I think it does tremendous work and it gives people what they want. Everybody to their own and I am not going to decry another person's God.

Let's go back to leafy Cheshire, because it was a totally different environment at that time. What kind of brickbats hit you?

I was stoned in the street, my house was set on fire. Well? they tried to set my house on fire, they set the outside shed on fire. It was dreadful, absolutely dreadful. And when the Moors Murders came up and were being investigated, we were investigated. That was terrifying. Anything that went wrong, we would be the first to be investigated. Now, I suppose because of the years of investigation, the police hold me in high regard and I'm quite proud of that. Because when you're involved in a cult, all sorts of weird and wonderful, strange and bad and good people are involved in the occult, just as there are in Christianity, and sometimes mud sticks and you have to be strong all the way

through. The temptation is there to get involved and you have to say, 'Why am I involved in this? Is it because I want to get involved with dope smoking or drugs or whatever?' And you have to say no. You have to stay clean. You have to come from the heart.

Is it correct that your immediate family disowned you?

Oh yes, completely, until about 1976 when my sister, who had been adopted by my aunt, wrote to the *News of the World* and said, I believe this is my sister. And, of course, we've become great friends now, very close. I just knew she would contact me. I had sent the birthday cards, the Christmas presents, but she didn't receive any of them because that part of the family were devout Catholics.

Once you were in the Craft with Alex, what did it come to mean to you?

We lived it, or I lived it. I lived the Craft from waking up, all the time. Everything was the Craft. When we moved to London, people said, 'How can you work the Craft from the middle of a city? 'Quite easily! I was religious, totally religious, and I would have died for the Craft.

Alex was very much into Qabalistic lore and presmably you and he were into spiritualism, into trance training? Did you concentrate on those aspects?

I didn't like it and, no, we didn't focus on

trance training. Alex was a medium and that was one aspect I really didn't like. I preferred the ritualistic work, because I got more out of it. I supposed Alex had a tendency to fake and I am a terrible doubting Thomas. I analysed and analysed and today I actually believe that most mediums are faking. Honestly faking, but it's coming from the sub-conscious. They're picking up power levels and different waves of vibrations and whatever. One can make every excuse in the book but, at the end of the day I didn't like it then and I don't like it now.

And, on the other side of the coin, what about the idea of revitalizing, restoring an ancient fertility ritual?
It never occurred to me that I was restoring or revitalizing something. I mean there was this controversy that it was Gardner that started the Craft off with Doreen Valiente. They got together and Gardner liked the idea of starting off a new religion. But when I was initiated into the Craft there were people that had no idea of Gardner's existence. I know people now who have been practising the Craft for over sixty or seventy years and their parents were practising too. And then the historians come along and say, 'There's no trace, you cannot trace it.' Maybe you can't but most of these people had to live as Christians, as Methodists, whatever, in their corner of the land but they were still practising and

they still had group meetings.

Is there a tendency today towards doing nothing and looking back towards archetypes rather than drumming up spirits and drawing double circles?
I think there are a lot of people doing what I'm doing now, talking about it and not getting on with it. But I think that is why I closed down and stopped having any publicity at all. For one thing my daughter was small and going through a hard time at school with people being rude to her about her mother.

Was any, or all, of the reasoning for moving from Cheshire to London because there was a more liberal attitude here?
No. Not at all. I became pregnant and all the witches were coming from London every weekend to work with us anyway. There were witches trained up well enough to carry on a coven in the north and so the next logical step, when a flat came available, was to move to London.

What kind of need do you think witchcraft served in the '50s and '60s. Technological materialism hadn't really taken over, militant feminism hadn't been invented, I can't imagine anyone knew what holistics were, certainly eco-politics hadn't been invented. What need did it serve?
Oh, come on. We had been put down by the Church, controlled by the Church. It was natural evolution and if it wasn't witchcraft it would have been some other

cult that did it. Now, because man's intelligence has grown, through the media, through science, the need has to be filled. But I look at witches today and witches thirty years ago. They were happy with simple spells and they worked wonderfully. Give a witch a simple spell today and it won't work for them because it's too easy, they need something complicated, the gobble-de-gook. In a way they are more ignorant today than they were then. People used to be far more superstitious because of the Church. Now they're not so superstitious, they want facts and witchcraft gives them an enjoyable way of finding those facts.

There's been an interesting change in a way. One has this group of men, Leland, Crowley, Gardner, Williamson and Alex who seem to have catalysed the Craft, and some of them were slightly odd-ball. That has now evolved into something that is very much driven by women. Does the fact that these guys were around to kick things into touch detract?
Probably . . . driven by women. Wow! Gardner was a showman and Alex was a showman. Alex was a powerful man before he got any publicity for witchcraft and he was quite famous in the north for his healing and his mediumship. He used to work in spiritualist churches, known as Paul Dallas? In those days when they had braziers to heat the church, a full-blooded Red Indian would materialise, using Alex who would lift the glowing red embers

with bare hands from the braziers take them round the church and perform fantastic healing's. He was the first man who did spiritual healing in a hospital.

Somebody suggested to me not so long ago that these men were largely kinky old goats who surrounded themselves with young women and then turfed them out when they reached the menopause. Did that ever strike you or deter you?
I totally disagree. The covens which I've belonged to have had beautiful men, beautiful old men, beautiful young men, and some ugly ones as well. I can't speak for any of these men. I can only speak from my personal experience with Alex and I think that when it started properly in the '60s and people were coming to him, of course his ego was flattered. He would be totally, totally exhausted. There would be hundreds of people. I can remember walking in to my living room and people were squashed against the walls and Alex was sat in his chair and just talking. And at that point he didn't have the ego that came later. The ego did come and it was a horrible thing to see this man, who was a spiritual man, a deeply religious man, become warped by the publicity, by the admiration. It was a dreadful thing to see because he had been so pure and he wasn't any more. It was a dreadful thing. Originally he was working the Craft, he'd found like-minded people. He'd been alone for years not knowing that there were other

witches in existence. Alex saw Pat Crowther on television. He went off to see her, she refused him initiation and has never stopped boasting about it since. Alex received his second initiation from Crowther's maiden, Pat Kopanski.

When you gave your interview to the News of the World *in 1975 you used, I think, words like disillusionment and disgust. Where were these sentiments directed?*

I'll tell you a truth now. I sat up the night before making it up! Not all of it because a lot of the stuff, the more unbelievable stuff, was true! But I has a slight vendetta against the *News of the World.* They'd destroyed my life and when the opportunity to do it came up, I thought, Yes, I'm going to take the money (*laughter*) I'm going to pay all these phenomenal debts off. As usual misquotes and clever editing by the paper threw a completely different light on the intended story. You can never win with the press.

But you went through a divorce. There must have been some disillusionment with Alex?

Yes, I suppose so. But then that happens in all marriages. I was heartbroken when our marriage did break but, having looked back, I think it was fate. You know, these things happen and we can go all metaphysical, but it did happen. The thing is the work was done, our work together was done. There was no longer any need for a King of the Witches. He

died in '88, still trying to be a public figure and there was no need. His kingship, the reason for his kingship, actually, was no longer necessary. His job was to bring the Craft into the public eye and it did become acceptable, so our work was done.

There was a level of publicity surrounding his death. Tell me what happened.

Before he died he was so poorly, and he was poor. He didn't earn money and he gave everything away. It had always been a habit of his to give things away, but there were people around him who wouldn't accept that he was dying and were constantly urging him on to have publicity. A man called Kevin Carlyon took taped interviews with Alex a couple of weeks before he died. Alex was on morphine and hallucinating and in terrible pain and coughing. And then, two weeks after he died, the man released these unedited tapes, selling them. He had also encouraged Alex to get the press wound up to Beltane saying that he was going to do something and, of course, he died, and I thought that was a good last joke. The people around Alex were greedy, they wanted to sell the story, sell anything to do with Alex. The people were sycophants, they were leeches and I despise them.

Do you think that the Craft, today, should still keep a level of secrecy and is it creating a rod for its own back by doing so?

'If it harm none, Do what thou wilt.' A Pagan visits a sacred site.

I think that by its very essence it is secret and it's so personal, so individual. I still agree with the Craft law where you don't get two covens meeting together unless it's for a Grand Sabbat. You just don't get those grand Sabbats now though. You get grand public dos and people trying to set up councils and what have you. I'm not at all interested. I'm not fighting for that cause any more. What the people of the Craft do with it, now that they've got the freedom to have it and practice without persecution is their decision.

How do you regard the so-called telly-witches, the Beth Gurevitch's of this world?
She's a money-making witch. If you put somebody like Doreen Valiente up against her, Doreen would floor her. I don't even consider her to be worth thinking about. One witch said to me some years ago, the Craft is going in two directions, a little bit like Christianity. You're going to get your outer Orders and you're going to get the enclosed Orders. I think you are always going to have groups that will never have publicity, that are training groups, that are working groups, that get on with it.

But is not the secrecy in a way fuelling the case for your detractors because they are saying, 'Look, there's secrecy here so there's something nasty to hide'?
None of my Circles have ever had anything to hide. You work with a group, you build up a group bond and you

develop together. Religious and spiritual realization is not something that you immediately want to go out and spread about. You want them to come from within yourself so that you can act as a better person. That sounds a bit horrid, doesn't it, but you jealously guard your spiritual elation. I've always believed that the light can only shine in the darkness so when you create a Circle and you are creating it in perfect love and consecrating it and making it holy, do I want a press camera there with a reporter when I don't know what kind of training he's had? I'm quite prepared, if people come along and ask me questions, to tell them what I'm intending to do.

You teach, as you say, so what is the purpose of the Craft today? Where has it reached?
I suppose the purpose is as it always has been, for personal fulfilment.

Forgive me but I would suggest that is slightly coy because, particularly in the States, the Craft has now become to no small extent politicized.
Oh yes, but that's not my way. You can say whatever you like about the Craft but I only speak about it from my experience. And if you say my words are coy, it's because I have not been a socializer, I've not been involved with these groups who are public, or set up public courses. Coy I may be but I'm quite happy being like that.

Remembering the dead at Samhain.

But do you think that there are political issues to be responded to by the Craft?

I don't care. I really don't give a damn, because for me the Craft is a very, very wonderful religious practice that I can thoroughly enjoy. I'm not brow-beaten by it, I'm not prepared to become political. One of the laws of the occult is that we are not allowed to be involved with politics. I'm not allowed to tell you what I vote. The Craft is a hearth religion.

Do you see yourself as a solitary witch these days?

No. I love working with groups. It's just that this last couple of years I've handed over to a Priest and Priestess who are doing my work for me. I've got other work to do and to some extent I'm going to go public because I think there is so much rubbish spoken about the Craft. A lot of the good sense is not being spoken and people might listen. They might want to listen.

To what extent has the Craft and the occult governed your life?

Totally. I've lived it. I haven't done anything else. Being involved with spiritual matters, living life has been terribly acute, intense, and yet when I discovered non-religious people, nothing was as acute for them. . .except maybe in Oxford Street!

How would you sum up your involvement

with the Craft and with Alex?

I was once asked was Alex a charlatan, and I said yes. The person was so shocked, he asked if Alex was a magician and I said yes. He was both, and a fool, and I loved him. It's as simple as that.

SANDRA (born Prague, 1940) Prominent Czech WITCH, now based in Munich, southern Germany. Born into a noble family and raised in large, ancient houses in a country with a long tradition of witchcraft, Sandra claims that she was aware from a very early age that she had unusual powers, although it took time for her to recognize how to control them.

She married a doctor and spent time with him in West Africa, where she discovered a great deal about the black magic traditions. Returning to Prague, which she believes is a place of special powers, she worked as an interpreter before moving to Germany in 1968 a few weeks before the Russians invaded Czechoslovakia – an event about which she had a premonition.

She describes herself as 'a very original, definitely white witch'. She also considers herself an 'old-style' witch, distinguishing herself from some 'modern' types of witch who have adopted PAGANISM as part of the feminist movement or other such trends. She values her combined role as mother and witch.

Her powers have not always been beneficial. She was always convinced that she would have three children, but long after the birth of her first two she found she was expecting twins. When one of these was stillborn, she feared that her negative feelings had killed the child.

Although she has appeared on German television, she strongly resists attempts to make use of her powers for entertainment purposes – when persistently asked by an interviewer for a 'demonstration' her refusal became so adamant that it is claimed her energy fused the studio lights.

Both her daughters are witches, though 'one more intensely than the other'. Sandra now runs Hexenladen, a shop specializing in the occult, in Munich and has published an autobiography.

SATANISM A phenomenon with little relevance to traditional WITCHCRAFT and firmly rejected by most PAGANS since it involves a hedonistic pact with Satan, a personality rejected in PAGANISM, since the Devil is a peculiarly Christian phenomenon. The principles of Satanism are largely removed from those of medieval witchcraft. Some Satanists worship LUCIFER but, by and large, they adhere to no particular deity and their creed is based on hedonistic occultism, rejecting ideas of MAGIC and trivializing notions of evil.

Among the most prominent members of the Satanic movement during the twentieth century are the somewhat comical Anton Szandor LA VEY, who founded the Church of Satan in California in 1966, and the infinitely more sinister Charles MANSON.

SATURNALIA The ancient Roman feast in honour of the god Saturnus which began on 17 December and continued for five days, climaxing at the Winter Solstice (see YULE). Derived from the worship of the pre-Greek fertility god, Kronos, the son of Ouranos and GAIA, in the harvest festival of *kronia,* it represents the Classical precursor of Christmas and is arguably the single most famous Roman festival. Although Saturnus is best known in his representation as an astral deity, he probably originates as a god of agriculture concerned with the sowing of seed. A Saturnus sanctuary (doubling up as an imperial treasury) existed on the Roman Forum from as early as 450 BC.

During the Saturnalia, masters and their slaves exchanged roles, with the former waiting at table and the latter giving orders. There was great feasting and candles were given as gifts that symbolized light amid the darkness of winter and the demise of the old year. The association of holly and ivy may have developed with the Saturnalia. Robert GRAVES describes how in Italy, on the morning of Yule (the last day of Saturnus' reign), his representative, a dark man called the Holly Boy, had to be the first over a threshold while women were kept at bay. This 'enmity' led to the old tradition of Ivy Girls and Holly Boys who played for forfeits and sang satirical songs at one another, and is the origin of the competition between the holly and the ivy mentioned in the Christian carol.

SAWYER, ELIZABETH The defendant in one of the more celebrated English witch trials of the seventeenth century and the subject of a publication *The Wonderful Discoverie of Elizabeth Sawyer, a Witch* (1621) by her interrogator, the Reverend Henry Goodcole, Visitor of Newgate.

SCEPTICISM TOWARDS WITCHCRAFT The repeal of the Witchcraft Act in 1736 (see WITCHCRAFT, ENGLISH AND SCOTTISH LAWS) represented the culmination of a process of amelioration which had begun in the late sixteenth century. As early as the 1570s, intellectual arguments were being voiced suggesting that witches were no more than a figment of vivid clerical imagination, and that many of those arrested and charged were guilty of no more serious crime than melancholia. One of the earliest records of a dissenting voice in England is that of John Tuckie whose trial appears in the Wells Diocesan Records (Somerset) for 16 May 1555 when he was accused of practising SORCERY. Tuckie observed, *No man or woman can do anything by witchcraft.*

The power of individuals to harm others through melting wax images or uttering occasional curses was considered doubtful by an accountable number of physicians and intellectuals. It was also regarded as inconsistent with Christian doctrine that, if the Devil had been relegated by Christ to the infernal regions, he could be restored to power by a solitary and otherwise harmless widow eking out an existence in rural Somerset or Essex.

During the seventeenth century the body of sceptics grew, their views represented by such leading writers as Thomas Ady, Samuel Harsnet, John Wagstaff and John Webster, all of whom followed in the wake of Reginald SCOT.

The repeal of the Elizabethan and Stuart witchcraft laws became inevitable when the level of doubt and cynicism among the intelligentsia who comprised the judges, lawyers and jurymen became so great that it was almost impossible to mount a successful prosecution in the courts.

SCORE, JOHN The English PAGAN revivalist who founded, and was the first editor of, the WICCAN newsletter in 1968 which promoted the theme of a world transformed through the re-emergence of the old religion of PAGANISM. The publication of the magazine had a direct bearing on the foundation, in 1970, of the PAGAN FRONT.

SCOT, REGINALD One of the foremost liberal Protestants amongst the sixteenth-century sceptics opposed to the Church's view of WITCHCRAFT as a form of Devil-worship. The author of *Discoverie of Witchcraft* (1584), Scot openly questioned the possibility of a formal compact between witches and the Devil, a notion which was strongly opposed by contemporary Continental writers.

Scot and others argued that the continental view of witchcraft was not supported by the Biblical texts in which witches appeared less as Devil worshippers than as WIZARDS, SORCERERS and diviners (see DIVINATION). The concept of witches entering a pact with Satan was, he maintained, a propaganda exercise promoted by the Papacy to distance witchcraft from its own sensitive position with regard to the relics of PAGANISM, retained and exploited within the teachings and ritual of Roman Catholicism. These included the magical aspects of the Eucharist, the maintenance of reliquaries, the treatment of the Virgin Mary as a goddess and the elevation of a pantheon of saints to nearly godly proportions. He was giving voice to a long-standing but largely silent body of opinion that argued that God would not have permitted witches the power to indulge in supernatural activity and that, if He had, He would not have wished them to become the objects of persecution.

Scot's publication was said to have exercised considerable influence over the opinions of his contemporaries in the magistracy and the clergy, and it acted as a rallying document for other sceptics. An indication of its popularity lies in the fact that, more than sixty years after first publication, it was reprinted in 1651, 1654 and 1665.

For several decades, however, writers on both sides of the English Channel were still strongly asserting that a covenant or conference with Satan provided the essence of witchcraft and that witches, both in the British Isles and the Continent, exercised devilish and wicked arts. Many commentators fully supported the continuance of the death penalty for all witches, without exception. During the greater part of the seventeenth century it is probably fair to say that the views of Scot were not generally supported (see also SCEPTICISM TOWARDS WITCHCRAFT).

SCRATCHING A procedure popular during the medieval WITCH-CRAZE. The victim of WITCHCRAFT could relieve his or her problem by scratching the suspected WITCH and drawing blood. The term scratching could imply a variety of actions, extending from light touching to serious physical violence.

SCRYER A term coined in medieval England for a person who raised spirits or perceived other visual images by means of a crystal, mirror or other reflective device. Conventionally the scryer was a child or youth of either sex. Among the most notorious scryers during the Elizabethan period was Edward Kelly, the associate of John DEE.

SCRYING The ancient art of DIVINATION using a crystal globe, in practice usually made of glass, or some other reflective device, such as a mirror, as a means of clairvoyance. The device is technically known as a speculum and, when made of rock crystal, is an object of considerable value. Black balls are also favoured scrying tools. Scrying is usually carried out in dim light, perhaps with the illumination of a candle flame placed behind the clairvoyant.

During the time of the WITCH-CRAZE, and prior to the repeals of the various Witchcraft Acts (see WITCHCRAFT, ENGLISH AND SCOTTISH LAWS and WITCHCRAFT, AMERICAN LAWS), it was hazardous to keep apparatus that was obviously linked with scrying. For this reason more innocent tools were employed, including fishermen's glass floats and black bowls filled with water.

SEIDKONA The priestess of an ASATRU PAGAN fellowship which tends to be more patriarchal in nature than WICCA. Known historically as a VOLVA, this type of priestess, who is essentially concerned with DIVINATION and prophecy, derives from the tribal SHAMAN or *shamanka*. Similar powers of shape-changing are observed in the seidkona and her power can be used to both beneficent and maleficient purpose. Historically, in her darker aspects, she frequently seems to have adopted the form of a horse. The *Landnamabok*, the book of the settlement of Icelandwritten by Ari the Wise in the eleventh century and subsequently added to by others, describes the trial of a seidkona in Iceland for trampling a man to death while in this guise. There also exists a similar account of the death of one of the early kings of Sweden.

Horse fetishes were often kept as fertility icons. The author Turville-Petrie (*Myth and Religion of the North*, 1964) describes how a farmer's wife was given a dismembered phallus of a horse which she dried and preserved in a cloth packed with herbs. The object was kept in her linen chest, but was brought out each evening for a family ritual which involved prayers to a horse deity, presumably Freyja or her brother, the fertility god Freyr.

According to Norse tradition the first seidkona was the VANIR goddess Freyja. It is arguable that her well-documented association with cats provides the origin for the popular image of the witch with her black cat.

SEIDR A form of WITCHCRAFT once practised widely in northern Europe and described in several

of the Eddaic prose sagas. Allegedly the knowledge
of this craft was given to the AESIR gods by the
VANIR goddess, Freyja.

In practice a wooden platform was erected on
which sat a seeress or prophetess, known as the
VOLVA or SEIDKONA, who practised a rite of
DIVINATION, although in some instances the powers
generated appear to have taken on maleficent
dimensions against a victim. The volva either
worked alone or was backed up by a choir. She
entered into a trance-like state during which she
communed with the world of the gods and was
subsequently able to answer questions put to her by
her audience. These questions invariably related to
future events, the state of the next harvest, fecundity
of animals, fates of individuals in the audience and
the outcome of feuds.

The best known poetry associated with this kind
of prophecy is contained in the *Voluspa* with which
the *Codex Regius*, the thirteenth-century Icelandic
manuscript containing the *Poetic Edda* and kept in
the Museum of Copenhagen, opens, literally the
prophecy of the volva. Here, the seeress foretells the
fate of the gods and the Norse apocalypse in
evocative and beautiful song. It begins:

Hear me all ye hallowed beings,
both high and low of Heimdall's children:
Thou wilt, Valfather, that I well set forth
the fates of the world which as first I recall.
(after Hollander).

One of several accounts of the activities of such
seeresses, the *Eiriks Saga Rauoa*, includes a
description of the visit of one of these women to a
farm in the Icelandic settlement in Greenland. She
came dressed in animal skins including catskin
gloves (cats were among the animals sacred to the
goddess Freyja), sat upon her high seat and invited
someone from the audience to sing the spell that
would stimulate her trance.

Whether the traditions of these travelling
seeresses derive from the activities associated with
the deity in the wagon described in the *Flatey-yarbok*
saga of King Olaf Tryggvason (Codex 1005, Royal

Danish Library) is unclear. The latter personality
was the fertility god Freyr but the description in the
Flatey-yarbok also bears strong similarity to the much
earlier account by the Roman writer, Tacitus, in
Germania, when he describes the goddess Nerthus
being driven in a covered cart to a sacred lake to be
washed. It is possible, although with the
incorporation of changes of gender, that these
various descriptions refer essentially to a similar
kind of divination activity with its origins buried in
a distant Celtic or Germanic tradition.

SERVANTS OF THE LIGHT (SOL) A British
magical fraternity started in the 1970s. SOL arose as
a splinter organization from the Society of the Inner
Light (SIL) founded in 1922 by Dion FORTUNE. It
first emerged as a training school run by Dolores
ASHCROFT-NOWICKI and is considered to be one of
the groups known collectively as the WESTERN
MYSTERIES.

SEYMOUR, CHARLES RICHARD FOSTER
(1880-1943) A twentieth-century Irish occultist and
PAGAN whose influence is only currently being
appreciated. A professional soldier, he became a
member of Dion FORTUNE's FRATERNITY OF THE
INNER LIGHT in the 1930s, subsequently writing a
significant piece titled *The Old Religion – A Study in
the Symbolism of the Moon Mysteries* which was
published in 1968 under the initials F.P.D. These
initials were a form of acronym for the French
proverb *Foy pour Devoir*, Faith for Duty. Monographs
that he originated for the Fraternity magazine have
now been compiled into a publication, *The Forgotten
Mage*. It appears that, while eschewing the limelight,
he was well read and sustained a particular interest
in the Celtic deities, preparing some of the
important groundwork through which they have
been accepted in modern Pagan circles. He was
initiated into CO-MASONRY in 1941.

Seymour's priestess and collaborator was the
witch Christine Hartley who had also joined the Co-
Masons in 1941.

SHAMAN (fem. *shamanka*) A person who functions as a seer, healer and transporter of souls through the art of shamanism, a form of ritual often associated with the primitive, nomadic religious belief described as ANIMISM. The term originates with the Tungus tribes of Siberia but is used generally among the nomadic peoples of the Arctic regions. In the broader context a shaman is an intercessor with the spirit world and is found in many religious disciplines of the world including modern PAGANISM.

The shaman is the oldest form of priest or witch who, in a trance-like state of ecstasy, liaises with 'master spirits' or with ghosts of ancestors and who is usually an individual of particular intelligence and dexterity. The shaman mediates not only with the spirit world but with the birds, animals and trees, seeing that which ordinary people may be unable to see and at a level of intelligence and expertise which, in a primitive, preliterate society means that he or she is often the artist of the tribe. The shaman is thus the honest broker between the world of the supernatural and the temporal earth.

The trance-like performance of the shamanistic ritual may frequently be induced by dancing and drumming, but is also facilitated by the use of hallucinogens and the climactic moment comes while the shaman is in a state of ecstasy, capable of foretelling events and of extraordinary physical feats, including self-mutilation.

The role of the shaman may change with circumstance and local tradition. The black shaman, the archetypal 'black witch' who performs ritual with full and sacred regalia, dispenses rough justice on behalf of the spirits of the UNDERWORLD. The white shaman, dispensing no harm and without ritual trappings, intercedes with more benign spirits.

Details of authentic shamanistic ritual in the northern hemisphere, as distinct from public performances, are almost wholly lacking but, wherever there is evidence of shamanism, its rituals very often set out to emulate the behaviour of animals. Rarely is this authentic behaviour, but rather that which might occur if human logic were applied to the animal. In Arctic bear festivals the shaman has traditionally dressed in skins and taken on the creature's instincts as he imagines them within the scope of human emotions such as elation, fear, rage and sorrow. It is possible that such impersonations are the subject of many of the anthropomorphic figures portrayed in European Ice Age art.

SHERWIN, RAY See CHAOS MAGIC and ILLUMINATED OF THANATEROS.

SHIPTON, URSULA (1488-1561) More generally referred to as 'Mother Shipton', a seeress, born Ursula Sontheil at Knaresborough, Yorkshire, who was effectively unknown during her lifetime. She only came to public prominence in 1641, some eighty years after her death, at the time when prophecy was enjoying a vogue as a result of the publication of the so-called Merlin prophecies, known from Thomas Heywood's *Life of Merlin*. She married a Toby Shipton and was, allegedly, the author of a celebrated prophecy which began *If eighty eight be past, then thrive* and which, it is claimed, was discovered in the Abbey of St Benet in Norfolk. Living in the reign of Henry VIII, she is also said to have predicted the fall of Cardinal Wolsey, whom she referred to as the 'Mitred Peacock' and to have made the assertion that England would return to Roman Catholicism.

Mother Shipton's utterances were first published as *Two Strange Prophecies* (1642). During the following years popular interest allowed the licence of their expansion to no fewer than *Fourteen Strange Prophecies* (1649). According to Keith Thomas, during the eighteenth and nineteenth centuries Shipton's predictions were often published alongside those of Nostradamus. It is, however, unclear how much of that which has been attributed to Ursula Shipton down the years is fact and how much romantic fiction.

SHROUD, RITUAL OF A ritual relying on the belief that dew is the breath of the God and practised by witches in the Isle of Man. As described by Cecil WILLIAMSON, it requires the placing of sticks which project about three feet (a metre) from the ground and a square cross grid made from twine, the whole constructed on an area of flat turf. Across this device, in the evening, is laid a clean white sheet, secured with pegs and left thus overnight. Before dawn the dew-wet sheet is folded, placed in a suitable vessel and carried to the client who is hypnotized, unclothed and swathed totally in the sheet. It is then lightly bound with cords, the client is placed on a bed board and left thus until the sheet dries out.

SIGIL An object, design or image that, in WITCHCRAFT or other occult disciplines including SORCERY, may symbolize a specific deity or less clearly defined principle. The sigil represents essentially a visual stimulus. Sigil magic is, arguably, a form of sorcery and much of it is derived from the work of Austin Osman SPARE. A sigil may be generated magically, often being facilitated through a device such as a GLYPH or a MANTRA and, as such, may wholly replace other 'props'. Believers suggest that a sigil may be empowered during such physical releases as orgasm, urination, sneezing or the edge of unconsciousness resulting from hyperventilation.

SIL See SOCIETY OF THE INNER LIGHT.

SILVER STAR See ASTRUM ARGENTINUM.

SIMOS, MIRIAM (born 1951) Better known under the name 'Starhawk', one of the most prominent feminist PAGAN activists in the United States as well as being a subscriber to Judaism and a teacher. Born in St Paul, Minnesota, and brought up in the Jewish faith, she first developed an interest in WITCHCRAFT at the age of seventeen while studying at the University of California in Los Angeles. She is the author of *The Spiral Dance: A Rebirth of the Ancient*

Religion of the Great Goddess which, although derived from Gardnerian WICCA (see GARDNER, Gerald), represents a radical departure from it, incorporating strictly feminist principles into modern witchcraft. The most prominent of her later books, *Dreaming the Dark*, expands on these principles.

She professes a commitment to the intertwining of MAGIC, politics and the erotic. Her first COVENS, Compost and Raving, in San Francisco began as hierarchical structures with formal rituals but evolved to a more collective functional operation. Both have now disbanded and she is involved with sister covens, the Wind Hags and the Holy Terrors, as well as with her own community, the Reclaiming Collection. She has taught Wicca at an institute run by the evangelist Matthew Fox.

She has spent the last twenty to thirty years attempting – in her own words – to 'create a culture', an ambition born of deep dissatisfaction with contemporary culture in the United States. Her feminist activism in the 1970s awoke her interest in the GODDESS movement when she and some of her colleagues began to see the development of their spirituality as part of their liberation as women, moving away from male-dominated religions. Starhawk herself had been very religious as a young girl, but found that there was no place for her in the Jewish hierarchy. She regards the noticeable shift in the position of women over the last decades as one of the achievements of her movement.

Starhawk's community has developed a spiritual tradition with rituals shaping the year, welcoming newborn babies and marking coming of age and death. They also have a system of mutual support and training which enables members to reclaim and recreate their tradition.

In order to create and maintain a viable culture, free of repression and victimization, she believes three things are necessary. Firstly, to have a real relationship with the land we are on, the place we are in, an understanding of such elements as soil and water and a sense of wonder about aspects of nature. The Goddess tradition as she sees it involve

Miriam Simos – Starhawk

a strong sense of mystery and an acceptance that the universe is 'bigger than we are' and that there are many things humankind cannot understand. But where understanding is possible, it is important to accept things as they are, not to impose a philosophy and try to force things to fit it.

Secondly, it is vital to connect with our own heritage and tradition. We learn from nature the value of diversity; this should enable us to appreciate the differences in human beings – particularly in the culturally and racially diverse United States where one person's 'ancestors' may come from all over the world. Starhawk does not accept splits and divisions between individuals or between groups of people – her own experience of being able to work within both feminism and Judaism has taught her that these differences can be reconciled.

Thirdly, she advocates the freedom and creativity to interpret and honour ourselves and our own experience, which becomes the core of our spiritual lives. If something is not working in our lives we need to be free to let go and move on.

Ritual and magic are an integral part of Starhawk's work. To make ritual work, she believes,

requires someone who can lead and direct the energy of a group, changing their consciousness at will. Such a person serves as the anchor for the group, entering a state of deep meditation in order to hold the collective energy and make the ritual more intimate. Starhawk emphasizes the need to be willing to explore, to experiment, to go deeper within the self. Magic requires us to have a positive image of what we want – it is not enough to work towards 'no nukes' without having a positive alternative to offer.

Starhawk believes in the existence of a magic realm – the AVALON of Arthurian tradition – which was once much closer to the physical realm. She believes the two realms are now approaching each other again and that we can learn to listen to the other world, which gives vitality to the physical one. It is not a matter of escaping from reality but of receiving the benefit of energies flowing back and forth.

Starhawk feels generally hopeful for the future, believing that the growing strength of PAGAN communities is no coincidence – it may be the Earth's way of starting a healing process. If current trends continue, humanity may help to atone for past mistakes.

She lives in San Francisco, where she continues to work as a writer, lecturer, feminist activist and priestess in the Goddess religion.

SKYCLAD The WICCA practice of performing ceremonials naked in the belief that clothing impedes the release of powers from within. The term may derive from a Jain sect in India, the d*igambaras* (meaning 'skyclad') which held that no clothing should be worn if the role of the true ascetic was to be fulfilled.

GARDNER observed, *It is easy to imagine that a witch who firmly believes that it is essential to be naked could not whip up the final effort to attain the ecstasy without being naked. Another, however, who did not share this belief might, though partially clothed, exert sufficient energy to force the power through her face, shoulders, arms and legs, to produce some results; but who can say that she could not have produced twice the power with half the effort had she been in the traditional nakedness?*

Contrary to Gardner's assertions, there is little evidence that witches in earlier times performed their ceremonies nude.

In the United States in particular, some COVENS have ceased working skyclad. In Britain it is an almost universal practice in WICCA; indeed it is considered a key feature of the Craft by most Gardnerians and ALEXANDRIANS.

SOCIETY OF THE HORSEMAN'S WORD A

mystical and magical cult derived from the so-called 'horse whisperers' who, allegedly, were connected with, or had access to, the OCCULT knowledge of an ancient order of horsemen that may date back to Romano-Celtic times.

The Society was in existence until recent times, actively practising in rural areas of Scotland. However, until the late nineteenth century, its focus may have been amongst the horse-breeding and racing communities in Suffolk.

It was claimed that the craft ran in families and that an experienced whisperer was able to adopt semi-magical control over a horse by uttering combinations of ritual and magic words into its ear (see also SULLIVAN, James). It is unclear to what extent, if at all, the technique of the Horse Whisperer has survived into modern times, although it has recently been made the subject of a popular novel.

SOL See SERVANTS OF THE LIGHT.

SOLO WITCH A person who practises the Craft
(see WICCA) alone and who, generally, has not been initiated or made a formal tie with a COVEN. Also known as a HEDGEWITCH, such an individual believes that he or she is following the ancient tradition of the old-time village wise person. The solo witch practises spellcraft for the purposes of healing and other objectives and teaches the

Mysteries. The magical working is always carried out alone or with a close magical partner. Books are the usual source of inspiration and teaching. In Britain the works of Marian Green and Rae Beth have been influential; in the United States those of Scott Cunningham and Ray BUCKLAND.

While the majority of solo witches work for good, there is reasonable evidence that in some instances their activities were, and continue to be, of a more maleficent nature and purpose.

SOLOMON, KEY OF Arguably the most
significant among the many medieval and Renaissance manuscripts of magic, and properly titled *Clavicula Solomonis*. Largely based on the apocryphal *Testament of Solomon*, the *Key* is known in Latin, French, Italian and German contemporary manuscripts dating from the sixteenth century although these are translations of an earlier work probably composed in Hebrew.

The *Key* falls within the late Hebrew Qabalistic (see QABALAH) tradition and provides a doctrinal discourse including OCCULT formulae for the conjuration of spirits in the enactment of both Black and White Magic. The best known English translation is that of S L MacGregor MATHERS (1889) although, while retaining but condemning the element of blood sacrifice, he physically removed much of the other Black Magic content within the medieval manuscripts. The formulae for conjuration rely largely on fasting, prayer and various devices, including inscribed circles, swords, wands, candles and holy water.

Because of the ambivalent nature of this and comparable works they were generally circulated only in manuscript form, although Reginald SCOT included the *Key of Solomon* as part of a general expose in a revised edition of *Discoverie of Witchcraft*.

Much of the subsequent nineteenth and twentieth century literature on ceremonial magic is derived from the *Key of Solomon* and there has been a revival of interest in the *Key* by modern occultists.

SOLOMON, TESTAMENT OF An apocryphal book of the Old Testament, the only known source of which is written in Greek and which ostensibly relates the discovery by Solomon that the building work on his temple was being frustrated by the demon, Ornias. It narrates Solomon's subsequent dominion over the seventy-two demons whose labours he harnessed to complete the construction. The underlying beliefs demonstrated in the *Testament* correspond closely to those of the Greek magical papyri and it was probably written less as a sermon on the dangers of demonolatry than as a discourse on popular demonology and MAGIC.

The work appears to be based on a mixture of Judaic, Pagan and Gnostic elements and includes, although is by no means limited to, a collection of magical formulae.

One of the most recent editions of the Testament, that of C C McCown (1922), derived from fifteenth or sixteenth century manuscripts, places the work as a Jewish oral tradition which was adapted by an unknown Greek Christian writer at sometime during the third century AD.

With the *Book of Enoch* (see ENOCHIAN MAGIC) the *Testament of Solomon* was frequently employed by medieval European magicians and wizards, and Solomonic incantations were regularly employed to cast out or invoke spirits of both benign and malevolent persuasions. The credentials of these manuscripts relied on the popular Hermetic tradition that the knowledge of all things in the natural world, lost by Adam at the Fall, was nonetheless inherited by the great figures of Jewish Biblical history.

SORCERER A person (male, the female equivalent being a sorceress) who practises SORCERY or, alternatively, diabolism, the term being derived originally from the Latin *sortiarius* meaning a diviner and, later, from the French *sorcier* which refers to both a sorcerer and a WITCH.

'SORCERER' (TROIS FRÈRES) Amongst the oldest known prehistoric representations of an anthropomorphic animal figure that, arguably, represents the Stone Age equal of the 'Lord of the Hunt', an engraved figure depicted in three close variations on the walls of the cavern system of Trois Frères in the Vezère region of Southwest France. The works have been dated to the Upper Palaeolithic period, circa 15,000 years BC.

The body, legs and feet are those of a man, the arms are cat-like, ending in paws, as are the genital organs, while the creature bears the tail of a horse. It possesses the ears and antlers of a stag and the face bears large, round, staring eyes. The figure is poised in what appears to be the action of dancing.

In the opinion of many observers, including the respected anthropologist, Mircea Eliade, the so-called 'Sorcerer' depicts a masked figure in ceremonial costume impersonating a spirit who provides game and establishes the rules for the chase.

SORCERER'S APPRENTICE, THE Once claimed to be the largest mail order store for the OCCULT operating in England with over 25,000 customers, and supplying books and a range of equipment and products associated with the occult arts. Based in Leeds, it is operated by Christopher Bray who became prominent in the 1980s as one of the public faces of the occult scene. He used the Sorcerer's Apprentice to establish a fighting fund for PAGANS faced with legal action and he worked extensively for public acceptability for the Pagan movement. He narrowly escaped death when his headquarters were fire-bombed in the early 1990s.

SORCERY The oldest form of European WITCHCRAFT which evolved from a mixture of Christian, PAGAN and other theological elements. It relies on the notion that the cosmos is a single entity permeated by links that connect all natural phenomena and events. By controlling or manipulating these links, the practitioner of sorcery achieves a desired objective.

In modern witchcraft, sorcery is regarded as equating with black magic or diabolism and is frequently performed privately for the benefit of one individual at the expense of another. Among the best-known illustrations, at simple level, is the sticking of pins into a doll in order to cause pain or injury. Sorcery frequently involves the performance of one action so as to induce another but, at a more sophisticated level, it requires the invoking of deities or spirits. It also frequently exploits the charged emotional condition of the victim and his or her fear of its effects.

In the twentieth century, sorcery has had its greatest affect in African countries and in its export to the West Indies through the slave trade.

SOUTHERN COVEN OF BRITISH WITCHES
The group alleged to have existed in the New Forest area in the 1950s and earlier, into which Gerald GARDNER was initiated. It has been suggested that the Rosicrucian Theatre in Christchurch, run by Dorothy CLUTTERBUCK, provided a front for their operation (see also NEW FOREST COVEN).

SPARE, AUSTIN OSMAN (1888-1956) An English occultist and artist who became noted for his works produced while, allegedly, in a state of trance. In about 1910 he joined, briefly, with Aleister CROWLEY's ASTRUM ARGENTINUM order, derived from the HERMETIC ORDER OF THE GOLDEN DAWN. His beliefs in re-incarnation led him to a philosophy that the mystical purpose of humankind was to trace, through states of trance and the use of SIGILS, previous existences to their primal roots, so-called atavistic resurgence.

He claimed links with a spirit medium identified as Black Eagle, an American Indian, but he also alleged possession by the artist, William Blake, whose work he appears to have emulated. Spare showed preference for sexual orgasm as the vehicle for entering states of mystical ecstasy.

He developed a magical system described as Zos, essentially practical and based on the premise that the human body is the ideal vehicle through which to manifest the spiritual and occult forces of the universe.

SPECULUM A crystal ball, mirror or other device with a polished reflective surface used in SCRYING as a focus of attention while entering a trance-like state. During the witchhunting craze, innocuous objects had to be employed and the black glass floats used by fishermen were an obvious favourite.

SPRENGEL, ANNA (died 1890) The alleged German ADEPT from whom, in 1887, it is claimed that W W WESTCOTT received the authority to found the ISIS-URANIA temple of Golden Dawn (see HERMETIC ORDER OF THE GOLDEN DAWN). Westcott obtained a cipher manuscript from a fellow Mason, A F A Woodford, which formed the basis of Golden Dawn ritual. According to one version of events retold by Arthur Machen, Woodford purchased a secondhand book between the leaves of which he discovered the manuscript, claimed to be of fifteenth century origin, but which subsequently turned out to be an eighteenth century forgery. The book also concealed an address, that of Sapiens Dominabitur Astris of Nuremberg, otherwise Anna Sprengel. In an alternative scenario recounted by Francis King, the cipher manuscript was inherited by Woodford on the death, in 1885, of a mystic, Frederick HOCKLEY. In his book *The Golden Dawn* R A Gilbert indicates that it was another, distinct document revealing alchemical secrets (see ALCHEMY) that had come through Hockley from a Dutch or Scandinavian alchemist, Sigismund Bacstrom, and was circulated among Golden Dawn members.

Sprengel conferred on Westcott, first the status of Adeptus Exemptus ($7 = 4$), the grade representing one of the higher ADEPTS. The motto $7 = 4$ is interpreted as a balancing of spiritual and material substance. As the spiritual ladder is climbed from 0 to 7 (or higher in some magical orders), so the material ladder is descended. $7 = 4$ is generally the highest mortal level beyond which the individual on which it is conferred is regarded as divine. Sprengel authorized Westcott to to establish a new Temple in England and, in subsequent correspondence, permitted him to use her device on official correspondence. Westcott was joined by two other founder members, W R Woodman and S L MacGregor MATHERS, both of whom possessed Rosicrucian pedigree.

MacGregor Mathers, who later became chief of Golden Dawn, subsequently claimed that the Sprengel letters to Westcott were fraudulent and that all knowledge of the Order had come through him.

SRIA See SOCIETAS ROSICRUCIANA ANGLIA.

STANG In Robert COCHRANE's form of WITCHCRAFT, a ritual tool used in witchcraft and constructed in the form of a forked wooden staff, usually of ash wood, symbolizing the presence of the HORNED GOD, when it stands at the northernmost point of the CIRCLE. It is generally decorated with upwardly pointing crossed arrows and a garland. Cochrane and his followers assert that in the past a conventional, old-fashioned, iron-shod pitchfork with an ash haft was often employed for the purpose, being inconspicuous, and it is also claimed that the besom broom was a convenient disguise whereby the give-away forked tip was concealed beneath the bunch of reeds and twigs.

The function of the stang is several fold but it acts as a male fertility symbol when pushed into the earth, and as the guardian of the Circle, the link between the deities and the human ring. According to Evan John Jones it should be garlanded for the BELTANE and LAMMAS SABBATS but that the arrows should be bare for SAMHAIN and IMBOLC or, possibly, decorated with yew. At Beltane it is suggested that the garland should contain birch, hawthorn, hazel and willow while at Lammas it should consist of stalks of grain. It is also suggested by some authors that the actual wood of the stang should, more properly, be hazel.

As a symbolic altar of sacrifice the stang is decorated only with crossed arrows and is accompanied by a sickle placed at its foot to symbolize the ancient principles of sacrifice and dismemberment of the dying and rising god. The cup or chalice (the female aspect) is placed to its left and the ATHAME (the male aspect) to its right with the stang, arguably representing the World Ash Tree YGGDRASIL of Norse and Germanic tradition, acting as a bridge between the two (see also WORKING TOOLS).

STAR CHAMBER A special court, established in England during the reign of Elizabeth I, that often heard cases against persons accused of the crime of WITCHCRAFT. The court of the Star Chamber kept its own records and followed its own practices and was unusual in that as the guardian of the state against all manner of disturbances, including treason, it was permitted to extract confessions through torture. It was described as: *the curious eye of the State and the King's council prying into the inconveniences and mischiefs which abound in the commonwealth.* Composed entirely of judges, its procedures were informal and its punishments summary and swift. The remit of the Star Chamber did not include capital punishment but it could dispense prison sentences, floggings, slicing off of ears and noses, branding and the pillory.

STARHAWK See SIMOS, Miriam.

STELLA MATUTINA A magical Order derived from the old, defunct HERMETIC ORDER OF THE GOLDEN DAWN. The established Golden Dawn collapsed in 1903 following a radical split in which rebellious members of the governing Second Order, including A E WAITE and M W Blackden, set up a new temple which retained the name ISIS-URANIA and followed a vaguely Christian path of mysticism, but rejected ritual MAGIC and astral workings. The magically-orientated members of the original London temple, led by an eminent physician, R W

FELKIN, formed a rival Amoun temple and changed the name of the Outer Order from Golden Dawn to Stella Matutina.

Felkin subscribed to the belief that the Order must attempt to restore communication with the mystical ROSICRUCIAN forces or Secret Chiefs, the so-called Third Order of Golden Dawn, who would provide new spiritual direction. To this end Stella Matutina applied much of its energies to making astral contacts with Rosicrucian entities and with the supposed original Arab teachers of Christian ROSENKREUZ, and Felkin travelled extensively in the hope of making physical contact with living Rosicrucians. From 1910 onwards Felkin was in close contact with a German Rosicrucian group led by Rudolph Steiner and a proposal was tabled to establish an international league comprising the Continental Rosicrucian groups and Stella Matutina. This ambition never materialised but, under Steiner's influence, Felkin revised the organization of Stella Matutina along open lines similar to those of the THEOSOPHICAL SOCIETY.

Felkin emigrated to New Zealand but, in 1919, was obliged to close down the Amoun Temple because its London membership had become obsessed with mediumship to the extent of lunacy and self-destruction. This closure represented the effective demise of Stella Matutina.

According to Francis King, the Outer Order may have been known as the 'Order of the Mystic Rose in the Outer' in the period from 1900 until 1903.

STONEHENGE The Bronze Age British monument in the form of a megalithic circle located near Amesbury in Wiltshire and dating from the pre-Celtic period. Probably designed as a solar temple, the first wooden phase of the monument was begun by Neolithic settlers circa 2800 BC and the site went through as many as six subsequent stages of development, climaxing in the erection of the stones circa 2150 BC. Archaeological evidence suggests that all work on the site had terminated by 1100 BC and there is no suggestion that the Celtic Druid

priesthood ever worshipped there subsequently. The use of Stonehenge by modern PAGANS, including Druids, is therefore based more on seventeenth century romance and less on archaeological evidence.

Greek and Roman writers, including Julius Caesar, indicated that the Druids worshipped in forest clearings and groves but, in 1659, John Aubrey, one of the first English archaeologists, writing of Druids in prehistoric Wiltshire in his *Monumenta Brittanica*, associated them specifically with Stonehenge. His theories, although unsubstantiated and already the subject of dissent, were picked up by William Stukeley, a Lincolnshire doctor and antiquarian who, in 1740, published *Stonehenge, a Temple restor'd to the British Druids*, in which he compounded the myth, through obsessive conviction, that the circles of Stonehenge and AVEBURY had been built by the priesthood of the ancient Celts and were therefore exclusively Druid temples. Among his contemporaries, Inigo Jones was equally convinced that it was a Roman monument, while Walter Charleton, the physician to Charles II, claimed that it had been constructed by Danish invaders. It is, however, Stukeley's unfounded but attractive theory that has persisted in the popular imagination of modern Druids who, when authority is granted, celebrate the Midsummer solstice there. Some modern authors, including Michael Dames, have made unconvincing attempts to renew the argument for establishing a connection.

STRIGA In early Italian tradition, a night spirit, also known as a *stria*, which drank blood. The word became applied as a common derogatory term for a WITCH.

STROKING A form of magical healing that derived from the ROYAL TOUCH popularized most notably by King Charles I. Stroking was not a royal prerogative and became an aspect of the healing art practised by CUNNING PERSONS. Predictably, charges of WITCHCRAFT and MAGIC were levelled against its practitioners when they were of common rather than royal stock.

Stroking subscribed to the Galenic medical theory that required the healthy body to maintain an equilibrium. When, at times, the equilibrium was disturbed it could be rectified by the evacuation of excess humours. If the surgeon's purging or bloodletting failed, the balancing could be achieved by magnetic means, moving the unwanted humours down the limbs and out through the fingers and toes.

The technique of stroking, essentially the laying on of hands, was often thought more effective by the accompaniment of a prayer or charm. It focused particularly on the disease of scrofula, the so-called King's Evil, an ideal target for all sorts of quackery since the symptoms of the disease were known to display regular periods of remission and even to heal spontaneously, but strokers also gave attention to the blind, the deaf and the lame.

The technique took on grotesque dimensions when, for a time, it was considered particularly valuable if the victim of disease was 'stroked' by the hand of a freshly hanged man. On occasions a sufferer could be seen being lifted up to a gallows for this purpose.

Towards the latter part of the seventeenth century it became particularly advantageous for seventh sons (or, better, seventh sons of seventh sons) to engage in stroking, although why their powers were rendered effective through this curious social position remains unclear. Persons who claimed to effect cures by touching or stroking could earn a substantial living from the practice, sometimes dealing with over a hundred cases a day.

SUCCUBUS A particularly Continental and somewhat mysogynistic notion, referred to extensively in the MALLEUS MALEFICARUM, of a female demon or spirit who performs acts of enforced sexual intercourse with mortal men. The guilty experience of 'wet dreams' was attributed to the activities of succubi. The male counterpart was the INCUBUS.

SULLIVAN, JAMES The Irish horse whisperer, born towards the end of the eighteenth century, who achieved notoriety for his skills in taming horses by semi-magical means. He practised strictly in private, although apparently rarely resorted to physical means of control. Among his best known successes took place at Curragh in 1804 and involved taming a hitherto unbroken stallion known as King Pippin (see also SOCIETY OF THE HORSEMAN'S WORD).

SUMMERLAND The mythical place recognized by nineteenth-century theosophists, including Helena BLAVATSKY, as one of the highest of the astral planes, a paradise to which the spirits of the dead are transported. Summerland is the Land of Eternal Youth, where the spirit is rejuvenated and given sustenance and prepared for rebirth in the temporal world.

SUMMERS, MONTAGUE (1880-1948) An author and Christian scholar who wrote extensively on the subject of WITCHCRAFT from the standpoint of Roman Catholicism and also made extensive translations of manuscripts and of sixteenth- and seventeenth-century publications relating to the OCCULT. Most notable amongst these was his translation of the MALLEUS MALEFICARUM. He was said to be a close acquaintance of Aleister CROWLEY and claimed variously to be a member of the Catholic priesthood, Father Summers, and an Anglican clergyman. He was often outspoken in his polemics against witchcraft, which he allied firmly and irrevocably with Satanism, believing implicitly in the reality of the Devil as an entity. He also supported the role of the Catholic Church in its persecution of witches.

SUMMER SOLSTICE One of the four Lesser SABBATS celebrating the longest day of the year when the sun is at its zenith and also known as the Midsummer Festival. The occasion when, traditionally, witches gather the herbs necessary for the preparation of potions and spells. In some traditions of WICCA, the Summer Solstice marks the transition from the reign of the Oak King to that of the Holly King.

SUMMIS DESIDERANTES AFFECTIBUS A papal Bull issued in Germany in 1484 under the seal of Pope Innocent VIII. The Bull represents the culmination of the efforts of the Catholic Church to formulate a style of prosecution for witches. At the time of publication it had the effect of confirming full papal support for the work of the INQUISITION. As a document it was also accepted by many Protestants.

SWIMMING (OF WITCHES) The practice of submitting an alleged WITCH to ordeal by water to test guilt or innocence, first used in English witch trials from circa 1590. The accused was trussed and towed across a pond. If he or she sank they were pronounced innocent (but regularly drowned). Those who floated were summarily convicted.

The ordeal represented the corruption of a Christian belief whereby it was presumed that water, as the instrument of Christian baptism, would absorb those who were true Christians and reject those who had made their pact with the Devil (see also ORDEAL BY WATER).

SYNOD OF PARIS In 829 AD, on 6 June, the Synod determined that a person found guilty of the MALEFICIUM should incur the death penalty. In England this resulted in new edicts by Alfred the Great (reigned 870–899) and in the following century by Athelstan (reigned 925–939) against anyone found guilty of being a witch.

A priest carrying the ritual stang, male fertility symbol and link between deities and human worshippers. In some traditions the stang is kept bare for Samhain and Imbolc but garlanded during Beltane and Lammas celebrations.

TABLE, RING AND DISC Devices of medieval origin which equate approximately to a modern ouija board. A gold ring is suspended on a silk thread and allowed to gyrate freely over a disc inscribed with the alphabet. It is claimed to spell out answers to questions posed during its use by a MAGICIAN.

TALIESIN (1) The renowned poet of Celtic legend who was otherwise known as Gwion Bach. He is said to have acquired access to OCCULT knowledge when he inadvertently swallowed some drops of a magical potion being brewed in a cauldron by the goddess of inspiration, CERIDWEN. The potion was ostensibly destined for her son Afaggdu to compensate for his extreme physical ugliness.

Gwion Bach is said to have fled from Ceridwen, adopting an assortment of guises until, as a grain of wheat, he was pecked up by her while she took the form of a hen. When, later, he was disgorged from her crop it was to be reborn as Taliesin, the poet.

The name Taliesin is given to one of the earliest manuscripts of Welsh Celtic poetry written in about 1275 and which was discovered with a manuscript copy of the *Mabinogion*.

TALIESIN (2) The nom-de-plume of a contributor to *Pentagram*, the official organ of the WITCHCRAFT RESEARCH ASSOCIATION who, in 1966, was partly responsible for a major confrontation between Gardnerian Wiccans (see GARDNER, Gerald) and other, more radical, groups. Taliesin scorned the Gardnerian view (currently being proclaimed by Doreen VALIENTE) as one of 'sweetness and light coupled with good clean fun under the auspices of a Universal Auntie'. He claimed to represent a traditionalist group operating in the west of England following a strictly Celtic tradition and employing the hallucinatory properties of the mushroom *Amanita muscaria*. In this respect he allied firmly with Robert COCHRANE, who was also writing defamatory articles of a similar nature in *Pentagram*.

TAROT A pack of seventy-eight cards, the name of which is a French corruption of the Italian *tarocco*. They had first appeared in Italy in about 1440. These cards were used originally for games, but became increasingly employed in the arts of MAGIC and DIVINATION. In 1781 it was claimed by the French occultist, Court de Gebelin, that the cards stemmed from a Hermetic source (see HERMETICISM) and reflected the lore of the Egyptian priests of Khemnu at Hermopolis, the so-called *Book of Thoth*.

At about the same time they were first employed in divination by one, Alliette. Later claims, most notably by Eliphas LEVI suggested that the tarot was derived from the Tree of Life symbols in the Christian and Judaic versions of the QABALAH.

The Tarot pack became a tool closely identified with the HERMETIC ORDER OF THE GOLDEN DAWN and its interest in the Qabalistic Tree of Life. Among the more noteworthy packs are the Marseilles, the oldest; that of the artist, Frieda Harris, who executed Aleister CROWLEY's designs embodying the doctrines of the *Book of the Law*; the nineteenth-century Oswald Wirth version; and the more modern Waite/Rider pack.

Doreen Valiente

The modern pack resembles a deck of ordinary playing cards with the addition of a court card and twenty two cards of the 'major arcana', also known as the 'greater trumps', each of which is numbered and includes a pictorial representation reflecting an aspect of human experience. Thus the images include the Lover, Temperance, the Hanged Man, Death, the Devil and so on. Arguably the most significant is that of the Fool. Each pack of cards possesses a unique significance and bears astrological or magical links.

Tarot cards are today employed for divination and as an aid to private meditation.

TEMPLES (CELTIC) Archaeological evidence suggests that, in pre-Roman Britain and Europe and through the Romano-Celtic period, these sanctuaries took one of two forms. Either they were clearings or groves in the forest, similar to the Greek concept of the *temenos*, the share of land apportioned to the god, or they were built as modest, round wooden structures which may or may not have been roofed over, their foundation post-holes usually marked with votive offerings. These buildings were typically surrounded by sacred enclosures which probably played an equally significant role in ritual and worship. Less frequently the temples took a rectangular outline. In most instances the central focus of the sanctuary was a tall, often massive, wooden post.

In Europe a number of Celtic sanctuaries were constructed of stone and possessed pillars with a series of niches, with carvings of severed human heads, that contained human skulls, reflecting the Celtic belief that the head was the repository of great power and spirituality.

THELEMA The OCCULT religious movement founded by Aleister CROWLEY. In the broad sense *thelema* is the Greek word for will. Crowley's concept of Thelema is based on the philosophical writings of Frederich W Nietzsche (1844-1900) who rejected accepted moral values, arguing against the existence of God and that individuals were free to create their own values, based on the strong imposing their will on the weak.

Crowley supported the belief that human progress was only possible by discovering ones own true will and making it effective. However, he went on to assert that, in accepting the Laws of Thelema, one had also to accept that that the LIBER AL VEL LEGIS is a divinely inspired *Book of the Law*. The *Liber AL Vel Legis* offers a number of principles: that the true self is discovered magically and that the strong will rule over the weak in the new Aeon when morality will become irrelevant. It must be considered, however, that the *Liber AL Vel Legis* contains a considerable level of drug-induced gibberish and much of it is highly obscure.

THEOPHILUS A priest who, according to an eighth-century manuscript, the *Ingeborg Psalter*, composed by an adviser to the court of the emperor Charlemagne and allegedly based on a sixth century Greek manuscript of uncertain provenance, achieved promotion to the office of bishop, after making a pact with the Devil to renounce Christ. The *Ingeborg Psalter* with its reference to Theophilus, represents the earliest known historical account of a formal pact with the Devil.

The legend of Theophilus was well known in Anglo-Saxon times and may have provided the origin for the Faust tradition.

THEOSOPHICAL SOCIETY Founded by the clairvoyant Helena Petrovna BLAVATSKY and Colonel H S OLCOTT in New York in 1875 with a strong focus on oriental spiritualism, the promotion of universal brotherhood, the study of comparative religion and the investigation of unexplained laws of nature and the powers latent in man. The headquarters moved to India in 1877 and are still found at Adyar, Madras.

It is an essentially OCCULT intellectual club that drew its membership from the educated ranks of the middle and upper classes whose peace of mind had been disturbed by the revelations of Charles Darwin. It particularly attracted Freemasons.

On the death of Olcott, the social reformer Annie BESANT became the international head of the Society. Its London lodge, whose first president was the seeress, Anna KINGSFORD, was founded in 1883 and attracted, among others, the celebrated spiritualist medium Mabel Collins and W B YEATS, the latter maintaining a scepticism about Madame Blavatsky. The Society has also maintained a strong Scottish lodge.

It has published a periodical entitled *Lucifer* and the aims of the Society are:

To form the nucleus of a Universal Brotherhood with no distinction on the grounds of race, creed or colour.

To promote the study of Aryan and other eastern literature, religions and sciences and vindicate its importance.

To investigate the hidden mysteries of nature and the physical powers latent in mankind (*Rules of the Theosophical Society*, 1882).

According to Blavatsky a secret fraternity of masters or Mahatmas, located in Tibet, oversee the spiritual development of each individual. She claimed that *by combining science with religion, the existence of God and immortality of man's spirit may be demonstrated like a problem of Euclid.*

The Society perceives a universe of seven interconnecting planes which are reflected in the seven metaphysical bodies of the individual. The planet on which we live is also part of an evolving series of seven.

The following of the Society has declined but it is still active in about 60 countries.

THORNDIKE, LYNN An influential American scholar, and the author of *History of Magic and Experimental Science* (8 vols.). The first of these was published in the 1920s and the last after World War II. They cover the scope of the history of magic in the West and are considered to comprise a very useful and intelligently written reference work.

TRADITIONAL CRAFT (USA AND CANADA) A term more or less exclusively applied to Gardnerian (see GARDNER, Gerald) and ALEXANDRIAN WICCA in North America, where these branches are well established with formal initiatory lineages going back, in Britain, to Gardner and Alex SANDERS and retain the central practices of these lines. The term differentiates these lineages from the more eclectic developments of Wicca, which are myriad in the United States.

TRIPLE GODDESS The principle female deity of WICCA, based on the early Celtic images of the fertility or mother goddess in three forms which were paralleled in the Roman Matres. In Greco-Roman mythology the three personalities or *avatars* of the MATRES correspond to Artemis/DIANA, the youthful and independent goddess of the hunt; Selene/Luna, the goddess of the moon and the Mother; and HEKATE, the Crone or HAG of the nocturnal hunt, death and destruction.

In Wicca the three forms are envisaged to be aspects of the one who is also identified as the moon goddess. The phases of the moon – waxing, full and waning – are reflected in the changing imagery of the goddess through virgin, mother and crone which, in turn, allegorizes birth, sexual maturity and death. The altered imagery also reflects the changing of the seasons. The crone, who traditionally makes her seasonal appearance at SAMHAIN, also equates with the wise woman (see also CERIDWEN). As the pastoral and agricultural culture of the Celts became established in the Danube basin, so this goddess became the tutelary deity of crops and harvests, and her festivals became aligned with the significant seasonal changes.

TROIS FRÈRES See 'SORCERER'.

TROYES, BISHOP OF The cleric who was tried and convicted in 1318 after evidence had been presented that he made a wax image of the Queen

of France, performed various OCCULT acts with it
and burned it. The Queen died.

TURNIP A source of 'sacrament' in the Satanic or
BLACK MASS, a parody of the communion wafer of
the Christian Eucharist. The turnip was cut into
slices or cubes and stained black.

 The turnip has long enjoyed an association with
the Devil and the white bryony (*Bryonia dioica*), with
its massive tap root, is commonly known as the
'Devil's Turnip' because it is perceived, as is the
mandrake (*Mandragora*), to grow into a distorted
human form.

UNITED ANCIENT ORDER OF DRUIDS A friendly society which derived from the ANCIENT ORDER OF DRUIDS and which administers funds for members but carries out little, if any, ritual. The Order wields considerable influence in several third-world countries, including Guyana.

UNIVERSAL DECLARATION OF HUMAN RIGHTS (ARTICLE 18) *Everyone has the right to freedom of thought, conscience and religion; this right includes freedom to change his religion or belief, and freedom, either alone or in community with others and in public or private, to manifest his religion or belief in teaching, practice, worship and observance.* A tenet of the European Commission of Human Rights which is also a guiding belief of the PAGAN FEDERATION.

UNDERWORLD In WICCA tradition, the land ruled by the Lord of Death, the dark winter aspect of the HORNED GOD, who controls mortality throughout the natural world. Some Wiccans see it as the place to which the GODDESS descends in search of the answer to the most fundamental human conundrum of death. She is provided with the answers she seeks and returns with the NECKLACE of Rebirth as the youthful MAIDEN.

This concept is loosely derived from the story of the *Brisinga men*, and the golden necklace which the Norse goddess Freyja obtained from the Underworld where it had been fashioned by dwarfs. It may also be traced, in some respects, to the Mesopotamian saga of Inana's Descent to the Underworld to challenge the forces of darkness embodied in her half-sister and alter ego, the Queen of the Underworld, Ereshkigal.

In some Wicca, the account of the descent of the Goddess into the Underworld is related at the SABBAT of the AUTUMN EQUINOX. The Lord of the Harvest, JOHN BARLEYCORN is now become the God of the Underworld to whom the Goddess, in her aspect as the HAG, travels for the dark months of winter. The festival of death is then celebrated at SAMHAIN, when the temporal and spiritual worlds come into close alignment.

VALIENTE, DOREEN (born 1922) One of the most respected leading WITCHES of the twentieth century, born in London, with family connections in Dorset, and in the New Forest area of Hampshire. Her father's name was Dominy, a family name frequently met with in the area around Cerne Abbas in Dorset. She is the widow of a refugee from the Spanish Civil War, Casimiro Valiente, who went on to serve with the Free French forces in World War II. They were married in London in 1944. In 1956 they moved to the south coast in Sussex and her husband died in 1972.

Doreen Valiente is a practising witch and clairvoyant, although no longer regarding herself as WICCA. She is a great admirer of the late Dion FORTUNE. She was friend and adviser to Gerald GARDNER and was, for a time, the High Priestess of his NEW FOREST COVEN, assisting him with the revisions of his BOOK OF SHADOWS. She has subsequently been initiated into other branches of WITCHCRAFT in Britain. She is the author of several titles, most notably *An ABC of Witchcraft* and *The Rebirth of Witchcraft*. She possesses a private collection of witchcraft artefacts, a fine library of OCCULT books and has made frequent radio and television appearances. She continues to live in Brighton, Sussex.

VANIR The race of deities in Germanic and Nordic belief concerned with the peace and fertility of the earth. Conflicting with, and distinct from, the AESIR, they are generally considered to include the god Njord (closely identified with the sea from which came much of the sustenance of the Nordic peoples) and his offspring, the god Freyr and his twin sibling, Freyja. The struggle between the two races may reflect the contrasting life styles of the warrior and the farming peasant in northern Europe. There is some evidence that a SACRED MARRIAGE, not unlike that found amongst ancient near eastern cultures, formed an integral part of Vanir worship. They appear to have endorsed marriage between siblings and they were also regarded as MAGICIANS or *seidr*. Among their forebears may have been the first-century Danish goddess, named by the Romans as Nerthus, although there is no proven connection.

The worshippers of the Vanir focused their attention on the earth and the ancestors interred therein, the great ship burials probably being closely identified with Njord. Their orgiastic rites included ecstasy and sacrifice.

The Vanir deities, being chthonic or earth gods and goddesses, are of particular importance to the modern cult of ASATRU and to the ODINIC RITE.

VOLVA A type of priestess in old Norse culture essentially concerned with DIVINATION and prophecy, and who is derived from the tribal SHAMAN or *shamanka*. She is also known as a SEIDKONA. The term volva derives from the word volr denoting a cylindrical object, this deriving from a root meaning *to turn*.

INTERVIEW WITH

DOREEN VALIENTE

✳

Are you a polytheist or a duotheist, or neither?
I should say neither, because I don't
think anybody can be dogmatic about
theology. We don't know what is the great
power behind this Universe. It's only that
we consider there must be one, manifest,
I think, as the Chinese say, in two ways,
the yin and the yang. I think that's the
way most Pagan religions express it.

*I put that to you because one of the tenets of
Wicca is essentially ritual rather than creed.
Can you worship the Goddess and the God
without actually believing in their existence,
other than through the apotheosis of the
Priestess and Priest?*
In some respects I don't have a lot of
sympathy with Wicca. There's a lot more
to witchcraft than what has come to be
called Wicca which, as a matter of fact,
doesn't mean witchcraft at all but it's
come to be used for what I prefer to call
the Old Religion. This usage has become
so popular now that I suppose there's not
much we can do about it. I remember
someone, years ago, saying witchcraft is
as simple or as complicated as you care
to make it. I think that's true. People can
regard the Goddess and the God as actual

superhuman beings or they can regard
them as archetypes which I think is the
way I regard them. Dion Fortune wrote
very profoundly about this sort of
question and she said that the Gods and
the Goddesses are actually the creation of
the human mind. But that doesn't mean
that they don't exist because they are the
personification of forces that are real. I
think it was Sir Wallace Budge who said
that Amun, the great God of ancient
Egypt, to the initiated Egyptian, was the
one God and all the others, of whatever
kind, were different manifestations of
Amun, the 'hidden one'.

*You became aware that you possessed psychic
powers as a child and, by your late teens, early
twenties, you also knew that you had abilities
of clairvoyance and you describe how, in 1952,
you became destined for a career in magic. You
rode home on the bus 'glowing with triumph'.
You had read Dion Fortune, you had read
Crowley. Why, in that case, did you steer
towards Gardner and a fertility religion, why
did you not become an Hermetic revivalist, a
Blavatsky, or a Horniman or an Annie
Besant?*
Well, because I was so fed up with all the

preaching of all the other occultists whilst I wanted to see something that worked. If you were discussing anything with theosophists they were quite horrified at the idea of you wanting to do something that worked. You could talk about it for ever and ever, and they endlessly did, but say to them, I'm going to draw circles to see if I can get in touch with so and so and they were horrified. I mean, if there is anything in magic then people should be able to use it. I'd read about it and I'd heard a lot about it. I talked about it, but I was fed up with talking about it. I wanted to see somebody or meet somebody that worked it and the only person that I met who worked it was Gerald Gardner.

Clairvoyance is something that has stayed with you. You begin Rebirth *with the persecution of Helen Duncan. You believe that you were in communication with John Brakespeare. Was Helen Duncan a martyr, a Joan of Arc figure, to whom you looked up with youthful fervour?*
Not really. She was a well-known spiritualist but I didn't idolize her. I didn't idolize anyone. If there was anybody I thought of in that respect it was Dion Fortune because she wrote some marvellous books. In fact I think her fictional books are much more meaningful because there is a lot that is conveyed in fiction that can't be conveyed in non-fiction. Old Gerald Gardner found that out when he first started writing in a fictional way about

witchcraft. He wrote *High Magic's Aid*, which is a good book and I think he put a lot in there which you don't find quite so inspirationally in his non-fiction books. I still think *Witchcraft Today* is a good book, though. It was an epoch-making book.

But which comes first for you, pursuing the powers of clairvoyance or devotion to Paganism?
Oh, I think devotion to Pagan religion is more important because that includes clairvoyance, it includes magic, and it includes delving into all sorts of things. Look, we're surrounded by books here. I've got books on everything from I Ching to Buddhism and Tantra and the Qabalah. I've got a very good book over there that I've just acquired, Cornelius Agrippa's works on occult philosophy. I'm delving into everything but I'm seeing it from the standpoint of a witch.

*In your 20s and 30s you were clearly influenced by Crowley, by Gardner. Let's put Crowley to one side for the moment. Here we are, more than forty years on, and you are a woman of mature years (*roars of laughter from Doreen*) who must have reflected many times on that youthful influence or perhaps even infatuation. What do you make of Gardner now? And, yes, this is a loaded question.*
He was a remarkable man and I think when they made him they broke the mould because in some ways he was an awfully manipulative old rascal and in

other ways he was a man who had real knowledge and real experience of magic and he was willing to try things, he was willing to suspend disbelief. He would say, well, let's try things, let's draw circles and find out. You know, there aren't too many people about like that.

We've got to hand it to old Crowley too. He was the most utter old reprobate and con man in his private life but he tried. He did the things. He didn't talk about them. He was willing to see if he could raise a spirit in the Triangle of Art and he was willing to consecrate a talisman and see if it worked, and there haven't been people like that since the Golden Dawn.

I ask because the rebirth was catalyzed by four, maybe five individuals – Leland, Crowley, Gardner, Williamson and Sanders. All dominant, chauvinistic personalities – not necessarily charismatic but driving and dominant. Yet probably all of them were pursuing causes which had aspects of dubious morality and were not averse to blatant chicanery to achieve it. I know it's the pot calling the kettle black in some respects but Williamson describes Gardner as clumsy, vain, tight-fisted, and very very economical with the truth. Doesn't all this take the gilt off the gingerbread a bit?
I think you've got to be able to detect the grain of gold amongst the dross, you know. Gerald could be the most devious, manipulative old devil that ever walked in shoe leather but, on the other hand, he

did it for a purpose. I always remember the first time I came to London to do a ritual with him, at the Winter Solstice, and he suddenly sprang it on me that he hadn't got a ritual but that I could write something! And of course I realize now that the old devil did it on purpose, to see what I could do. He was rather like the Zen Buddhist masters are supposed to be. He would land you in something to see what you could do!

But these men were chauvinistic in the extreme. They saw the Craft as a means of acquiring willing and malleable female acolytes. You yourself were an acolyte of Gardner. Now a contemporary of yours, an august Pagan lady, describes them as 'kinky old goats'.
What I objected to in Wicca was that it was a fertility religion so that when a woman had the menopause she was out, but the old bloke, if he could still function, could have young girls.

Surely that was one of the things that offended you?
Yes, yes. The Priestess had to retire gracefully when she was no longer young and pretty but the old boy could go on as long as he was . . . I was going to say something vulgar there, but being a perfect lady, I wouldn't dream of that (*more hilarious laughter*). Of course, that was the attitude of old Crowley. He had 'scarlet women', as many as he could get hold of. They came and went and, in

spite of the stuff in the *Book of the Law*, in practice she was just his puppet to be used and cast aside when he found another one, one with better looks and more money. But, no, I don't think Gerald was like that. He had taken some of that attitude from Crowley because he was a member of OTO at one time, but he also realized the importance of getting back the idea of the Priestess and he wasn't as chauvinistic as all that. Kinky, perhaps. He was fond of flagellation. But he was also a very marvellous person. I was very fond of him and we've got to hand it to him in this respect, he was the one who stuck his neck out. He was the one who was willing to be publicly described as a witch at a time when it was definitely a term, very much, of opprobrium and only just legal. In fact I was told it was only made legal because the authorities thought witchcraft had entirely died out and there was no point in keeping the term and, of course, they were very soon disillusioned, but that was what old Gerald did. He stuck his neck out and he should be recognized for his courage.

Kate Westwood uses a lovely turn of phrase. She says, whatever our history, or lack of it, modern day paganism is but a thread newly spun from an ancient tapestry. Does not the fact that those modern day male apostles of the Goddess resorted to chicanery, to personal sexual licence, to in some cases telling downright lies in pursuit of a cause, does not

that tarnish the thread?
It depends how far you let it tarnish you. I've been told by people who were members of Alex Sanders' coven that one of his favourite public boasts was that he had sexual relations with every member of his coven, male and female. Well now that, to me, is just using the Old Craft for your own peculiar gratification and I don't agree with that at all. There has been a lot of that sort of thing, I'm afraid, but there's always two sides to every story. Sanders opened the door for a lot of people who couldn't get into a coven in any other way. Because he was the publicist, he got himself into the newspapers on every conceivable occasion. He must have had the most photographed bum in England. People went on from his organization, like the Farrar's did, They got to the point where they saw through Alex but, at the same time, they realized that there was something real there and they went on and formed their own coven on a better level. So, you see, these people served their purpose. Crowley, old reprobate, yes, con man, total sexual exploiter, but he opened the door for people to get the secrets of the Golden Dawn which he published in The Equinox and in Magick which previously had all been shut up and locked away with a great key. So he did service to the cause of knowledge. Gerald was a thoroughly kinky old goat and into flagellation but, from research, flagellation was part of the ancient

Mysteries. Look at the famous fresco in the Villa of the Mysteries in Pompeii. They are actually in the act of ritual flagellation. The same thing was done in ancient Egypt. So was Gerald a kinky old goat, or is it us that have grown so alienated from the realities of ancient Paganism that we can only think of this sort of thing as kinky?

While we are on the subject of things ancient, Margot Adler has said, 'Pagans are scholars without degrees.' If you look in the pages of Pagan Dawn *or* Talking Stick *or* Cauldron, *you will find certain articles which claim to be academically researched but which under any accepted academic rules would be thrown out because they contain so much that is presented as hard fact but which is, in reality, little more than idle speculation and, in some cases, just demonstrating plain ignorance. How much damage do you think this does to the credibility of modern Paganism?*
I would say undoubtedly it must do some damage. You get people writing the most utter rot about wonderful previous incarnations as the Queen of Atlantis. Yet you also get scholarly investigations from people who are into it in an intelligent sort of way. The sillier things do harm but you have to take the rough with the smooth.

Margot Adler also said that Pagans are an assemblage of alienated intelligentsia and natural anarchists. Are you an anarchist?
I think anybody who wants to rule anybody else must be sick. There are so many people around these days who are into power for its own sake. The old magical adage is the person whom you should be out to rule first is yourself. Yes, I suppose I am a natural-born anarchist.

But do you think you need some level of government, or the whole thing falls apart?
Well, if you don't keep to the rules there's no point in trying to play chess or any other game. You have got to have a framework, you've got to have the rules. The curious thing is that they will make a rule of having no rules!

I think it depends what you mean by anarchy. I would hate to think that Paganism was an organized religion because, to my mind, that is an unmitigated curse to humanity. You've only got to look at the state of the world today and the number of wars being waged in the name of organized religion to see the proof of that, and the number of people whose lives have been ruined by organized religion. Well, if what we do is anarchy, long may it flourish.

But at the same time you've got to have some kind of framework and I think the Pagan Federation is doing a good job because they have combated the attempts of our enemies to try and get witchcraft banned, and we have been in quite serious danger of that. Some of the more extreme Christians, not all, can be dangerous and if we don't watch out they might well succeed in getting witchcraft banned because we've had all this stuff about ritual satanic abuse with children snatched at dawn. There are people in America who have suffered even more, lost their jobs, in some cases been driven to suicide. It's not funny and these people can create the atmosphere of another Salem if they get the chance. You can do this and I can do that, but we're both witches and if the local vicar wants to get us banned, we've got to both stand together. That's the sort of organization we want to have but, with regard to having some hierarchy with some sort of Dalai Lama at the head of it, well, God forbid! I don't want to be the Dalai Lama of witchcraft.

Do you think there is a future for Paganism in politics?
Yes, from the point of view of feminism and the green issue, that could be very much a live thing. We like to do our rituals in woods and talk about the Old Green Man. Well, dammit, if we don't watch out, there aren't going to be any woodlands for him to be green in. Politics from the green point of view and the feminist point of view and the ecology? Oh yes, we should be, we must be, we can't help ourselves being involved in that sort of politics. It's no good sitting in little ivory towers and letting people outside do as they damned well please. There are plenty of nasties in the world outside.

In 1982, Ginny Brubaker [mid-west festival organizer] said, nobody is as isolated or as pure as they were - everybody is stealing from everybody else. Good for the survival of our religion as a whole but in another ten years nobody is going to know what a Gardnerian was.
Ha! My response to that is, jolly good thing. All this rot about Gardnerian witches and Alexandrian witches and all the rest of them is really so silly because a witch is a witch is a witch and I don't think we should be compartmentalized like this. Of course, you know the joke about how many Gardnerian witches does it take to change a lightbulb? And the answer is we don't know because old Gerald never put it in the *Book of Shadows*. The complementary question is how many traditional witches does it take? And the answer is, we couldn't possibly tell you because you aren't one of us! I try to look back to what the old-time witches really did and what they really thought. Most of them probably could neither read nor write but they had a tremendous bond with nature and they could do all sorts of things which, believe me, we can't do. I don't think my old great-granfer Peckham could read or write. He used to sell pea and bean sticks and he also made a kind of horse liniment, and he had a famous notice stuck up in the New Forest: 'Pay & Bane Stiks. Good Oss Ile fer Sale' When I said I didn't go much for Wicca I didn't mean I had anything against people who

practised the Gardnerian form of the Craft, but I would like to see it expanded, see it broadened, to take in more of what the Old Religion was like. I don't suppose they wrote anything down. What would be the point? They couldn't read it anyway, although I think there are some, very few, records of people reading out of a book at witch meetings. But they had phenomenal memories. The basic format of the religion I really think goes back a very long way. What some people rather naively thought in the days when we started working with Gerald Gardner was that we were seeing rituals come down virtually unchanged from the Stone Age. Well, come on, tell us another! But the spirit of that ritual very probably has come down from the Stone Age. And we can enter in to the feelings of those people, and into their hopes and their fears which are probably very much like our own. After all, human nature hasn't changed very much. And I want to see witchcraft broadened. I want to be true to those old people who followed the Old Religion in the past. Let's not have this frightful antagonism like, for example, there was with Robert Cochrane and the Gardnerians, which is how I fell out with him as you remember. I thought this was so stupid. We've got enough natural enemies as it is. Not that I have anything against the Christians but it's the Christians that have got something against us (some of them – some are a bit more intelligent) and they really would

bring back the prohibition of witchcraft if they could.

You were once very much in favour of secrecy in the Craft. It was part of your dissent with Gardner. Is secrecy now not a bit of an anachronism. Throw out the element of secrecy and surely you take much of the wind out of the sails of your detractors.

I think you should keep people's secrets and people's confidentiality. You shouldn't, as some people very unadvisedly did, some while back in America, force people to go public. I don't think it's right because they have family commitments, they have business commitments, and we have to take cognisance of practical realities of life. People have to look after their kids and pay their mortgage and they don't want to lose their job and have their kids taken away from them. From that point of view I really do think a coven should keep secrets. But with regard to publicizing the details of their ritual, a lot of it has already been publicized. I think Stuart and Janet Farrar in their book (*The Witches Way*) did a very good job in that and I revealed what I had of Gerald Gardner's original *Book of Shadows* to them because I wanted to get it into print before I joined the great coven above. But, of course, you can print as much as you like and there will always be something there which, so to speak, you can't put into print. There's been a lot of silly cloak and dagger stuff about. Aleister

Crowley once said a rather profound thing, *That which can be taught shall be taught, and that which cannot be taught may at last be learnt.* You can study books for a very long time but, unless you practice the thing, you won't really find out the core of it. There are things which can't be taught by their very nature. You cannot teach people how to have a mystical experience.

What do you think about the telly-witches – Sybil Leek, Beth Gurevitch, Susan Leybourn, Carlyon. They have very clearly proselytized in a roundabout way.

Well, with regard to one of those ladies – no names, no pack drill – who was in the habit of describing herself as the Queen of the White Witches, I really do not know where she got this from. I'd never heard of her before she started making these claims and neither, as far as I know, had anybody else and I'm very sceptical about anybody who starts calling themselves the Queen or the King of the Witches. There never was any such title until, I think, it was Alex Sanders started coining this phrase. I don't think there is any historic foundation whatsoever. But you also mention Sybil Leek. She was an awfully nice person. She had this wonderful familiar called Mister Hotfoot Jackson. He was a jackdaw that fell out of the nest and she nursed him up and he grew to be a fine big bird. I have had his hot little feet on my wrist! I approved of her because she didn't exploit going public in any grasping sort of way. Some have, but they don't last very long.

Pagan revival, we have already said, was spearheaded by a number of men with great drive and dominant, if not charismatic, personalities. It may be argued that there are many good technicians today, but no shining stars, no publicly visible visionaries. Has the momentum been eroded?

I wouldn't worry too much about that because, as Dion Fortune said, some of the best minds in occultism were completely unknown outside their own orders and I wouldn't be surprised if some of the best, and the most effective witches, are completely unknown to the outside world. The idea of secrecy may be overdone and even degenerate into a lot of cloak and dagger nonsense but the basic idea of secrecy, I think, is instinctive. There's the essential secrecy of the magician, the four powers of the magus, to know, to dare, to will, to be silent, and I believe it's effectively true.

Where is it going? Obviously there is a future for Pagan belief in a technological world in which Christianity is seen to be increasingly an irrelevance. But how does the Craft earn its keep as it were?

Oh, I think it earns its keep in feminism and, particularly, in green issues, in ecology, and also it's going to earn its keep in giving people that other road. We've got Christianity, orthodox belief if you like, on the one side. You've got, on the other side, total scientific materialism. And then you've got the other road, rather like the one the Queen of the Fairies showed Thomas the Rhymer, the middle road. People will follow that road and whether it's publicly or whether it's privately, it'll be there. I think that's how the Craft will earn its keep. It's going to give people that particular way of realizing themselves spiritually, which is neither going to be an organized religion nor is it going to be the intellectual, scientific materialism. In my opinion real religion is something personal, to you, individually. That's my feeling about it

A final, personal question. This quotation will be very familiar to you because you wrote it. Ancestral voices fill the skies. Starlight and witchfire in my eyes, and echoes of lost centuries across this elfin ground . . . all around I feel them close in ghostly company. *What has your faith done for you in respect of the anticipation, the fear, or lack of it, of death?*
I was very ill some years ago. I had peritonitis and the doctor told my husband – he was alive then – that I had a fifty-fifty chance of survival. I got to the point, in hospital, when I think I was on the way out. I found myself in a dark wood. This was very real to me. It was a winter wood and I could see starlight round about and I was making my way towards a stockade and inside there was a beautiful blue light and I knew that if I could get in there I wasn't going to come

out again. And I wanted to get in there. I'd had enough of this life and I was very willing to go. The trouble was there was something pulling me back, as if I had a sort of elastic rope tied to the back of me and I was trying to break this. I was trying desperately to get into this stockade and, after a while, two presences came out. I don't know how to describe this because I couldn't see them and they didn't speak in articulate speech but they were there; they were persons. They weren't angels or anything like that, just people, and they took hold of me and they said, now look, you can't come in now, you've got to go back. And they just sort of jollied me along until I went back into my body in that hospital ward. They sent me back. They said, you've got something to do. So I've experienced that astral world, I've experienced the pull of that astral cord. When I came back and started to get better, though, I can tell you I felt a darned sight worse than when I was dying (*laughter*). I have a confidence in Witchdom, the Land of Faery. The spiritualists call it Summerland. That experience of the stockade in the wood and the blue light and the starlight . . . that experience was entirely Pagan. It was nothing to do with any Christian heaven or anything else, or any spiritualist Summerland with white robed angels. I was off to my own kind.

WAITE, ARTHUR EDWARD (died 1942) An influential English occultist and a strong proponent of Christian mysticism. In 1890 he became a member of Golden Dawn (see HERMETIC ORDER OF THE GOLDEN DAWN) but, with his mystical leanings, was essentially against the magical aspects of the Order. In 1901 he was initiated as a Mason and the following year became a member of the Societas Rosicruciana in Anglica (SRIA, see ROSICRUCIAN SOCIETY). In company with William Ayton and Marcus Blackden he left the original Golden Dawn in July 1903 during the period of infighting, for which he claimed considerable responsibility, and which effectively brought its demise as a functioning body. In doing so he became part of the triumvirate heading the reconstituted governing body, the Second Order, which took over and continued with the name of the ISIS-URANIA Temple but which maintained the old Golden Dawn rituals, more or less unchanged, until 1910 when they were fundamentally re-drawn. The original Golden Dawn members, who felt the direction should be more closely focused on MAGIC and astral contact with the Secret Chiefs, formed the Amoun Temple of STELLA MATUTINA.

In 1915 Waite founded a new Order, the Fellowship of the Rosy Cross, including an Inner Order, the Ordo Sanctissimus Roseae et Aureae Crucis, which he staffed largely with Masons and Theosophists and equipped with rituals described by R A Gilbert as 'ponderous and unexciting'. The FRC survived until his death when it was disbanded.

WALDENESIANS Also known as the Waldenses, these were members of an extremist heretical sect founded in about the eleventh century by a Lyons merchant, Peter Waldo, and resembling the later Protestants in some of their aspirations. They suffered persecution until the seventeenth century, although their influence extended into many parts of Europe. Today they survive as a sect in the Piedmont region of northern Italy. They rejected many fundamentals of the Catholic doctrine, including the notion of purgatory, the invocation of saints and transubstantiation. They professed pacifism, accepted a life of poverty and were linked with the heretical sect of Albigenses.

WALPURGISNACHT The Christian feast day named after the Anglo-Saxon missionary, St Walpurga, and coinciding with one of the four Grand SABBATS, BELTANE, taking place between 30 April and 1 May to mark the return of spring. This is the occasion in WICCA when the GODDESS has become restored to her aspect as the youthful MAIDEN.

WARLOCK A term equating with WITCH but applied by the Christian Church in a derogatory sense to distinguish a male witch from his female counterpart. Derived from the Old English words *waer* (truth) and *logan* (to lie), the original meaning determined a traitor or oath-breaker although, from the mid-fifteenth century, warlock became an expression specifically associated with witches. The term is little used by modern PAGANS.

WARRIORS OF PAN A little-known PAGAN organization founded in southern England during

TOP LEFT: *The pregnant Mother Goddess, representing the fecundity of the earth.*
TOP RIGHT: *Traditional witch bearing the insignia of her trade.*
BOTTOM LEFT: *The Tarot archetype of the Water Nymph.*
BOTTOM RIGHT: *The 'wolf woman' – a primitive shamanistic image representing fertility.*

the 1930s which followed many of the principles of the Scouting Movement, although with less emphasis on the imperialism and militarism of the latter. Pan was open to both adults and children, although the work of the two age groups was distinct and separate. Members were recruited either as Warriors or Handmaidens and met at summer camps located adjacent to ancient sacred sites, where they benefited from fresh air away from urban life and learned an amalgam of Pagan and woodcraft doctrine.

WATCHTOWER One of four symbolic edifices standing at the compass quarters, north, south, east and west, of the WICCA Circle and reflecting four aspects of consciousness which the Wiccan initiate must achieve in order to reach a perfect inner state (see also FOUR ELEMENTS).

WAX IMAGES Devices used in sympathetic MAGIC since ancient times (see FITH-FATH).

WCC See WICCAN CHURCH OF CANADA.

WEAVER (CRAFT) The style of WITCHCRAFT evolved by the English witch Shan JAYRAN of House of the Goddess in South London. Inspired by the work of the PAGAN feminists Starhawk (see SIMOS, Miriam) in America, Shan Jayran evolved the concept of Weaver during the late 1970s and early 1980s. It is strongly feminist-oriented and may or may not include male consorts. It is, however, open to both men and women, as well as having a place for children.

Emphasis is placed on the individual rather than on a hierarchical organization, there is a strongly practical approach and the theosophy emulates that of Taoism in respect of working and meditating with light/dark concepts.

WEIGHING (OF WITCHES) A bizarre method of trying and judging an alleged witch by placing him or her on a pair of scales opposite the Holy Bible. If the accused weighed lighter, it was considered to be an indication of guilt.

WELSH TRADITIONAL WITCHCRAFT The style of the Craft (see WICCA) pursued in parts of Wales where there is strong Celtic influence and where a secret unbroken line of witches is suggested, though unproven.

WESTCOTT, W WYNN (born 1848) A qualified medical practitioner who joined the Freemasons in 1872 and became a member of the Societas Rosicruciana in Anglia (SRIA, see ROSICRUCIAN SOCIETY) in 1880, rising to the position of General Secretary in 1882. He was an acknowledged authority on alchemy and on Qabalistic (see QABALAH) and Hermetic lore, and was a regular speaker to Anna KINGSFORD's HERMETIC SOCIETY. In 1892 he became the Supreme Magus of the SRIA.

As one of four founder members of Golden Dawn (see HERMETIC ORDER OF THE GOLDEN DAWN) he went under the various magical pseudonyms of Non Omnis Moriar and Sapere Aude. He claimed to have acquired a cipher manuscript in 1887 from a colleague, A F A Woodford, which he decoded and which was found to contain details of rituals that were to become the foundation of Golden Dawn. The account cannot be verified and the authorship of the manuscript is thought to have come from another SRIA member. He is also said to have invented a secret Hebrew name for Golden Dawn. Westcott favoured pursuance of the so-called Western philosophical path, which stood in stark contrast to the anti-Christian position of other theosophists headed by Helena BLAVATSKY. He retired from Golden Dawn in 1897.

WESTERN CEREMONIAL MAGIC A system of OCCULT belief based on three theoretical principles: Implicit in the doctrine is the notion that the universe exists both on physical or temporal and

A Yule altar.

spiritual planes, and that there exist other intelligences than those resulting from physical incarnation.

Psychic correspondences exist between the macrocosm of the universe as a whole and the microcosm of the human individual. These correspondences indicate that a principle present in the cosmos is also present in the human soul. The properly trained magician will call upon the universal forces, whether from the outer cosmos or the inner man, and will add strength to his invocation according to prescribed principles, including characters, numbers, patterns, colours and other attributes which relate to the spiritual entity involved.

The human entity is capable, subject to correct discipline and training, of anything through the strength of his or her own will.

WESTERN MYSTERIES The collective title for certain OCCULT and magical groups which have descended from the FRATERNITY OF THE INNER LIGHT founded in 1922 by Dion FORTUNE. At least five groups or fraternities have survived, including the Society of the Inner Light, which is the direct descendant of the Fraternity of the Inner Light. Involving initiation, a near-ascetic discipline, and run by trained leaders or ADEPTS, Western Mysteries are essentially intellectual in nature. They are so-called because they claim to subscribe to the mystery traditions of Egypt and Eleusis, as well as involving Mithraic, Druidic (see DRUIDRY) and Qabalistic (see QABALAH) magical ingredients. Meditation is an important aspect of membership.

Followers of the Western Mysteries generally and SOIL members specifically believe in reincarnation on an evolving upward journey not unlike that of the Buddhist concept. They subscribe to the broad notion that the universe has evolved into entities that possess varying degrees of material and spiritual existence and which exist on different planes, of which the material plane is at the lowest level. Members may also often be practising

Christians. Homosexuals are generally excluded. Fraternities meet in a prescribed temple and, by and large, confer three ritualized degrees on their members akin to those experienced in Freemasonry.

WESTLAKE, ERNEST (1855–1922) A Quaker who, with his son Aubrey (1893-1985), was the most important founding member of the Order of WOODCRAFT CHIVALRY. Father and son attempted to reconcile elements of Christianity with Classical PAGANISM to generate a modern nature-loving religion. They purchased an estate at Godshill in the New Forest as the main meeting place for the Order. Ernest Westlake died in a car crash and was succeeded by his son.

WHEEL OF THE YEAR The term given in WICCA to the annual cycle of the natural world, marked by the eight seasonal SABBATS which are represented by the eight spokes of the Wheel. The Wheel commences and ends with the autumn festival of SAMHAIN. The principal dates during the year are:

31 October (Fire festival)	Samhain (Hallowe'en)
21/22 December (Solstice)	Yule
1 February (Fire festival)	Imbolc (Oimlec)
21 March	Spring Equinox
30 April (Fire festival)	Beltane
21/22 June (Solstice)	Midsummer
1 August (Fire festival)	Lammas (Lughnasadh)
21/22 September	Autumn Equinox

See also entries under individual festivals.

WHITE GODDESS, THE The book by Robert GRAVES which describes itself as *an historic grammar of poetic myth*. Graves admits in his postscript that the bulk of the writing, 70,000 words of unsolicited enlightenment on a subject which had meant little enough to him, was completed in three weeks, given the original title of *The Roebuck in the Thicket* and pointedly ignored by the scientific academic fraternity. It was later renamed after the white goddess of Pelion, the moon deity identified with the mountain of that name at Magnesia in Greece, to whom the SACRED KING annually fell victim.

The book has aroused substantial interest since its first publication in 1946 and has been sold widely. It claims the existence of a paramount goddess of the moon and of poetry, appearing in three aspects to equate with the waxing, full and waning moon, who was previously worshipped in the Mediterranean region and across Europe. As a speculative thesis it must be regarded as a brilliant literary and poetic creation. Its factual and historical content is, however, often unprovenanced, subjective and in many places inaccurate.

WHITE, RON 'CHALKY' One of the co-founders of the REGENCY group of witches in the 1960s, all of whom were friends and associates of the radical traditionalist Robert COCHRANE.

WICCA (1) The Old English term for a WITCH, first appearing in a manuscript dating from the ninth century when it was applied to identify a SORCERER. During the purges of the sixteenth and seventeenth century, it was associated with anyone practising diabolism.

WICCA (2) The principal branch of the PAGAN revival to which most WITCHES adhere and which principally sustained modern WITCHCRAFT between the 1940s and the 1980s (although since the mid 1980s there has been a growing interest in other forms of PAGANISM to the extent that the opening statement may, according to some authorities, no longer present an accurate view). Wicca first emerged, publicly, in the late 1940s and commenced, effectively, with the repeal of the Witchcraft Act in 1951. The movement was started in England by Gerald GARDNER and spread first to the United States, then to other English-speaking regions of the world and, more latterly, to non-English-speaking European countries.

Also known as The Old Religion, The Craft of the Wise or, simply, The Craft, it relies on a syncretzsation of beliefs some of which are drawn from known ancestral religious practices, including those of the Celts, some from the tenets of Freemasonry and others from Classical themes. In terms of modern cults it is most closely related to DRUIDRY. Its religious calendar celebrates eight seasonal festivals or SABBATS (see also WHEEL OF THE YEAR).

Wicca may be regarded as a mystery religion, subscribing to a path of INITIATION. Its principles include a profound communication with the natural world and the implicit understanding that each and every individual possesses innate psychic abilities which, if properly channelled, can both foresee the future and influence events in the present through the application of MAGIC. Its symbolism is that of Qabalistic (see QABALAH) and ritual magic.

It is emphasized by Wiccans that theirs is more than a religion, it is also a Craft. A fundamental feature lies in that its members practise magic and achieve practical objectives through psychic abilities which are applied for beneficial purposes, be they for healing or for good in other ways.

There is an important distinction that a member of the Wicca faith is a witch, but a witch is not necessarily a Wiccan. In Wicca there is, in some COVENS, little sense of an hierarchical gulf between an active clergy and a passive congregation, familiar in more orthodox religions, while in others a hierarchy is more apparent.

Each Wiccan becomes a priest or priestess at their initiation, the only restriction being that the initiate must be at least eighteen years of age. In common with many other branches of modern Paganism, Wiccans do not proselytize and the Craft essentially takes the form of an OCCULT spiritual discipline that is adopted by a limited number of people. Its object is to follow a spiritual path which generates personal fulfilment and which allows for the development and use of psychic and magical strengths.

Around the world Wicca is divisible into four main branches, Alexandrian, Gardnerian,

Hereditary and Traditional (for further details see under these respective headings) and more or less all other traditions have evolved from these. In practice the distinctions between Alexandrian and Gardnerian have largely merged. Some Wiccans, however, prefer to follow a solitary path, worshipping alone and subscribing to no particular branch (see SOLO WITCH and HEDGEWITCH). In Britain these solitary witches are not usually called Wiccan, but are witches in a wider sense.

In general Wicca asserts that human consciousness is not dependent on the physical world of the body but can extend beyond its temporal limits. Emphasis is placed on the equal values of the spiritual and temporal worlds and, in contrast with the Christian faith, it does not equate pleasures of the flesh with sin and damnation but considers that physical incarnation is a gift which is to be enjoyed and explored to the full. Wicca beliefs, however, are not fixed but are to be interpreted and modified according to the experience and understanding of the individual practitioner. Its rituals are thus presented in outline form which, although they will have certain common threads, are to be developed according to personal preferences.

WICCAN In Old English the plural of the noun *wicca,* but now taken to mean a person who follows the path of the post-1940s mystery religion of WICCA.

WICCAN, THE A magazine, founded in 1968 by John SCORE and published quarterly at the time of the Fire Festivals (see WHEEL OF THE YEAR) by the PAGAN FEDERATION. For many years it was the main organ of thought and communication of UK Gardnerian witches. With the founding of the PAGAN FEDERATION it also became the organ of that organization. Since SAMHAIN 1994 it has been entitled PAGAN DAWN and edited by Christina Oakley.

WICCAN CHURCH OF CANADA The organization founded by Richard and Tamara James in Toronto. In 1987, the WCC purchased the collection of Gerald GARDNER's letters from Ripley International, the company that obtained them from Monique WILSON, Gardner's high priestess and beneficiary, in the early 1970s.

WICCAN-BASED PAGANISM A less committed and more accessible style of GODDESS-oriented worship than true WICCA. Of comparatively recent development, Wiccan-based Paganism often incorporates aspects of other tribal or PAGAN beliefs and is of a generally eclectic nature. It is less formalized in its ritual and does not necessitate initiation ceremonies (see also WEAVER CRAFT).

WIER, JOHANN Author of the treatise entitled ON MAGIC (1563) in which he argued that the indiscriminate prosecution of WITCHES was unjust. Wier suggested that those indicted were no more than harmless old women suffering from mental disorders. The establishment rejected his views and arraigned Wier himself on charges of WITCHCRAFT.

WILD HUNT, THE An alleged nocturnal phenomenon during which processions of phantom beings rode through the countryside on their way to a SABBAT. First described in the BISHOP'S CANON of circa 900 AD: *Some wicked women . . . seduced by illusions and phantoms of demons, believe and profess themselves in the hours of the night to ride upon certain beasts with Diana, the goddess of the Pagans, and in the silence of the night to traverse great spaces of the earth, and to obey her commands as of their mistress, and to be summoned to her service on certain nights.*

WILKINSON, LOUIS UMFRAVILLE The close friend and literary co-executor of Aleister CROWLEY; also a novelist writing under the pseudonym Louis Marlow. His father was the headmaster of a preparatory school in Sussex and he himself reached Oxford University before being sent down on the grounds of blasphemous conduct.

Wilkinson had no direct interest in the OCCULT but greatly enjoyed Crowley's company and, acting upon his posthumous request, read the *Hymn to Pan* and the Anthem from the *Gnostic Mass* at Crowley's funeral at Brighton Crematorium, causing a furore in the local press and prompting one national newspaper editor to label the occasion as a BLACK MASS.

WILLIAMSON, CECIL (born 1909) The founder of the Museum of Magic and Witchcraft at Castleton, Isle of Man (see WITCHES MILL MUSEUM, ISLE OF MAN), which was later sold to Gerald GARDNER, and of the WITCHES HOUSE MUSEUM at Boscastle in north Cornwall, which was formerly located at Bourton on the Water in Gloucestershire. He claims to have been formerly a wartime MI6 agent, his father was a naval officer and his mother spent much of her time following the Fleet. Born before World War I, according to Williamson's own testimony his first brush with WITCHCRAFT came at the age of seven when he was staying at North Bovey on Dartmoor and witnessed an elderly woman being harassed by a group of drunken farm labourers suspecting she had put a curse on their cattle. After the war, his father gained a job at the Admiralty and his parents moved to a house in Mayfair while he attended a preparatory school where he suffered from bullying and where he claims to have met a witch who showed him how to counter the unkind attentions of his peers. He also claims that some of his teenage years were spent working in the poverty of London's Docklands, where he developed strong socialist leanings. His grandmother, who was an astrologer, owned property at Dinard in Normandy where he spent summer holidays and where he became acquainted with the rituals of something akin to Freemasonry. He returned to the West Country, becoming deeply interested in the work of local wise women or Aunty Mays. From there he continues to run the Witches House Museum.

Williamson has become something of an eccentric elder statesman in the Craft (see WICCA) scene and writes frequently for journals including *Talking Stick*. His observations are often of a controversial nature.

WILSON, JOE See ROEBUCK.

WILSON, MONIQUE Allegedly a niece of Gerald GARDNER but more probably his high priestess who, at his death in 1964, inherited the Gardner museum in the Isle of Man. During the 1970s she sold the collection to a Canadian organization, Ripley's International, who transported it to Toronto. In 1987, Gardner's letters were purchased from Ripley's by the WICCAN CHURCH OF CANADA.

WILSON, STEVE See CHAOS MAGIC.

WINTER SOLSTICE One of the four lesser SABBATS held on or about 21 December and stemming from a PAGAN festival designed to mark the rebirth of the sun after the shortest day of the year. The occasion is also intended to ensure fertility and thus, during the medieval period, participants dressed in costumes to emulate stags and bulls. For the WICCA tradition, see YULE.

WITCH A person of either sex who practises the art of WITCHCRAFT. The term derives from the Indo-European root *weik* which infers something concerned with MAGIC or religion. This provides the basis for the Old English nouns *wicca* (pronounced *witcha*) meaning a male witch and *wicce* (pronounced *witcheh*) meaning a female counterpart. The verb *wiccian* means to cast a spell, to bewitch or to work SORCERY.

The term witch is considered by modern etymologists to have no connection with the Old English verb *witan* meaning to know or to be wise.

James I of England (see JAMES VI OF SCOTLAND), strongly antagonistic towards witches and the Craft (see WICCA), authorized corruptions in the translation of the King James Bible (1611) so as to provide Biblical sanctions to justify the EXECUTION of witches under civil law (see BIBLE). The Hebrew *kashaph* was at first correctly rendered by the translators as WIZARD, implying a MAGICIAN, but, on the instructions of the king, they altered the translation to witch. The Old English root *weik* may also be found in a separate context to mean *bending* and thus gives rise such words as *weak* and *witch elm* in modern English usage, none of which have any link with witches or PAGANISM.

The desire to become a witch during the medieval period probably stemmed from various sources, but one of the most frequent was that of extreme poverty with the promise that, if one liaised with the Devil, he would provide much needed material comforts and betterment of living conditions when all else had failed. This alliance was highly ambivalent since few of those indicted would have claimed themselves to be engaged in diabolical pacts. Witchcraft provided a sense of power to the under privileged and was also an escape for a person who had been branded a sinner by the Church, on the maxim of 'in for a penny in for a pound'.

Irrespective of good or evil intent, he or she was branded by the Christian church as a heretic who practised diabolism and who had rejected Christ for the Devil. The Church orchestrated a great fear and hatred of witches in the minds of the public that resulted in the WITCH-CRAZE of the seventeenth century.

The modern Wiccan neither practises nor recognizes diabolism but is involved with a revivalist religion drawn from various sources including the ancient cults of nature. He or she is largely a member of a COVEN and is involved in initiatory rituals (see INITIATION) and SABBATS. Witches still have no corporate identity, other than a commonality of belief, and the practices of individual covens vary widely. Some are hierarchical in their organization, others espouse a more anarchic approach.

WITCH OF ENDOR The fabled woman of the Biblical Old Testament who conjured the spirit of Samuel before the Israelite king, Saul, (1 Samuel 28.8ff). He was terrified when he saw *Gods ascending out of the earth*. It is one of the few instances in the Bible where the existence of witches in a positive and benevolent role is acknowledged and, significantly, the passage is the only instance throughout the Old Testament where an admission is made that the dead rise again. Although the 'shade' of Samuel appeared at the command of the witch, he seems to have conveyed nothing of value to Saul.

WITCH The tongue-in-cheek acronym of a feminist political protest organization, the Women's International Terrorist Conspiracy from Hell, some of whose members subsequently became converts and joined the Craft (see WICCA). WITCH was founded at Hallowe'en 1968 by a group of women who were involved in political and surrealistic protest activities. Its original manifesto included the statement: *WITCH is an all-women everything. It is theatre, revolution, magic, terror, joy, garlic flowers, spells. It is an awareness that witches and gypsies were the original guerrillas and resistance fighters against oppression, particularly the oppression of women, down through the ages. . . . They (witches) bowed to no man, being the living remnants of the oldest culture of all – one in which men and women were equal sharers in a truly co-operative society, before the death-dealing sexual, economic and spiritual repression of the Imperialist Phallic Society took over and began to destroy nature and human society.*

The members have asserted the claim that WITCHCRAFT is inseparable from politics and that any group of women can form a COVEN and call themselves WITCHES. In the eyes of many feminists, however, the association with witchcraft is an unwelcome distraction from their more secular political aims, while the militant and anarchic stance of WITCH has alienated, conversely, many more moderate WICCANS. Although the title WITCH has been retained the aspirations of the group have changed according to circumstance and need.

WITCH-BOTTLE A medieval device used to counter the effects of WITCHCRAFT and allegedly cause physical harm to a WITCH. The procedure involved collecting a specimen of the witch's urine which was then either boiled or buried. The witch would then suffer considerable discomfort, being unable to urinate, and would thus be forced to confess his or her crime. The use of the witch-bottle was usually advocated by CUNNING PERSONS or WIZARDS living within the community.

Excavations in recent years in both London and East Anglia have unearthed many examples of witch-bottles which were found to contain not only traces of urine, but also hair and nail-parings from the intended victims.

WITCHCRAFT The meaning of the term has varied according to history and perceptions, and the concept of what witchcraft actually is has sometimes been eclipsed by what witchcraft is presumed to be.

Early witchcraft The activity which, in Europe, evolved from the art of nomadic tribal shamanism (see SHAMAN). In certain aspects it was practically indistinguishable from SORCERY, augury or DIVINATION and is still to be found in primitive societies worldwide based on reverence for the spirits or gods of the natural world and on sympathetic MAGIC. This is arguably closest to the form of WITCHCRAFT described in the books of the Old Testament and was the witchcraft of the Anglo-Saxons and their successors. It is based on various influence, including Celtic, Germanic and Norse. Early witchcraft bears no association with diabolism, although it was portrayed by the early Christian Church as being a form of heathen worship, a view embellished by lurid accounts, including that of the WILD HUNT. If witches made nocturnal journeys it was to assemblies in which they were obliged to meet under the cover of darkness for their own security.

Medieval and post-medieval witchcraft

Perceptions during the period which, in the British Isles, covered the centuries from the accession of the Tudors until the repeal of the Witchcraft Acts in 1736 differed strongly according to whether the view stemmed from the Church, the public at large, or from practitioners.

The Church of Rome argued the existence of a witchcraft cult, membership of which involved the making of a blasphemous pact with the Devil. The roots of this attitude, which was also largely supported by the Protestant movement, lay in a number of political and social insecurities, and in the Church's inability to sustain widespread loyalty among the population or to explain or respond to a variety of problems including, most notably, diseases of persons, domestic animals and crops. Distinction was drawn between witchcraft, which was linked with diabolism and perceived to be a manifestation of the Devil insinuating himself into the persona of an individual, and sorcery, which was merely viewed as an abuse of things found in nature.

Typical of the Catholic Church's viewpoint is that of Jean Bodin, who describes in *Daemonomanie* how witches *come together in certain assemblies and at times prefixed when they do not only see the Devil in visible form, but confer and talk familiarly with him. In which conference the Devil exhorteth them to observe their fidelity unto him, promising them long life and prosperity.* The practice of witches was said to include:

despising any of the seven sacraments

treading on crosses

spitting at the time of elevation

breaking fast on fasting days and fasting on Sundays.

It was alleged that witches were met at markets and fairs and were commanded by a summoner to assemble at certain hours of the night to advise the Devil whom they had killed and how they had profited. They would then resort to dancing and the singing of bawdy songs. Reginald SCOT, citing Bodin, makes an interesting observation on what is perhaps the real origin of the concept of the witch's broomstick: *If they be lame, he saith the Devil delivereth them a staff, to convey them thither [to the assembly] invisibly, through the air.* He also noted that witches came together in assemblies of fifty rather than the thirteen popularly claimed.

By and large Scot viewed the anti-witchcraft hysteria emanating from such writers as rubbish. A typical object of his scorn was Danaeus who claimed that, at the SABBATS, the Devil provided powders and roots for magical purposes and gave every initiate a Devil's mark either with his teeth or claws. Members of the COVEN then kissed the Devil's bare buttocks and indulged in incestuous adultery and, when the inevitable consequences came to fruition, the newly born was cut into pieces, its blood drained into pots, its carcass burnt and the ashes mingled with the blood.

The Church's antagonism culminated in the spate of hysterical persecution which reached its climax in the seventeenth century and which declined, not primarily through change of religious attitudes, but because among the intelligentsia who comprised the judiciary it ceased to be chic to believe in witchcraft.

Scot's own observation was that witches were generally women: *who be commonly old, lame, bleare-eied, pale, fowle, and full of wrinkles, poore, sullen, superstitious and papists; or such as knowe no religion; in whose drousie minds the divell hath gotten a fine seat.* The public at large drew a blurred distinction, between the beneficent and maleficent magical activity in its midst. It recognized, on the one hand, wizardry and the practices of CUNNING PERSONS that involved finding lost goods, curing ailments, predicting future events and offering herbal remedies. The lay person also recognized and feared witchcraft, an activity sometimes involving the application of MALEFICIUM (itself an invention of the Church of Rome), designed to dispense harm to persons and property, and practised as a form of retribution by those who could find no other recourse against social injustice.

The separate concepts of beneficent and maleficent witchcraft merged during the reign of Elizabeth I, and throughout the period of the WITCH-CRAZE, swinging towards an activity with evil intent. There was no special term that distinguished malevolent magicians from those cunning persons who practised healing arts and located lost property but the term witchcraft generally implied an injurious activity causing harm to other people or their possessions by occult methods, in other words application of the *maleficium*. Scot comments: *It is indifferent to say in the English tongue, 'she is a witch' or 'she is a wise woman'.* As Keith Thomas describes it: *In this sense the belief in witchcraft can be defined as the attribution of misfortune to occult human agency.*

To its practitioners, wizardry or witchcraft was a job of work, no different from that of a lawyer or a surgeon and equally open to quackery, abuse and misuse. Some adopted it as a means of livelihood, some in the search for power over others, some as a last recourse when all else failed or when the Church had already condemned them as sinners beyond reprieve.

In reality, therefore, the witchcraft that was subject to extensive persecution in Europe and America in the sixteenth and seventeenth centuries was an activity of persons who applied innate or self-raised powers of magic to dispense forces for good or evil purpose. From the records of the Assize courts assembled by C L Ewan and later by A MacFarlane, it appears that, while witchcraft permeated every level of society, most of those actually convicted were women drawn from the lower social strata. Out of a record of 109 executions on the Home Circuit (Hertfordshire, Kent, Surrey, Sussex) only seven were men, and of nearly 600 defendants all but four were tradesmen, labourers, husbandmen and their wives.

If court records of the time are an accurate reflection, some individuals entered into fanciful pacts with the Devil but this was by no means universally true. There is also no demonstrable evidence that, during the medieval period, a 'witch cult' existed either in the British Isles or Europe, or that witches were, to any extent, organized into covens, certainly not consisting of groups of thirteen. According to Scot, assemblies existed that involved initiation rites but, generally, witchcraft appears not to have involved ritual Sabbats, nor did its practitioners see themselves as belonging to an 'Old Religion' They were mainly isolated individuals who conducted their affairs without clear links to earlier PAGAN traditions.

The activity of witchcraft probably included any unacceptable brand of popular religion even if it was practised without any formal breach with Christianity. Most of its practitioners, during and prior to the medieval period, strongly refuted any claims that they were other than Christian in their religious beliefs although they undoubtedly respected and made use of Pagan vestiges in the form of festival dates, fertility rites, wells and other sacred places of a pre-Christian pedigree.

Modern witchcraft (including Wicca) Since the revival of interest in PAGANISM during the twentieth century and, particularly, in the early 1950s, witchcraft has come to represent a religion based on reverence for the natural world, the duality of the God and GODDESS based loosely on Celtic deities, initiation and the use of MAGIC to beneficial and benevolent purpose. It possesses no association with diabolism and the notion that it possesses traditional and hereditary links with Tudor, Elizabethan or Stuart witchcraft is now firmly discounted among most Wiccans.

Distinction continues to be drawn between witchcraft and SORCERY. Witchcraft is argued to be an innate quality that stems from a psychological peculiarity and which requires no material aids in the form of words, spells or potions. Sorcery, in contrast, requires the employment of technical devices and formulae and can be practised by anyone who is suitably informed.

WITCHCRAFT (AMERICAN LAWS)
Until 1951 the laws on the English statute books were observed in North America. Since 1951 there have been no federal laws governing witchcraft but a number of state laws have been implemented regulating spiritualism and fortune telling.

WITCHCRAFT (ENGLISH AND SCOTTISH LAWS)
The first statute against witchcraft was passed in England in 1542 during the reign of Henry VIII and was repealed in 1547 on the accession of Edward VI. North of the border a similar statute was passed under Mary Queen of Scots in 1562. In Scotland, however, the law differed in that torture was allowed as a legal means of extracting confession. The 1542 Act in England treated witchcraft as a felony, involving positive acts of malevolence towards the public in general. The Act stated that it was a capital offence to practise WITCHCRAFT, enchantment or SORCERY, to find treasure, to cause physical harm to another, to provoke unlawful love, or for any other unlawful purpose.

The second English statute was passed in 1563 under Elizabeth I. It was more draconian than that of 1542 in that it decreed the death penalty for all convicted of invoking evil spirits irrespective of whether or not they involved the MALEFICIUM. It was more lenient, however, in that the death penalty was only served if the witchcraft involved the death of another person. Less serious results of witchcraft incurred a maximum one year jail sentence.

The third statute of 1604, passed in the reign of James I, incorporated a number of Continental notions of witchcraft, including those of a diabolical pact and Devil worship and was essentially the most severe law, making it a capital offence if the victim was injured and if all kinds of lesser magic were practised. It also became a felony to disinter bodies for magical purposes, in other words for NECROMANCY. The Act did, however, continue to draw a distinction between evil and benign spirits and in so doing spared the WIZARD or MAGICIAN from charges.

In England and Wales indictment proceeded under civil, not ecclesiastical, law so that those convicted were hung not burnt. In this respect the style of punishment differed from that in Scotland and on the Continent.

The first major English trial conducted under any of these laws took place at Chelmsford in 1566 when three women, Elizabeth Francis, Agnes Waterhouse and Joan Waterhouse were arraigned on charges of witchcraft. Joan Waterhouse was acquitted but her mother, Agnes, was convicted and hanged. Elizabeth Francis was also acquitted but was hanged after a subsequent conviction in 1579.

Essex was the county of England chiefly affected by the WITCH-CRAZE and among the most famous Chelmsford trials was that of Joan Prentis who, with two others, was hanged in July 1589.

Arguably the extreme severity of the Act of 1604 was instrumental in turning the tide of the witch-craze in England since it generated considerable scepticism among both common people and the magistrates.

In 1736 the remaining Witchcraft Acts in England and Scotland were repealed. The new law preserved the right to prosecute persons who allegedly possessed magical powers but it also denied the existence of those powers. The 1736 statute was effective until it was replaced by the Fraudulent Mediums Act of 1951 which gave freedom for the individual to practise witchcraft so long as it did not result in harm to persons or property.

WITCHCRAFT RESEARCH ASSOCIATION A body founded in October 1964 by a friend of the PAGAN and occultist, Robert COCHRANE, who went under the name John Math. It was set up with the object, ostensibly, of reconciling the various factions of WITCHCRAFT in Britain, the older traditions and the radical Gardnerians (see GARDNER, Gerald), which at the time were engaging in public and damaging infighting.

The launch was opened by Doreen VALIENTE, and the WRA went on to publish a regular quarterly journal, *Pentagram.* At the time this had some importance, and was intended to become a voice for various Pagan groups. From the outset, however, the organization was doomed to failure, beset by factional squabbling between Gardnerians and others with opposing views. The WRA was seen by Gardnerians as an attempt by 'radicals' to dominate the Craft (see WICCA) and, in practice, traditionalists like Cochrane and TALIESIN used the pages of *Pentagram* as a vehicle by which to denigrate the Gardnerian Craft.

The organization effectively ceased to exist after the close of 1965.

WITCHCRAFT RESEARCH CENTRE Founded by Cecil WILLIAMSON at the WITCHES' HOUSE MUSEUM and effectively run by him single-handedly, it deals with aspects of west country witchcraft with its emphasis on the old-fashioned solitary, country witch living and practising independently. It has no connection with the defunct WITCHCRAFT RESEARCH ASSOCIATION.

WITCH-CRAZE A spate of persecution that began during the sixteenth century, based on the assumption that witches entered into a diabolical pact having formally rejected the Christian faith (see MALEFICIUM). It presumed, among other erroneous notions, that witches made nocturnal excursions through the air to attend meetings, during which they desecrated the Eucharist, performed sacrificial slaughter of children and engaged in acts of cannibalism.

WITCHES' HOUSE MUSEUM Curated by Cecil WILLIAMSON at Boscastle in north Cornwall, the museum contains a collection of exhibits that are claimed to be associated with traditional WITCHCRAFT and folk MAGIC, mostly applicable to, and drawn from, the English West Country.

Although the museum contains a wide range of artefacts, documents and photographs, many of the exhibits are without proper provenance and are therefore of questionable authenticity and origin. The museum was formerly located at Box Bush House, Bourton-on-the-Water, Gloucestershire where it was founded as the Museum of Witchcraft.

Williamson was also the founder of the Museum of Magic and Witchcraft, later purchased by Gerald GARDNER, at Castletown in the Isle of Man – see WITCHES' MILL (ISLE OF MAN).

WITCHES' MARKS Abnormal protuberances on the body of an accused, such as warts, which were judged to be teats from which devilish FAMILIARS suckled. Persons arraigned as WITCHES were regularly stripped and searched for such marks.

WITCHES' MILL (ISLE OF MAN) A windmill at Castletown destroyed by fire in the nineteenth century, the extensive barns attached to which were opened as 'The Folklore Centre of Superstition and Witchcraft' in July 1951. The museum was founded by Cecil WILLIAMSON and the opening ceremony performed by Gerald GARDNER. The Witches' Mill dated from no later than 1611 when it is mentioned in a court record and was so called because, after the fire which destroyed it in 1848, the ruins were used as a dancing floor by the Arbory witches who lived in the vicinity.

Gardner subsequently purchased the museum from Williamson and added to it his own collection of OCCULT artefacts. After Gardner's death his high priestess, Monique WILSON, who inherited the museum, sold the contents to Ripley's in Toronto.

WITCHES' RUNE The chant which, in altered forms, often precedes the main ritual of a SABBAT. The original version written by Doreen VALIENTE and included in her own old BOOK OF SHADOWS is as follows:

Darksome night and shining Moon
East, then South and West and North
Hearken to the Witch's Rune

Here come I to call ye forth!
Earth and Water, Air and Fire
Wand and Pentacle and Sword
Work ye unto my desire
Hearken ye unto my word!
Cords and Censer, Scourge and Knife,
Powers of the witch's blade,
Waken all ye into life,
Come ye as the charm is made!
Queen of Heaven, Queen of Hell,
Horned Hunter of the night,
Lend your power unto the spell,
Work my will by magic rite.
In the earth and air and sea,
By the light of Moon and Sun,
As I will, so mote it be;
Chant the spell and be it done!
(By permission of Doreen Valiente)

WIZARD A term stemming from the Middle English word *wis* (wise) and first applied in the mid-fifteenth century to denote a wise man or woman commonly known as a CUNNING PERSON or a white WITCH who worked only for beneficent purposes. The sense was modified in the sixteenth and seventeenth centuries to refer to a high MAGICIAN and, from 1825 onwards, it equated wholly with a witch.

Many medieval wizards adopted an ambivalent attitude towards Christianity and, in fact, probably saw themselves as good Christians, believing that their powers stemmed from such Biblical personalities as Adam, Abel and Moses and including prayer and fasting in their methods.

Members of the Christian establishment, including such notable figures as Archbishop Thomas Becket, were not above seeking the services of wizards and the more modest ranks of clergy were also susceptible. A record in 1579 is typical, noting that Edmund Curteis, Vicar of Cuckfield, Sussex, was defrocked as a 'seeker to witches', having requested the aid of a local wise woman for some magical purpose.

WOMEN'S MYSTERIES A term used generically to describe a variety of OCCULT rites performed by feminists who do not expressly view themselves as WITCHES. Often the rites are put together, *ad hoc*, from the manuals of feminist WITCHCRAFT authors, including Starhawk (see SIMOS, Miriam), Zsuzsanna BUDAPEST and others. There are no fixed places or patterns of worship and parts of the ritual are frequently spontaneous. There is a general emphasis on the Earth Mother, life, death and MAGIC. Many of the principles would appear to derive from GARDNERIAN WICCA although, unlike the latter, the ritual is generally performed by all members without passive onlookers.

WOODCRAFT CHIVALRY, ORDER OF An organization founded in 1900 in New York State and based on the Birch Bark Roll books of Ernest Thompson Seton, it possessed strong parallels with the Scouting Movement of Baden-Powell in England, although it was less militaristic and imperialistic in doctrine. It attempted to reconcile Christianity with elements of Classical PAGANISM, so creating a modern nature-loving religion. Drawing a romanticized picture of the native American Indian tribes, it attracted many who were disenchanted with the jingoistic tones of the Scouts.

In 1917, its various tribes were amalgamated into the Woodcraft League of America.

At the same time, the Order of Woodcraft Chivalry was first established in England in 1917 by Ernest and Aubrey WESTLAKE, with its headquarters at Godshill in the New Forest, Hampshire. The English Order involved an hierarchical system based loosely on that of the Scouts, with initiates rising from the grade of Woodcub to Pathfinder. They were then invited to join the inner Sun Lodge, based at Godshill, whose rites bore strong similarity, in certain respects, to those of WICCA. These included the opening of a CIRCLE by moving in a DEOSIL or clockwise progression from east to north and nude ritual celebration (described as *gymnosophy*). There is some suggestion that the

members of the New Forest Woodcraft organizations may have been among the first recruits to Gerald GARDNER's pioneering Wicca COVEN which arose in response to the growing popular vogue for naturism and alternative forms of spiritual devotion in the 1930s. To what extent the Woodcraft organizations provided a blueprint for Wicca is questionable.

During the 1930s, the Westlakes ran popular summer camps that provided a mixture of spiritual and physical work. The Order of Woodcraft Chivalry is not to be confused with the similar but distinct organization, the WOODCRAFT FOLK. Woodcraft Chivalry eventually split into an assortment of small splinter groups, each following its own path.

WOODCRAFT FOLK An organization established in England the 1930s which derived partly from the Social Credit Party or Greenshirts founded by John HARGRAVE in 1929 and partly from another of his movements, the KIBBO KIFT KINDRED. Membership was drawn mainly from adult intellectuals with socialist leanings who came together for family summer camps and who, to some extent, merged in their activities with the Order of WOODCRAFT CHIVALRY. There is some argument that the so-called Nine Covens of George PICKINGILL were, in reality, rather more established branches of Woodcraft than clans of Hereditary witches (see HEREDITARY CRAFT).

The Woodcraft Folk are still active.

WOODMAN, W R One-time Supreme Magus of the ROSICRUCIANS.

WORKING TOOLS The eight magical tools presented to a WITCH at his or her INITIATION. In order of presentation they include the sword to symbolize the trained and focused will; the ATHAME or black-handled dagger which is the personal knife purchased by or crafted by the initiate; the white-handled dagger for use exclusively within the

Adler, M *Drawing Down the Moon* Boston 1986

Aswynn, F *Leaves of Yggdrasil* Llewellyn 1990

Beth, Rae *Hedgewitch* Robert Hale 1990

Bracelin, J L *Gerald Gardner: Witch* Octagon Press 1960

Chadwick, N *The Celts* Penguin edition 1987

Crowley, V *Phoenix from the Flame* Aquarian Press 1994

Crowley, V *Wicca, the Old Religion in the New Age* Aquarian Press 1989

Deutch, R *The Ecstatic Mother* Bachmann & Turner 1979

Drury, N *Pan's Daughter – The Strange World of Rosaleen Norton* Collins Australia, 1988

Ellis Davidson, H R *Gods and Myths of Northern Europe* Penguin 1964

Ellis, P B *A Dictionary of Irish Mythology* London 1987

Evans, G E *The Horse in the Furrow* London 1960

Farrar, J & S *The Witches' Way: Principles, Rituals and Beliefs of Modern Witchcraft* Robert Hale 1984

Ferguson, J *The Religions of the Roman Empire* London 1970

Fielding, C & Collins, C *The Story of Dion Fortune* Dallas 1985

Gardner, G B *Witchcraft Today* London 1954

Gilbert, R A *The Golden Dawn* Aquarian Press 1983

Graves, R *The White Goddess* Faber & Faber edition 1961

Green, M *The Gods of the Celts* Alan Sutton 1986

Hine, P *Condensed Chaos* New Falcon Publications 1995

Hollander, L M (trans.) *The Poetic Edda* University of Texas Press 1962

Johns, J *The King of the Witches* London 1969

Jordan, M *Encyclopedia of Gods* Kyle Cathie 1992

Jordan, M *Gods of the Earth* Transworld 1992

Jordan, M *Myths of the World* Kyle Cathie 1993

King, F *Ritual Magic in England* London 1970

Kittredge, G L *Witchcraft in Old and New England* 1956

Lane, Fox R *Pagans and Christians* Viking 1986

Leek, Sybil *The Complete Art of Witchcraft* London 1975

Lethbridge, T C *Investigating an Ancient Religion* Routledge & Kegan Paul 1962

Liddell, W E *The Pickingill Papers* Capall Bann 1994

Luhrmann, T R *Persuasions of the Witch's Craft* Blackwell 1989

Lurker, M *Dictionary of Gods and Goddesses, Devils and Demons* Routledge & Kegan Paul, 1987

Macfarlane, A *Witchcraft in Tudor and Stuart England* 1991

Markwick, M (ed) *Witchcraft and Sorcery* Penguin 1970

Matthews, J & C *British and Irish Mythology* Aquarian Press 1988

Pennethorne Hughes *Witchcraft (1952)* Longmans edition 1965

Piggott , S *The Druids* Thames & Hudson 1968

Powell, T G E *The Celts* Thames & Hudson 1958

Richardson, A *Priestess: The Life and Magic of Dion Fortune* Aquarian Press 1987

Robbins, R H *Encyclopedia of Witchcraft and Demonology* 1959

Robertson, O *The Call of Isis* Cesara Publications 1975

Russell, J B *A History of Witchcraft* Thames and Hudson, 1980

Sanders, M *The Witch Queen* Star Books 1976

Sandra *Ich, Die Hexe* Goldmann 1991

Scot, R *The Discoverie of Witchcraft* 1886 edition

Sharp, J A *Witchcraft in 17th century Yorkshire* 1992 pamphlet

Starhawk *Dreaming the Dark* Unwin Paperbacks edition 1990

Sturluson, S *Edda (trans. A Faulkes)* Dent 1987

Summers, M *Witchcraft and Black Magic* London 1946

Suster, G *The Legacy of the Beast* London 1988

Symonds, J *The Great Beast* London 1951

Thomas, K *Religion and the Decline of Magic* Weidenfeld & Nicolson 1971

Valiente, D *An ABC of Witchcraft Past and Present* Robert Hale 1984

Valiente, D *The Rebirth of Witchcraft* Robert Hale 1989

Waite, A E *The Book of Black Magic* Maine 1995

PERIODICALS

Cauldron, The – quarterly Pagan journal of the Old Religion catering largely for hereditary and traditional aspects of witchcraft

Pagan Dawn – quarterly journal of the Pagan Federation, formerly *The Wiccan*

Talking Stick – London-based quarterly occult magazine dealing with various aspects of witchcraft and magic

In Wicca the occasion marks the turning point in the depth of winter when the world may look forward to the miracle of genesis in the spring. In recognition of the promise of renewal of the natural world, evergreen boughs are cut and brought in to the house. This parallels the decorating of fir trees for the Christian festival, a practice which has its roots firmly in PAGAN traditions and which owes nothing to the Christian nativity story. The practice is more likely to have derived from a Mesopotamian rite, than from the north European notion of the world tree, YGGDRASIL, although it is claimed that the Norsemen revered the Yule log as a symbol of the world ash tree and began the practice of lighting a Yule log which was then kept burning through the period of festivities.

Yule derives from a Celtic festival, also observed in Norse and Anglo-Saxon traditions, the archaic title of which is *Geola* (pronounced *Yula)* and meaning 'yoke', literally the circle of the year completed. The word would also seem to have etymological links with the Norse *hweol* meaning wheel

The origin of the association between mistletoe and Yule also lies in Norse tradition since it was the weapon that Loki used, through the innocent agency of the blind god, Hod, to slaughter OTHIN's favourite son, Balder, in mid-winter. Balder was not, as has been claimed by some PAGAN authors, reborn at Yule since such regenesis of a dying god formed no part of the Norse religious tradition.

ZODIAC The astrological configuration which consists of a circle divided into twelve segments of 30 degrees, each representing one of the twelve signs named after constellations – Aries, Taurus, Gemini, Cancer, Leo, Virgo, Libra, Scorpio, Sagittarius, Capricorn, Aquarius and Pisces – traversed by the sun, moon and planets in varying cycles. When applying a horoscope, this 'mobile' zodiac circle is related to a second 'fixed' dial of twelve numbered 'houses' against which it rotates fully once in every twenty-four hours. The time of the day is therefore critical in reading a horoscope accurately.

The signs of the zodiac have been recognized since ancient times and are depicted in art from Pharonic Egypt. One of the most popular in Europe is the Great Zodiac claimed to exist in the landscape surrounding GLASTONBURY in Somerset, the provenance of which is, however, highly speculative.

YEATS, WILLIAM BUTLER (1865-1939) The Anglo-Irish poet and playwright, founder of the Abbey Theatre in Dublin and a leader of the Celtic revival, who was awarded the Nobel prize for Literature in 1923 and who became one of the early members of Golden Dawn (see HERMETIC ORDER OF THE GOLDEN DAWN) through the encouragement of S L MacGregor MATHERS. He was initiated into the ISIS-URANIA Temple in London in March 1890 and took the magical pseudonym Festina Lente, which, after achieving the grade of Adeptus Minor in 1893, he changed to Daemon est Deus Inversus, a motto that he borrowed from Eliphas LEVI. Hitherto he had been a founder member of the HERMETIC SOCIETY in Dublin in 1885 and, in 1888, had joined the THEOSOPHICAL SOCIETY where he became critical of Madame BLAVATSKY's claims to have acquired the teachings of departed Mahatmas.

Yeats was also mildly contemptuous of MacGregor Mathers, respecting his scholarship but not his tastes. He was elected Chief of Isis-Urania in April 1900 until his resignation in 1902, amid internal wrangling about the existence of OCCULT Groups within the Order which he believed ran contrary to the principles of Golden Dawn. In 1903 he joined the splinter group, STELLA MATUTINA, which advocated pursuing a path of magical workings and astral communication, remaining an active member until the 1920s.

In Ireland he founded the Order of the Four Treasures. In 1917 he married the medium and mystic, Georgie Hyde-Lees, having been rejected by the beautiful Maude Gonne to whom many of his poems had been dedicated.

YGGDRASIL The World Ash Tree of Germanic and Nors tradition that marks the centre of the nine worlds of gods, giants, dwarfs and men. The term originates in the fusion of *Ygg*, one of the epithets of OTHIN, and the Old Norse word *drasill*, a horse, meaning literally *the horse of Ygg*, a euphemism for a gallows tree. The expression derives from the legend that Othin hung himself from the tree, pierced by his own spear, for nine nights in the pursuit of OCCULT knowledge. To the same end he also gave his right eye in exchange for the right to drink from the Well of Urd (the Spring of Fate) beneath the Tree.

By hanging from the Tree, Othin rendered himself a sacrifice according to his own self-ordained rites of death and in clear parallel with the Christian crucifixion account. He acquired occult knowledge through his symbolic death.

Tradition has it that Yggdrasil will survive the day of doom, Ragnarok, and give shelter to those who will populate the new earth.

Some authors have suggested that the tree is not an ash but a yew, though there is scant support for this notion. There is little in literature to identify Yggdrasil with the Tree of Life known from the mythology of the ancient near east and Classical empires of Greece and Rome.

YULE (YULETIDE) In WICCA, the SABBAT festival held on 21 December that marks the WINTER SOLSTICE and in which the most common thematic focus is the birth of the new Sun God to the Mother GODDESS. In some Wiccan COVENS it focuses on a passing of power from the Holly King to the Oak King, adopted from a myth from English folklore.

CIRCLE; the wand symbolizing the phallic nature of the HORNED GOD; the PENTACLE; the incense censer; the scourge; and the cords.

WRA See WITCHCRAFT RESEARCH ASSOCIATION.

WYRD An Anglo-Saxon term defining the quality of personal actions both in terms of merit and demerit. The term may be expanded to the Web of Wyrd in which an individual moves. The dimensions of the Web of Wyrd, and the individual's control over these, which are determined by his or her level of consciousness. The concept is not dissimilar to that of KARMA in Buddhist doctrine.